MARTIN SCORSESE
A JOURNEY

MARTIN SCORSESE

A JOURNEY

MARY PAT KELLY

WITH FOREWORDS BY

STEVEN SPIELBERG

AND

MICHAEL POWELL

THUNDER'S MOUTH PRESS ■ NEW YORK

Copyright © 1991 by Mary Pat Kelly
Forewords © 1991 by Steven Spielberg
and the Estate of Michael Powell.
All rights reserved.
First paperback edition, 1992.
First printing 1991.

Published by Thunder's Mouth Press
54 Greene Street, Suite 4S
New York, N.Y. 10013

Interview with Haig Manoogian on page 51 and interview with
Peter Boyle on page 93 from *Martin Scorsese: The First Decade*
by Mary Pat Kelly.
Reprinted by permission of the author.

Excerpt from Martin Scorsese's remarks at the Center for
Advanced Film and Television Studies on page 71
reprinted by permission of the Center for Advanced Film
and Television Studies.

Library of Congress cataloging-in-publication data:
Kelly, Mary Pat.
Martin Scorsese: a journey / by Mary Pat Kelly; with forewords
by Steven Spielberg and Michael Powell.
p. cm.
Filmography: p.
Includes index.
ISBN 1-56025-044-5 (pbk.)
1. Scorsese, Martin. 2. Motion picture producers and directors—
United States—Biography. I. Title.
PN1998.3.S39K45 1991
791.43′0233′092—dc20
[B] 91-24017 CIP

Designed by The Sarabande Press
Printed in the United States of America

Distributed by Publishers Group West
4065 Hollis Street
Emeryville, CA 94608
1-800-788-3453

For my mother, Mariann Williams Kelly,
and in memory of my father,
Michael Joseph Kelly

The burning sands will become pools,
and the thirsty ground, springs of water, . . .

A highway will be there
called the Holy Way, . . .

no fools shall go astray on it.
No lion will be there, . . .

It is for those with a journey to make . . .

Isaiah 35:8-9

CONTENTS

CONTENTS

FOREWORDS

My movies are whispers. Marty's movies are shouts. There are a few things we have in common, though, even if they're not always apparent. There's our friendship, first of all. I've known him for the better part of two decades now, and for most of that time (he doesn't know this) I've been a bit in awe of him.

And then there's all the emotion; that's another thing. Both of us make movies that provoke strong reactions. Movies that make an audience respond. The difference is that Marty does this all on his own terms. He doesn't fret about what's going to "work," or not "work," for an audience. His concern is what's true to his characters and what's right for their feelings. If he can work that out—and he always does—then he goes right ahead, and lets the audience catch up with him. And if they don't, Marty doesn't wait around for them. I admire that, too. Maybe I even envy it a little.

Francis Coppola also takes those big chances. He goes his own way. That's the best way, and that's why I think Francis and Marty are the two best filmmakers working in America right now. They are artists, of course. But they are also great explorers, always taking risks, always crossing emotional frontiers, always striking out for fresh territory.

Being with Marty is like watching one of his movies. It's a kinetic experience. There's a greeting, warm and fast, and then you go spinning off on a dizzying ride full of ideas, memories, wisecracks, and personal investigations. For anyone who hasn't had the luck to spend some time with Marty, watching him act is a good guide to what it can be like. Think of the characters he's played (and played well, too): the gunman in *Mean Streets*, the passenger full of murderous rage in *Taxi Driver*, the volatile club owner in Tavernier's *Round Midnight*. You can't trust these guys. You can't trust what they're thinking and you can't predict what they're going to do. It's the same with Marty himself, with one big difference. There's something threatening about all these characters. But the only thing you risk being with Marty is a sudden, drastic loss of energy. It's hard keeping pace with the guy.

In his movies, Marty sets the pace, along with a punishingly high standard. He makes movies about things that a lot of us are afraid to admit we even think about. Movies like *Mean Streets* and *Raging Bull* and *The Last Temptation of Christ* make us confront troubling thoughts and stormy feelings, then make us understand them. Lots of directors can make movies that make you feel things easily, temporarily. Marty's movies can change you, and they cling to your heart forever.

Steven Spielberg

What was that flash of genius, just now, that illuminated the Croisette at Cannes and the SoHo district of New York? Scorsese's *Life Lessons*, one of the most perfect short films since Astruc's *Le Rideau Cramoisi*. Who nearly succeeded in making a new man out of Newman? Who made taxi a four-letter word? Who was the matador who tamed the raging bull? Who was it who turned the mean streets that had shaped him into a stairway to heaven? Martin Scorsese. Who was it who taught the bible-thumpers that the true meaning of God is love?

And he's only just started! This is all apprentice work. The great sermons are to come. We are going to see many more. We are going to see the hearts of men laid bare. We are going to be shown what waits for us on the other side of the wall called convention. We are going to learn a very great deal.

Martin Scorsese is a sensualist. He enjoys good wine, good food, good clothes. He is personally attractive. His friendship is valued by his friends. To his collaborators, he is a conundrum. He has never heard of logic. He knows very little about life. He knows that when you are dead, you begin to smell. Making a film is, for Martin Scorsese, a happiness and a torture. For us, his audience, it is a promise that sweetens the whole year.

Michael Powell

Michael Powell wrote this appreciation of Martin Scorsese's films not long before his death in March of 1990. *Requiescat in Pace.*

AUTHOR'S ACKNOWLEDGEMENTS

I am grateful to all whose voices speak in this book, especially to Martin Scorsese, who finally said to me, "What more can you possibly ask?" I also want to thank the members of his staff, past and present, especially Debra Schindler, Betsy Marino, and Raffaele Donato, as well as Robert De Niro's assistant, Robin Chambers, for their help. This book would not have been possible without the help of Julia Judge, Martin Scorsese's assistant. Thank you. Thanks to Marion Billings of M/S Billings Publicity and to Diane Collins and Elizabeth Petit of her office.

I received great support throughout from my sisters, Margaret, Randy, Susan, and Nancy, and my brother, Michael. Also from Roberta Sorvino and Elizabeth. Support came, too, from Sam Levin, Lynn Garafola, Dee Ito, Carol Rinzler, Joy Harris, Patricia Bosworth, Bob Hoyt, and Margaret O'Brien Steinfels. Loretta Barrett, my agent, gave the project invaluable attention and energy, for which I thank her. Special gratitude to Sister Marie Denise Sullivan, S.P., who was there at the beginning of all this.

The logistics involved in interviewing and editing were sometimes daunting. I wish to thank those who helped in transcribing and preparing the manuscript, especially Willia Osby, Ted Panken, Sheila Ward, Deb Spohnheimer, Barbara and Fred Feld. Margaret Campion, Ronni Hudson, and Lucia Sciorsci know how much they extended themselves for this project, and how much I appreciate their efforts. To Mary Bringle, my editor, who made it fun, thanks. Thank you to all at Thunder's Mouth Press who worked on this book. Special appreciation goes to Jean Casella for her skill and sensitivity and to Carol McGuire for her counsel.

My husband Martin Sheerin contributed photographs, for which I am grateful. My gratitude for all he gives cannot be contained in words.

MPK

New York, August 15, 1991

CAST OF CHARACTERS

MARTIN SCORSESE

CHARLES SCORSESE — Martin Scorsese's father; made cameo appearances in many of his films, featured in *Italianamerican, Raging Bull,* and *GoodFellas.*

CATHERINE SCORSESE — Martin Scorsese's mother; made cameo appearances in many of his films; featured in *It's Not Just You, Murray!, Mean Streets, Italianamerican, The King of Comedy,* and *GoodFellas.*

FRANK SCORSESE — Martin Scorsese's brother

FATHER FRANK PRINCIPE — Priest at Old St. Patrick's Cathedral when Martin Scorsese was growing up.

MARDIK MARTIN — Screenwriter who shaped the script for *Mean Streets* and collaborated on scripts for *Raging Bull* and *New York, New York.*

IRA RUBIN A.K.A. ALEX ROBESON — Murray in *It's Not Just You, Murray!*

HARVEY KEITEL — J.R. in *Who's That Knocking at My Door?,* Charlie in *Mean Streets,* Sport, the pimp in *Taxi Driver,* Alice's psychotic lover, Ben, in *Alice Doesn't Live Here Anymore,* and Judas in *The Last Temptation of Christ.*

THELMA SCHOONMAKER — Edited *Who's That Knocking at My Door?, Raging Bull, The King of Comedy, After Hours, The Color of Money, The Last Temptation of Christ, New York Stories: Life Lessons, GoodFellas,* and *Cape Fear.* Won the Academy Award for Best Editing for *Raging Bull.*

HAIG MANOOGIAN — Established the film department at N.Y.U. Taught Scorsese, and financed *Who's That Knocking at My Door?,* Scorsese's first feature.

JAY COCKS   Screenwriter and *Time* magazine critic. Long-time friend who worked with Scorsese on various drafts of *The Last Temptation of Christ.*

OLIVER STONE   Academy Award–winning director. Scorsese's student at N.Y.U. in the late 1960s.

CHARLES MILNE   Chairman of the Department of Film and Television at the Tisch School of the Arts at N.Y.U. Student at N.Y.U. in the late 1960s.

BARBARA HERSHEY   Bertha in *Boxcar Bertha* and Mary Magdalene in *The Last Temptation of Christ.*

ROBERT DE NIRO   Johnny Boy in *Mean Streets,* Travis Bickle in *Taxi Driver,* Jimmy Doyle in *New York, New York,* Jake La Motta in *Raging Bull,* Rupert Pupkin in *The King of Comedy,* and Jimmy Conway in *GoodFellas.* Max Cady in *Cape Fear.* Won the Academy Award for Best Actor for *Raging Bull.*

RICHARD ROMANUS   Michael in *Mean Streets.*

MICHAEL POWELL   Legendary English director whose films inspired Scorsese.

ELLEN BURSTYN   Alice in *Alice Doesn't Live Here Anymore.* Won the Academy Award for Best Actress for her performance in the film.

PAUL SCHRADER   Wrote the scripts for *Taxi Driver* and *The Last Temptation of Christ,* and worked on script for *Raging Bull.*

PETER BOYLE   The Wizard in *Taxi Driver.*

MICHAEL CHAPMAN   Director of Cinematography for *Taxi Driver, Raging Bull,* and the *Bad* video. One of the cinematographers for *The Last Waltz.*

IRWIN WINKLER   Producer of *New York, New York* and *Raging Bull,* and co-producer of *GoodFellas.*

LIZA MINNELLI   Francine Evans in *New York, New York.*

ROBBIE ROBERTSON   Lead singer of The Band. Initiated *The Last Waltz.*

DAVID FIELD   United Artists studio executive for *Raging Bull.*

CIS CORMAN   Casting Director for *Raging Bull, The King of Comedy,* and *The Last Temptation of Christ.*

JOE PESCI	Joey in *Raging Bull* and Tommy DeVito in *GoodFellas*. Won the Academy Award for Best Supporting Actor for *GoodFellas*.
CATHY MORIARTY	Vickie in *Raging Bull*.
PAUL ZIMMERMAN	Screenwriter for *The King of Comedy*.
SANDRA BERNHARD	Masha in *The King of Comedy*.
FREDDIE SCHULER	Director of Cinematography for *The King of Comedy*, and one of the cinematographers for *The Last Waltz*.
PATROCLOS STAVROU	Secretary to the President of the Republic of Cyprus; literary executor for the estate of Greek writer Nikos Kazantzakis.
ELENI KAZANTZAKIS	Widow of Nikos Kazantzakis, author of the book *The Last Temptation of Christ*.
DAVID KIRKPATRICK	As Vice President of Paramount he oversaw *The Last Temptation of Christ* project in 1983. Now President of the Motion Picture Group of Paramount Pictures.
KEITH ADDIS	Hollywood producer and Sting's manager; production assistant for *Taxi Driver*.
STING	Cast as Pontius Pilate for the 1983 production of *The Last Temptation of Christ*.
HARRY UFLAND	Scorsese's agent for over twenty years, until he became a producer. Executive Producer on *The Last Temptation of Christ*.
AMY ROBINSON	Teresa in *Mean Streets*. Co-producer of *After Hours*.
MICHAEL BALLHAUS	Cinematographer for *After Hours*, *The Color of Money*, *The Last Temptation of Christ*, and *GoodFellas*.
GRIFFIN DUNNE	Paul Hackett in *After Hours*, which he also co-produced.
ROSANNA ARQUETTE	Marcy in *After Hours* and Paulette in *New York Stories: Life Lessons*.
MICHAEL OVITZ	President and founding member of Creative Artists Agency (CAA). He has represented Scorsese since 1986.
PAUL NEWMAN	Eddie Felson in *The Color of Money*. Won the Academy Award for Best Actor for his performance in the film.

RICHARD PRICE	Wrote the scripts for *The Color of Money, New York Stories: Life Lessons,* and the *Bad* video with Michael Jackson.
JOE REIDY	Assistant director for *The Color of Money, The Last Temptation of Christ, GoodFellas,* and *Cape Fear.*
MICHAEL EISNER	Chairman and Chief Executive Officer of Walt Disney Company, which produced *The Color of Money* and *New York Stories: Life Lessons.* As President of Production at Paramount, supported Scorsese in his first effort to make *The Last Temptation of Christ.*
TOM POLLOCK	Chief Executive Officer of Universal Pictures, which produced *The Last Temptation of Christ.*
AIDAN QUINN	Cast as Jesus for the 1983 production of *The Last Temptation of Christ.*
WILLEM DAFOE	Jesus in *The Last Temptation of Christ.*
VERNA BLOOM	June in *After Hours,* and Mary, the Mother of Jesus, in *The Last Temptation of Christ.*
PEGGY GORMLEY	Martha, the sister of Lazarus, in *The Last Temptation of Christ.*
PAUL HERMAN	Pool hustler in *The Color of Money,* the Apostle Phillip in *The Last Temptation of Christ,* a cop in *New York Stories: Life Lessons,* and a wiseguy in *GoodFellas.*
VIC ARGO	McDate in *Boxcar Bertha,* mafioso in *Mean Streets,* the deli owner in *Taxi Driver,* and the Apostle Peter in *The Last Temptation of Christ.*
MICHAEL BEEN	The Apostle John in *The Last Temptation of Christ.*
ALAN ROSENBERG	The Apostle Thomas in *The Last Temptation of Christ.*
LEO BURMESTER	The Apostle Nathaniel in *The Last Temptation of Christ.*
TOMAS ARANA	Lazarus in *The Last Temptation of Christ.*
GARY BASARABA	The Apostle Andrew in *The Last Temptation of Christ.*
PETER GABRIEL	Composed the score for *The Last Temptation of Christ.* Made a cameo appearance in *New York Stories: Life Lessons.*
BARBARA DE FINA	Producer of *The Color of Money, The Last Temptation of Christ, New York Stories: Life Lessons, GoodFellas,* and *Cape Fear.*

NICK NOLTE	Lionel Dobie in *New York Stories: Life Lessons.*
NESTOR ALMENDROS	Cinematographer for *New York Stories: Life Lessons.*
JEFFREY KATZENBERG	Chairman of Walt Disney Studios. Worked closely with Scorsese during the Paramount attempt to mount *The Last Temptation of Christ.*
NICHOLAS PILEGGI	Author of *Wise Guy: Life in a Mafia Family.* Co-wrote, with Scorsese, the script for *GoodFellas.*
PAUL SORVINO	Paul Cicero in *GoodFellas.*
CHRIS SERRONE	The young Henry Hill in *GoodFellas.*
FRANK DILEO	Tuddy in *GoodFellas.*
RAY LIOTTA	Henry Hill in *GoodFellas.*
ELAINE KAGAN	Henry Hill's mother in *GoodFellas.*
WESLEY STRICK	Screenwriter for *Cape Fear.*

MARTIN SCORSESE
A JOURNEY

INTRODUCTION

"No, actually, I met Martin Scorsese twenty-five years ago in the mop room of the convent where I was studying to be a nun."

That rattled Antonio's espresso cup and halted the conversation we had begun on the terrace of the Excelsior Hotel on the Lido, headquarters for the 1988 Venice Film Festival, where Scorsese's *The Last Temptation of Christ* was to have its European premiere.

Antonio had already told me that for him Scorsese was "the most important American director—a European's sensibility, yet *molto* Hollywood." Although he was a film critic for a prominent Italian chain of newspapers, Antonio, like many of his continental colleagues, wrote from an intellectual perspective on art and culture. I was not to confuse him with the packs of paparazzi, tabloid reporters, and TV crews who jammed the hotel's lobby. They had come from all over the world, drawn by the controversy that boiled up when fundamentalist groups in the U.S. attacked *The Last Temptation of Christ* as blasphemous. The media hoped for a demonstration here in Venice, or at least picket lines. Banner headlines on the cover of the Italian magazine *Eva Express* proclaimed, "*Gesu Nudo.* Excommunicate Scorsese. Photos inside." In fact, everyone in *Eva* was mostly "nudo," caught unaware by *Eva*'s long lens. This included a matronly Mrs. Luciano Pavarotti, who had mistakenly assumed she was sunbathing in private. And *they* had the nerve to condemn Scorsese.

"That's what comes from religion," Antonio had said. "Why would a sophisticated artist like Scorsese choose a religious—*the* religious—subject?" His shrug implied that serious Europeans left such preoccupations to right-wing politicians and anthropologists interested in folklore.

And why were we at the festival? he had asked. I told him that I was a writer working on a book about Scorsese—an oral history, really—which would include interviews with his collaborators: actors, writers, cinematographers, his parents, early teachers. My husband was the photographer on the project.

And had I met Scorsese?

Yes.

Here in Venice?

No.

In Hollywood? In New York?

No. No.

And so we come to the mop room. In 1966, when I was a college undergraduate and candidate for the religious life, my two favorite subjects were James Joyce and the movies. No conflict there. Didn't Fellini, Antonioni, and Bergman use the cinematic equivalent of Joyce's stream-of-consciousness, non-linear narrative and many-leveled allusions? And didn't Joyce's work resemble the movies, with its flashbacks, flashforwards, montages, and cross-cutting? Joyce's epiphany theory also described what film at its best could do, create a pattern in which: "the relation of the parts . . . are adjusted to the special point, [so that] we recognise that it is *that* thing which it is. Its soul, its whatness, leaps to us from the vestment of its appearance. The soul of the commonest object, the structure of which is so adjusted, seems to us radiant. The object achieves its epiphany." (*Stephen Hero*) (I didn't say that word for word to Antonio—I looked it up later.)

At that time, I wanted to devise a topic for my senior thesis that would allow me to explore this idea further. By the greatest happenstance or providence, I found an article about a then-new phenomena, student filmmakers. Martin Scorsese's prize-winning film *It's Not Just You, Murray!* was described as an innovatively structured comedy that used parody. It sounded intriguing, and I wrote to him at New York University asking to see it. He sent a print. As it turned out, *Murray* reminded me a great deal of Joyce's story "Grace." Both were the work of young artists beginning their careers, with themes at the heart of their art. Both men found significance in everyday objects; both used parody and stylistic allusions; both concerned themselves with the salvation of an ordinary guy from the neighborhood and provided the audience with an epiphany the main character chooses not to see.

"All very interesting," said Antonio, "but you call that meeting Scorsese?"

"Wait—I have to tell you about the letters."

"Letters?"

"Yes—twelve and fifteen pages long, single-spaced on legal-sized sheets, jammed with such an enthusiasm for movies that words ran together and the pressure he applied to the keys left the paper riddled with holes."

"As he talks," Antonio said.

"Exactly!"

Scorsese sent me reading lists. He recommended *Famous Screenplays* as a source for "the conventional well-written screenplay," Ingmar Bergman's scripts, and those for *Hiroshima, Mon Amour, Last Year at Marienbad*, and *The Misfits*, all available by mail order from the Gotham Book Mart. He also told me to study the pictures of John Ford and Alfred Hitchcock, of John Huston and Howard Hawks. This last suggestion was surprising. In the 1960s, American students tended to look to Europe for the cinematic masters.

Of course he also included Fellini, Truffaut, Godard, Rossellini, Resnais, Antonioni—though where he thought I could get to see *Hiroshima, Mon Amour* in a rural Indiana convent, I don't know. But it was great to think I could learn about film by recalling the Hollywood movies I'd loved since childhood. The letters also suggested the best way to watch a film. Don't be swayed by critics. "Decide for yourself," he wrote. "Of all things, do not view a film and dissect it while you are watching. Just sit there and see whether or not you enjoy it." Then decide why or why not. It was possible to "recognize the greatness or importance of a film" without really enjoying it. And sometimes, after many viewings, a film may suddenly reveal itself and become a favorite.

He laid out the elements of film. First came the visual—images qualified by light and movement. Shots, sequences, dollies, zooms. Detailed examples from *Citizen Kane, The Third Man*, and *The Trial* accompanied each definition. Then he discussed sound, music, and "the greatest and most important element"—editing. He went on for pages and pages. "Excuse the typing, typographical errors and cross outs," he wrote, "I have to write down what I am thinking before I forget it."

Antonio nodded. He was caught up by the idea of the twenty-five-year-old film student, on the brink of a brilliant career, explaining with patience and great enthusiasm the basics of film and his ideas about it to an aspiring nun. But what about the mop room? That was the only space where I could improvise a private study and store all those Gotham Book Mart imports.

Later that day the press saw *The Last Temptation of Christ*, and afterwards Scorsese met with a small group of journalists. They were confused. The movie had not seemed scandalous or blasphemous. Antonio, in fact, had found it a little *too* reverent—"like a *signa*, the holy picture the priest gave to me at my first communion."

Then Scorsese began to talk in very simple terms about his own faith, his love of Jesus, and the long struggle to make *The Last Temptation of Christ*. "I made it as a prayer, an act of worship. I wanted to be a priest. My whole life has been movies and religion. That's it. Nothing else."

The journalists exchanged surprised looks. Was he serious? They could understand if Scorsese wished to demythologize Jesus, or even, as the protesters said, use the story of Christ to shock audiences (artistically, of course). But Scorsese was saying he had made the movie because he believed in Jesus and his teachings.

Somehow, as the interview went on, Scorsese's personal confidences broke the journalists' reserve. The woman from Finland said she had little religious background, but the film had made her see what she had

MARTIN SCORSESE AS HE TALKS WITH A SMALL GROUP OF FOREIGN JOURNALISTS AT THE 1988 VENICE INTERNATIONAL FILM FESTIVAL, WHERE *THE LAST TEMPTATION OF CHRIST* PREMIERED.

assumed was a bankrupt myth in a new way. The journalist from Holland was encouraged to see that Scorsese, with his Roman Catholic upbringing, and the scriptwriter Paul Schrader, raised in the Dutch Reform tradition, could find common ground. Even Antonio chimed in and the conference became an occasion for personal religious testimony.

The same spirit infused the whole festival. The large press conference that afternoon with Scorsese, Willem Dafoe (Jesus), Harvey Keitel (Judas), and Barbara Hershey (Mary Magdalene) featured a debate on liberation theology. The elegant audience at the Palace of Cinema that evening, who expected a *cause célèbre*, instead found themselves engaged by a challenging, serious movie. And at the bar of the Excelsior late that night, Harry Dean Stanton (St. Paul) was locked in intense discussion about what St. Paul had believed and what he did or did not have in common with the street-corner Southern Baptist preacher he played in *Wise Blood*. When a French radio technician asked him to buy him "one for the canal" in honor of *Paris, Texas*, Harry Dean asked him if he thought Jesus had really intended an organization like the church Paul helped to establish.

But the most evocative moment of the festival came quietly, away from the glitter and the glare. Many festival-goers who did not have press passes or coveted screening tickets wanted very much to see *The Last Temptation of Christ*. They had come to Venice not to see and be seen, make deals, or promote a film, but to listen to directors and to watch their movies. Finally a scrawled sign appeared on bulletin boards: "Special screening, 1:40 A.M." Somehow the word was passed and a crowd gathered in front of the now very deserted Palace of Cinema.

My husband and I joined the line. Next to me was the head of a student film society in Bologna. He began to explain why Scorsese's films meant so much to him and the other members of his group. Others in the line joined in, using simplified English, Italian, and French, along with gestures, to communicate. What would *The Last Temptation* be like? Why had he made it?

After the movie, we gathered outside again. The gray mix of sea and sky lightened to pink. Dawn came to the Lido. The birds started up and morning workers appeared. But no one went home. We stayed doing what everyone in Venice—movie stars or journalists, directors or paparazzi, deal makers or bartenders at the Excelsior—found themselves doing at

UNIVERSAL STUDIOS CHAIRMAN TOM POLLOCK,
LAST TEMPTATION EDITOR THELMA SCHOONMAKER, AND
BRITISH DIRECTOR MICHAEL POWELL, IN VENICE FOR THE
1988 FILM FESTIVAL.

some point during the festival. We stood around talking about Jesus.

Two years later, Scorsese would return to the Venice Film Festival with *GoodFellas* and win the Best Director's award. I am sure that film generated many great conversations around cafe tables, too. And if you are reading this, I am sure that Scorsese's films have inspired animated discussion for you, as they have for me with all kinds of people. I hope so, because that is the premise of this book. The movies, of course, speak powerfully for themselves. And now video cassettes and discs provide the means of seeing them over and over. Scorsese has even recorded commentaries for *Raging Bull* and *Taxi Driver*, available on a separate track of the Voyager Company's video disc. As the years go by, scholarly and critical studies of his films will begin to appear. Scorsese has accumulated impressive archives, valuable not only in tracing his own career, but also as a source for the history of movies over the last thirty years. Hopefully Scorsese will some-day emulate his admired friend Michael Powell and write his autobiography. *Scorsese on Scorsese*, a collection of speeches given in England, is a start.

In this book, I wanted to stay with the movies and the people who worked on them. My model as I began writing was that dawn seminar in Venice. At the core are the interviews with Scorsese—in his office, on the sets of his movies, and in a series of classes at New York Unversity. But I also hope the book has that sense of a tale told by many voices. I hope, too, you can feel the personal connection the people I talked to feel with the movies they have helped to create. Films as diverse as *Mean Streets, Alice Doesn't Live Here Anymore, Raging Bull*, and *The Last Temptation of Christ* compelled great commitment from the people who worked on them, because they knew Scorsese was never merely producing a product; he was the priest of the imagination, presiding over a ritual putting together of elements.

This brings me back to James Joyce and Scorsese. Both men spent their childhoods convinced that they had a vocation. Joyce never made it into the Jesuits, but Scorsese actually entered the New York archdiocesan seminary. He stayed only one year, but intended to join an order of priests after high school.

As an altar boy at Old St. Patrick's Cathedral on Mulberry Street, Scorsese was, at an early age, initiated into to the priestly caste. He assisted the priest in the complicated and precise set of actions that made up the Mass. He stood apart from the congregation. Only the altar boys heard the sacred words the priest whispered, "*Hoc est enim Corpus meus*" ("This is my body"), and, "*Hic est enim Cali Sanguinis meis* . . . " ("This is the Chalice of my Blood . . . which shall be shed for you and for many unto the forgiveness of sins"). After speaking these words, the priest genuflected, then lifted up the host and elevated the chalice. An altar boy shook a set of hand bells. Scorsese participated in this sequence over and over again, each time reliving the same dramatic buildup: the transformation, then the revelation, and then the bells.

Since the Second Vatican Council the Catholic liturgy has become less of a performance, more of communal act celebrated with the people in their own language. But even in Scorsese's youth, the Mass, though solemn, was never stark. The music, the flames of the candles, the colors of the vestments, the statues and stained glass windows of the church made a rich mosaic. Everything carried special significance: Gold was for great feasts such as Christmas, purple for the seasons of penance, red for martyrs, white for the Blessed Mother and the great saints, and green for ordinary Sundays and days when no special saint was commemorated. The brief biographies of the saint of the day featured stories of heroic martyrs, missionaries, great scholars—extraordinary people whose lives were much more dramatic than those of anyone in the parish. Every article of clothing, every piece of altar linen, each sacred vessel, even the candles had to meet the specifications of the Catholic Church: pure beeswax, unalloyed gold, 100 percent cotton. The clouds of incense that Scorsese, as an altar boy, sent rising over the heads of the family and neighbors burned from special coals. Everything had to be perfect, for when all the actions were performed correctly, and the sacred words spoken, the bread and wine were no longer what they appeared to be. They had become the body and blood of Christ, who was truly present, just as he had been at the Last Supper, on the cross, at his birth.

This is a profound concept to embrace at age seven, but once held, it transforms the imagination and creates artists such as James Joyce and Martin Scorsese. Every Catholic school child learns the difference between a sign and a symbol. A sacrament is a sign that effects what it signifies. It is not *like* something else, it *is* something else. The language which defined the sacraments and mysteries of the faith came from St. Thomas Aquinas, who based his theology, as well as his theories of art, on Aristotelian philosophy. As James Joyce said, the "sensualist" Aquinas won out over more Platonic theologians. Christ's presence in the sacrament of the Eucharist was not symbolic; it was real. The Church held onto this doctrine against attacks from every direction. The bread and wine were not props in some reenactment of the Last Supper meant to remind the congregation of Jesus. Jesus was not *thought* into being. He was there. Nor did his presence depend on the worthiness of the priest. If the priest was ordained and the words, actions, and elements were there licitly, Christ really became present and offered himself as food. At his first communion, Scorsese received the host and Jesus became part of him. A sense of wonder and mystery marked the child who took religion seriously.

At a very early age, he imbibed a sacramental view of the world. He believed that transcendent moments could be reached through material means—the bread and wine of the Eucharist, the waters of baptism, and the oils used in the ordination of priests.

Another reality surrounded and permeated the world of the senses. That supernatural reality could be reached through the things of nature.

Jesus, in whom the union of the natural and supernatural reached perfection, was himself "the Sacrament of the Encounter with God." As a child, Scorsese saw the sacraments as the way to this deeper, more profound, truer world of the spirit. He began to see the artist as one called to a similar task—to arrange the elements of experience until they became signs, effecting what they signified.

The transformation that happened in the Eucharist was called transubstantiation. Scorsese would have learned this word by the third grade. It meant that when the correct form—in this case the words of consecration said by the priest—combined with the proper matter, bread and wine, the substance changed. The objects might remain the same—the bread and wine looked like bread and wine—but the essence was transformed; it was made radiant.

The priests of the imagination—Joyce in his writing, Scorsese in his films—can also be agents of transformation. They create moments of epiphany by finding the visual arrangement of parts that reveal an objects's potential significance, its radiance. And that, too, is a kind of transubstantiation. The image of a yellow taxi emerging from the swirling smoke at the start of *Taxi Driver* comes immediately to mind. But the Joycean quality of Scorsese's work goes beyond such individual images. Scorsese finds his stories and characters in limited, confined worlds—Little Italy, Forty-second Street, a fight ring, a bandstand—close to his own background, just as Joyce's Dublin provided material enough for a lifetime. Scorsese chooses, as Joyce did, to explore this material on a level beyond the rational. He seeks to signify rather than to explain, to create moods and moments rather than to build from conventional plots and structure. This approach requires the audience to respond from the soul as well as the mind, and accept the diffuse and emotional quality of such a response. The effect of Joyce's language cannot be pinned down through analysis. Neither can Scorsese's images be summed up in verbal equivalents. In a sense, both men want their works experienced on a spiritual level.

For a Catholic schoolchild in the 1950s, every soul was a cosmic battleground on which the forces of God and the devil contend. It did not matter whether that soul belonged to you or to a failed hood, a street-corner kid, a driven musician, a prizefighter, housewife, prostitute, or taxi driver; in the drama of salvation each one was as important as the Pope himself. When Scorsese says Jake La Motta's story in *Raging Bull* is about redemption, he speaks in a way that is second nature to him. If Scorsese's characters concern themselves with the existence of God, guilt and expiation, and man's ultimate end, that is because Martin Scorsese grew up discussing these things with friends over Chinese food.

Scorsese's characters define and seek redemption in different ways. But all want to go beyond the narrow role that a materialist society assigns them. Murray finds transcendence by "living good"; for J.R. in *Who's That Knocking*, salvation lies in a "pure love"; and Charlie, a later development of the same character in *Mean Streets*, wants to be saved by saving Johnny Boy, who would be happy just to exist. Travis Bickle in *Taxi Driver* thinks that if he sweeps away the garbage, he will be cleansed. Music and the road seem the way of redemption for the members of The Band in *The Last Waltz*, for Alice in *Alice Doesn't Live Here Anymore*, and for Jimmy Doyle in *New York, New York*. Women like Francine Evans (*New York, New York*) and Teresa (*Mean Streets*) will be saved if they can love without destroying themselves. Jake La Motta in *Raging Bull* tells himself that if he can stand up to all the punches, his redemption will be assured. Rupert Pupkin wants simply to be the "King of Comedy," Eddie Felson (*The Color of Money*) wants to recapture his pool-playing excellence, and Paul Hackett (*After Hours*) just wants to get uptown.

Temptation comes from the fallen world outside and from the passions within. Somehow lust and pride and jealousy are more palpable than grace. But in Scorsese's films his characters do steal sacramental moments—Johnny Boy and Charlie in the Russian Orthodox graveyard, Francine and Jimmy in the snow, Iris and Travis at breakfast.

Raging Bull closes with a parable from the New Testament. Jesus cures a blind man, but the Pharisees tell the man that he has been cured by a sinner. The formerly blind man says, "I don't know if he is a sinner or not a sinner. All I know is I was blind and now I see." This same cure figures prominently in *The Last Temptation of Christ*. The story comes from a very long description in the Gospel of St. John. There are dialogues between Jesus and the people, Jesus and the blind man, the Pharisees and the blind man's parents, the Pharisees and the blind man, that start to sound like a comedy routine. One point of debate is, Why is he blind? Who sinned? Was it the man or his parents? Neither, Jesus says, and proceeds to cure him. Offended by the miracle, the Pharisees castigate the parents. "Don't bother us," the parents say. "Talk to him. He's of age." Finally the man has enough. "I was blind," he says, "and now I see." Obviously there's more going on here than simply a story about physical sight.

Scorsese follows this passage from St. John at the end of *Raging Bull* with "Thanks Haig," a tribute to his N.Y.U. teacher. Haig Manoogian, as Scorsese says, made him "see value in my own experiences." This "seeing" allowed Scorsese to comprehend and ultimately to make a sacrament of experience—a sign that effects what it signifies. Matter is mysterious. Under the right circumstances it can even become the body of Christ.

Scorsese's Italian-American background did not encourage introspection the way Joyce's Dublin, full of the "agen bite of inwit," did. But the theological concepts he learned from the Irish nuns and Italian priests at Old St. Patrick's Cathedral stretched his mind, challenged his imagination.

None of this is to deny the negatives of Catholic education, especially pre-Vatican II. Certain failures of both the system and of individuals, especially with regard to sexuality, the dignity of women, and social justice, are undeniable. But I am speaking of early days, when the imagination is pliant, the nuns like you, the priests are friendly, and your parish is a place like Old St. Pat's, proud of its history.

Every Scorsese film yields moments of transcendence, but the viewer must be open, must take part. If Scorsese had presented a merely symbolic Jesus—so neutral that any interpretation could apply—there would have been no controversy. But the Jesus on the screen in the crucifixion scene of *The Last Temptation of Christ* is graphically present. We see the blood. We hear the pounding of the nails. The world tilts, the suffering of Jesus becomes so palpable that we must experience it in and of itself. The pain is too immediate to be a symbol or concept. A man is dying and he is Jesus. Scorsese had said at the Venice Film Festival press conference, "I wanted him to be a character you cared about when he died."

Scorsese, with his sacramental background, could not portray Jesus, or any of the characters in his movies, as projections of his own mind. He looks to reality. He arranges the material hoping for that moment of transcendence. The accidents remain the same, but the essence changes, and we go through the flickering image to the soul of another person. Why else do artists struggle but to make present reality, to bring us a step closer to unapproachable light?

But the sacraments are meant to create and affirm the community.

Scorsese takes the matter of images, music, performance, and imposes a form on it. He adjusts the elements. The image attains its radiance. We apprehend its truth. A Scorsese movie grips us, pulls us beyond ourselves and enlarges our view, and somehow brings us closer together.

The question arises, Why does Scorsese expend such energy on prodigals? Why Jake La Motta, Johnny Boy, Eddie Felson, Lionel Dobie, and Henry Hill? One answer may be found in the parables (which also have a prominent place in *The Last Temptation of Christ*). "What shepherd, having a hundred sheep, would not leave the ninety-nine to search for one that is lost? What woman, having ten pieces of silver, and losing one, does not light the lamp and sweep the floor to find it?," Jesus asks. He goes on to tell the story of a dissolute son who disgraces and leaves his family. When he returns out of desperation, willing to become a servant in his father's house, his father instead embraces him and orders a great feast. This annoys the more conventionally good older brother. "But he was lost," the father says, "and now he's found." Scorsese films reveal a similar sort of compassion.

I started with the mop room and now I will end in a convent chapel. Soon after returning from Venice, we visited my father's cousin, Sister Erigenia, one hundred years old. She had been a nun for more than eighty years—most of those as a first grade teacher. She lived with sixty other nuns—thirty of them over ninety. That Sunday at Mass the priest read those same parables to them. I looked around the chapel. No prodigal sons here. These women would have a right to complain if a sinner showed up and got the best table. But that's not how Sister Erigenia saw it. "Jesus wants us to know the depth of God's love. Love always looks for the lost one, and aren't we all the prodigal sometimes?"

Before leaving Venice, after the festival, I had found myself standing near an outside wall of St. Mark's Basilica, in a small alcove away from the crowded entrance. Two plaques commemorated former patriarchs of Venice—Pope John XXIII and Pope John Paul I, shepherds both. I wondered if the church would have received *The Last Temptation of Christ* differently had either of them been alive.

Scorsese's films are made for those described by Isaiah, who in burning sands search for the Holy Way. *Mean Streets, Raging Bull, GoodFellas, The Last Temptation of Christ*—indeed, all of Scorsese's movies—are for those with a journey to make.

ONE

ELIZABETH STREET

ITALIANAMERICAN (1974)

"I GET MY TIMING FROM MY MOTHER."
—MARTIN SCORSESE

MARTIN SCORSESE discovered his parents while shooting the documentary *Italianamerican* in 1974. "I had seen them as parents, not as people." he later said. "Suddenly they became people. And I saw the story of their life as a love story."

Certainly, many artists trace their artistic inspiration to their families. But Scorsese not only roots his movies in the rich material of his past—he actually puts his parents on the screen. In the documentary, they are themselves, but Catherine Scorsese also plays characters in *It's Not Just You, Murray!* and *Mean Streets*, and her husband joins her in *New York, New York* and in subsequent films. At first they appear as extras or in very small roles. But in *GoodFellas*, both Scorsese parents play important parts, and Mrs. Scorsese, in her performance as the gangster Tommy DeVito's mother, steals a scene from Joe Pesci, Robert De Niro, and Ray Liotta. Even when they are not featured, the Scorseses frequently visit the sets of their son's movies, both in New York and on location.

In *Italianamerican*, Scorsese reveals the emotional structure of his family and the source of the stories he tells. He shot *Italianamerican* in his family's apartment on Elizabeth Street on the Lower East Side of Manhattan. The Scorseses had worked for many years in New York's garment industry: Charles Scorsese pressed couture gowns. Catherine Scorsese made samples for designers. Martin Scorsese and his brother Frank grew up in this apartment, on the block where their parents had been born.

In the first moments of *Italianamerican*, Scorsese's voice directs the camera and sound men and positions his parents. It is his last moment of control. In an animated off-camera conversation, his mother asks, "Where should I sit? Marty, is this okay? Charlie, move over." The first shot shows Mrs. Scorsese surrounded by cables and lights. She asks, "Is it time to start?" but the movie has already begun. This is no ordinary documentary. Nothing is distanced. The camera is not allowed to be invisible or detached. This is *Italianamerican*. Like any other guest, the camera must participate, and the crew must eat the spaghetti sauce that simmers in Mrs. Scorsese's kitchen.

Both the sauce and the kitchen play important roles in the film. Scorsese's camera follows his mother as she leaves the living room conversation

MARTIN SCORSESE'S PARENTS, CHARLES AND CATHERINE SCORSESE, TALK WITH MARY PAT KELLY AND LYNN GARAFOLA IN THEIR ELIZABETH STREET APARTMENT IN 1987.

to chop onions or roll meatballs. She hurries back to finish a thought or story, then heads for the stove to stir the sauce or add another spice. As she cooks, she explains. Occasionally her voice takes on a Julia Child tone, but the expressions are all her own.

In the kitchen mother and son exchange confidences. She seems upset. After some coaxing, Scorsese finds out the reason. His father had talked about the large number of bars that filled the neighborhood when the Irish lived on the Lower East Side. It's not nice to talk that way about the Irish. It's true, what his father says is true, but to say it in a film . . . ? Scorsese reassures her. Mrs. Scorsese returns to her sauce. But this is the quintessential moment. A son learns reality from his father but his mother teaches him to shape it. In Scorsese's movies, humor often lightens harsh situations. Digression and emotion can count for more than the plot.

MARTIN SCORSESE: The movie *Italianamerican,* a film I made about my parents in 1974, is, I think, the best film I ever made. It really *freed* me in style. I was able to shoot this footage, in 16 millimeter, of my parents in their apartment on the Lower East Side. We were having dinner on a Saturday and a Sunday and I shot it in six hours. My friends made up some questions about immigration, about how the family came over, because it was made as part of a series called "Storm of Strangers" for the National Endowment for the Humanities for the bicentennial of 1976. It had to be twenty-eight minutes long, they said. One was on the Irish, one on the Jews, Chinese, Polish, etc. They asked me to do the Italians. I said no. But finally I said, "Yes, I will, if we don't do it the way that you normally see. I don't want to go back to 1901 with stock footage and a narrator saying, 'In 1901 . . .'" But I did wind up taking some of the footage from the archives; it is really interesting. I said, "Let's ask my parents these questions." My parents worked in the garment district all their lives. They stick to the emotions. That's what I wanted to hear, some emotion.

My mother talks a great deal, and my father is quite reticent, usually. He sat on one side of the big couch in the living room and my mother sat on the other side. The camera panned over. And she said, "Well, what do you want me to say?" I said, "Well, just, you know, talk." There were no questions. So she looks at my father and says, "Why are you sitting over there?" Then I *knew.* I said, "This is going to be easier than I thought. In fact, I'm going to lose control of the thing if I don't watch out." It's a whole other thing up there with your parents, trying to control them. It's quite extraordinary, and I felt it came out in the film.

My father says, "What do you mean? I'm sitting over here because I want to sit here." She says, "What are you doing? Look, this man is married forty-two years and he sits over there. Why don't you come over to me? Why don't you talk to me?"

We're sitting there, watching this, and my father says, "What do you say to a person after forty-two years?" And I said, "Cut. That's it." Then we go into the kitchen, the dining room, and ask some questions while they're eating. I was able to learn things about my parents I didn't know. I learned where they came from. I learned how they lived in the twenties and thirties in New York. They were born in 1912 and 1913 on Elizabeth Street, downtown. And I saw it as the story of these two *people*. I had seen them as parents, not as people. Then suddenly they became people, and it was a love story.

I get my timing from my mother. She is a great storyteller, humorous, emotional. My father tells good stories too, but his are more somber. She has the emotion. But the structure is not straightforward. Even now I get interested in the emotion of a shot and sometimes forget to give the audience the plot information they need.

Italianamerican tells a series of stories. But because of the structuring of the questions and their answers, a bigger story came out overall. And that was a work-in-progress. It was terrific. It was fun. It was learning. We shot medium shots of people talking, and intercut with some music over stills of them. To me it seemed very, very strong. It smashed all those preconceptions about what a film should look like and how a film should be presented. It also freed me, in a sense. It streamlined the style for *Taxi Driver*. And in *Raging Bull*, we didn't give a damn. We didn't care about transitions, really. What I should say is, we didn't care about *artful* transitions.

In certain parts of *Italianamerican*, my mother is talking, and we put in twenty frames of black. Then we cut back and she's taking another breath, and she keeps going. It looks like the film was off for a second. Who cares? It doesn't matter. I said, "This is amazing."

• • •

Mr. and Mrs. Scorsese no longer live on Elizabeth Street, but they still go downtown for the best bread in the city and to visit old friends. Their memories of those days are fresh, and they share them gladly. Their interaction, the way they tell their stories, reverberates in their son's work. In the following conversation, Mr. Scorsese carries the thread of the story. Mrs. Scorsese provides the emotion. Sometimes these lead her onto tangents, but the story circles back, like a jazz riff. Sometimes they may disagree on details. Was Mr. Scorsese's heart attack in the airport as they left Chicago or at Kennedy when they arrived home? Each remembers a different place, but they agree on how it *felt*. There was confusion, worry, and an overcharging cab driver to inject a banal note.

Visiting with the Scorseses is like watching one of their son's movies. To get the flavor of Scorsese's style, listen to his parents. Sharing a meal helps. Mrs. Scorsese expresses herself in her cooking—not in gourmet one-upmanship, but in a generous bounty of calzone and pizza, chicken with garlic and lemon, ricotta cheesecake and pound cake dusted with powdered sugar. If the stories stir painful memories, then food soothes. The conversation constantly draws a guest (or audience) into the center of the family and its experiences. And though the riffs may go off in a different direction, the Scorseses always finish together.

MR. CHARLES SCORSESE: I was born on Elizabeth Street, in the Lower East Side of New York. My father and mother came from Sicily, *di Palermo*—actually, from a town called Polizzi Generose. It means "generous." The name came after a certain war, when soldiers went there, and these people took care of them and gave them everything they wanted, and so the soldiers called them "generous people."

MRS. CATHERINE SCORSESE: Mine were from the town of Gemina. I visited my mother's half-sister there a couple of years ago. She was old. I could only stay for a day. She said to me, "No, you've got to stay longer. I've been waiting for you for years." I said, "I can't. I have the ticket to go back. I'll come back to see you." "You'll never see me any more," she said. Poor thing. She died after that.

MR. SCORSESE: They got the butcher up from bed to come make sausages for us.

MRS. SCORSESE: Now her son is bothering us to go back to Italy. He built a beautiful house there, he sent us a picture. She's got four sons, two in Italy, two in Chicago. And when we made *The Color of Money*, I finally got the son's telephone number in Chicago, and I said to Charlie, "Marty's going to make a picture up there, so let's see if we can find him." I called him up, "This is the first time I'm talking to you. We're going to be in Chicago. My son is going to make a film."

To make a long story short, we finally got there and they came over—and you should see what they brought! A grocery store! A gallon of wine, a gallon of vinegar, five pounds of coffee, cheese and olives. They came to the set to see Marty direct. They were looking all over for the director and there was Marty standing right there saying hello to them. They were looking right over his head. They said in Italian, "But he's, you know, short." I said, "What did you expect? We're not big people!"

It was Marty who got us back in touch with the family in Italy. He called me from Italy once and says to me, "I want to know Grandma's sister's family name." He wrote it down. And a funny thing, when he got into town, he was asking people where he could find this name, and everybody shunned him. So Marty called me back, "What's happening? You gave me this name, and everybody ignored us." It turned out someone by that name had been arrested one time, and he escaped.

MR. SCORSESE: No, he disappeared. They thought Marty was the FBI or something.

MRS. SCORSESE: Marty found out, when he came home, that I had given him the wrong name. He said, "You know, they could have killed us."

MR. SCORSESE: No, they wouldn't bother him. They thought he was the FBI. They wouldn't bother him.

MRS. SCORSESE: Marty said, "They shut the doors! It was terrible, Mother. I got so scared. So we had to leave." I had given him the wrong name, but then our real cousin found out that Martin was looking for him.

A woman from Elizabeth Street went there, to the same town. Someone there says to her, "Where do you come from?" "From Elizabeth Street."

"Oh," he says, "Do you know Charlie Scorsese?" "Sure, I know him. He lives across the street from me. But he moved and I don't know where he moved. But I know where he goes to take a shave." So he says, "Oh, good. Give him this letter." Anna—the woman's name was Anna—she left her number at the barbershop, and I said, "Who the hell is Anna?" I called up and she lived in Brooklyn. She said, "I lived across the street from you. Listen, I have a letter to give to your husband. But I have to come to your house and read it." What can I tell you? That's how we got in contact with the family in Italy.

Let me tell you how I started in the garment industry. When I graduated from junior high, I wanted to become something, go to high school and become something. My mother said to me, "No, you can't go to high school, because it will cost me money and I can't afford it. You have to go to work." My mother had nine children. We all had to help out. So naturally, I looked for work. There was this friend of ours, my mother used to make a nice cup of coffee for her. She saw me at home one morning, and she said to me, "You graduated?" I told her I was finished, but I couldn't get a job. She said to me, "Would you like to come with me? I work in a doll clothes factory." I said, "What's the difference?" She asked, "Do you know how to run a machine?" I said yes, so she got me in. I learned a lot. You start to learn, then you get better and better and better.

I stayed with the dolls quite a while, until I was about seventeen. But I wanted to go into dresses, so I met another friend, and she said, "What are you doing? Listen, I own a dress factory on Second Avenue. It's walking distance. Do you know how to run the machine? Would you like to try over here?" I say, "Why not? I can't lose anything." The first day I think I made four dresses, a quarter a dress, something like that. And I started to get better and better.

Then I started to keep company with Charlie, who lived across from me on Elizabeth Street. He used to play his guitar, sitting on the fire escape.

MR. SCORSESE: I used to do arias.

MRS. SCORSESE: He was a big showoff.

MR. SCORSESE: I used to serenade her from across the street.

21

CATHERINE AND CHARLES SCORSESE AT THEIR WEDDING IN 1934.

MRS. SCORSESE: Anyway, I said to myself, "Now I'm starting to keep company . . . "

MR. SCORSESE: Sundays in Washington Square Park, we used to go to play.

MRS. SCORSESE: It was beautiful then.

MR. SCORSESE: It was nice then. We'd get together with all the guitars and ukuleles.

MRS. SCORSESE: Oh, it was beautiful. It was so much fun.

MR. SCORSESE: I always looked at the N.Y.U. college buildings and I used to say, "I hope some day one of my sons will go there." Sure enough, God granted me that wish.

MRS. SCORSESE: So anyway, I figured, "I want to get a nice job because I want to save some money." My brother-in-law was working in a dress factory. So he said to me, "Come and try my place. You won't regret it." So I went up the next day and he introduced me to the boss. He was so wonderful, Mr. Silverman. Rest in peace where he is. I worked for the man thirty-nine years, they used to call him the Jersey King because he was the king of the jersey fabric.

So then I got married in 1934. It's going to be fifty-eight years. My first child, Frankie, was born in 1936, and Marty was born in 1942.

MR. SCORSESE: I was a presser and I enjoyed pressing. I got a kick out of it when the things came out right. When I started to work there were no steam lines, so I worked with a sixteen-pound iron, a bucket of water, a sponge, and a cloth. When you pressed it *was* pressing. When they came up with the steam all you were doing was wet-washing the whole thing, but I enjoyed that, too. It was a challenge to me. I used to press samples, it was satisfying and a challenge to me.

When they told me, "Make it like this here, make the lines look this way or that way," I would say, "Sure." They'd walk away and when I finished it,

I'd tell them, "This is what you want?" "Yeah." But I did it *my* way. As long as I gave it to them the way they wanted.

It was always a challenge in the dress line. They used to come to me for every little thing. They gave me dresses, the detailed work which was tedious. I did the fine stuff.

But pressing was seasonal, so I'd take unemployment insurance for thirteen weeks, then they'd extend it to another six weeks. There were about eight of us, all pressers. We were all out of work, and we would hang around this poolroom on Elizabeth Street. At about twelve o'clock in the afternoon one day, a couple of detectives came over and they said, "What are you guys doing here?" I said, "Well, we got a day off. Business is slow, we're off." "What do you do for a living?" "Presser." Right down the line. "Presser, presser, presser." "What are you guys, wiseguys?" We said, "What do you mean, wiseguys?" "Let me look at your hands." We all had callouses on our hands. We were really all pressers. They didn't want to believe us because they thought we were giving them the business. Ah!

I enjoyed my work. When I hung up a dress and it looked like it was pressed I was proud of it. But I didn't make much money in the early days with piecework, I was too much of a perfectionist. But later, I went into gowns. I spent five years in one place, one of the greatest dress houses in the world, the International Dress House. Then they went out of business after so many years. I was making a lot of money, twenty dollars an hour. I could make seven hundred to eight hundred dollars a week. The boss would get sick when he gave us our pay! But *he* wasn't paying us, the *jobber* was. The boss was taking thirty-five cents on every dollar we were getting, but he told me he was jealous that we were making so much money.

Every dress that was made that I liked for my wife, I used to get the samples. Today those same dresses cost you a thousand dollars, and I used to get them for nothing. She was a nice size then.

MRS. SCORSESE: I was a size five. I weighed ninety-four pounds when I was married!

MR. SCORSESE: Yeah. The first time I took her out we were walking on Second Avenue, and I saw a dress in the window. I'll never forget it. It was a brown dress with a leopard collar. I'm walking with her, and I say, "Do you

MARTIN SCORSESE'S MOTHER, CATHERINE, AT AGE
SEVENTEEN, WEARING THE BROWN DRESS HER HUSBAND
BOUGHT HER—"RETAIL"—ON THEIR FIRST DATE.

like that dress? Let's walk inside." We walked inside and I bought it. I
think I paid about fifteen dollars.

MRS. SCORSESE: When I started to keep company with him, his sister
took me to Jersey, to her sister-in-law's place. And I wore that dress. I was
seventeen years old. It looked beautiful on me, because it fit just so. I used
to wear my hair a little higher. She took a picture of me as I walked across
the yard, and it came out beautiful. I'm in motion, walking. So I said to
Charlie the other day, "You know, there's a picture of me when I was
seventeen years old, and I wore the brown woolen dress with the leopard
collar. I don't know where it is." I said, "I think your sister Rose has it." And

sure enough, that week, Rose sent me the picture. But it was a small snapshot. So I said to Charlie, "Christmas is coming. I'm going to play a trick on the boys. Instead of sending them Christmas cards, I'm going to have this photo enlarged, five-by-seven." I sent them one each.

MR. SCORSESE: They couldn't believe she was so thin.

MRS. SCORSESE: They couldn't believe that I was so thin. It was so beautiful. I loved it.

MR. SCORSESE: I bought that dress for her the first day that we went out. She never had to buy another dress retail in her life.

MARTIN SCORSESE: When the Sicilians came over to New York, the first ones must have settled on Elizabeth Street. Then they wrote to their friends in Sicily, "Come over, we've got rooms for you." And they all settled there, on Elizabeth Street. The Neapolitans, somehow, wound up on Mulberry. Each group wanted to be together. So they kept telling their friends, "We've got rooms for you here." The Sicilians brought with them a village culture. A medieval culture or older, based around dukes. The dukes were the *capos* of each village. The *capo* took the place of the government in Sicily. There was no such thing as police. I mean, how could you trust them? After two thousand years, four thousand years of being the penal colony of the world, how could a Sicilian trust the authorities?

There was no such thing as law. It was a feudal system. And they did the same in New York. Village to village. And so you had the man, the *capo*, who would preside over family disagreements—sit down, have a cup of coffee with them, and say, "Now you can't fight like this. It's very bad for the rest of the family. You've got to come together." At the same time, he may have been a killer, too. We don't know. I can't say that. But they were the law in many different respects.

My parents went from Elizabeth Street to Queens, where I was born. But when I was seven I had to survive this major trauma: We moved from Corona, where there were at least a few trees, back to the Lower East Side.

FRANK SCORSESE: The neighborhood was very violent—the gangs, the fights. It could break out instantly. In the middle of the night, you could hear all kinds of fights and violence. You would pull the shade down and go back to sleep, because "this was none of your business." In the event you opened your mouth, you were next. You lived by the sword, you died by the sword. But people felt safe there because they took care of their own.

My brother was a sickly boy. From the day he was born, he had to go for shots for his asthma. Marty had a tough childhood. But I used to keep him close. Take him to the movies. He was six years younger, so I'd look out for him.

My Dad used to caution me in how to be streetwise, the dos and don'ts. He used to say, "Don't see anything, never say anything about anybody, never borrow money, don't borrow cigarettes. You need money, we'll give you money."

. . .

The young Queens immigrant found two refuges, both huge, dim, quiet buildings where miraculous dramas unfolded—Loews cinema on Second Avenue and Old St. Patrick's Cathedral on Mulberry Street. First came the movies.

MARTIN SCORSESE: During the first five or six years of my life, I was mainly in the movie theater. I had asthma as a child and was not able to participate in children's games or sports of any kind, so my parents took me to the movies. My brother did too. It became a place to dream, fantasize, to feel at home.

MR. SCORSESE: I took Marty to the movies a lot. Marty was more for cowboys and Marty, the first time he saw . . . what's that one? My little rosebud? *Citizen Kane*, that's it. *Citizen Kane*, he went crazy for that. And John Wayne? Forget about it!

MRS. SCORSESE: That was his idol.

MR. SCORSESE: And John Huston. Marty used to love movies, but he never said a word. Sometimes I used to go two times a day with him. It was only fifteen cents. And with his asthma, he couldn't play out with the kids, so we'd go to the movies. They stuck in his mind.

■ ■ ■

The high, rose brick walls around Old St. Patrick's Cathedral enclose an entire city block, bounded by Mulberry, Prince, Mott, and Spring Streets. The only trees in the neighborhood shade the tombs in the church's small, two hundred-year-old graveyard. The cornerstone for the first church in the New World to be dedicated to St. Patrick, the patron saint of Ireland, was laid in 1809.

St. Pat's was a church big enough for everyone, but during its early years it belonged to the Irish. When the first Italian immigrants arrived they attended Mass in the church basement. Italian Catholicism, with its folk traditions, seemed too lush and superstitious to the Irish clergy.

It was 1937 before Old St. Patrick's had its first Italian pastor. In the 1940s the Italian community refurbished the building and claimed its history and traditions for its own—including the catacombs where famous New Yorkers are buried. They began to send their children to the Sisters of Charity, who taught in the oldest parochial school in New York.

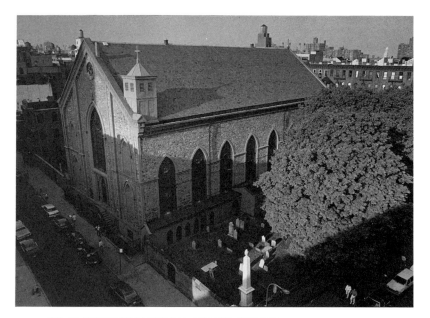

OLD ST. PATRICK'S CATHEDRAL AND THE SURROUNDING NEIGHBORHOOD
ON NEW YORK'S LOWER EAST SIDE.

MARTIN SCORSESE: I became enamored of the church when I was seven. We had Italian priests and Irish nuns. I went to Catholic school and the nuns taught us that this terrific thing happens; at 10:30 every morning God comes down to the altar, and it's great. Also, I had to survive, so religion became a kind of way of survival, too. I tried to understand what the priests were talking about, and deal with that, and after a while, *be* like that—be like a priest, especially the young priests.

My feeling about God was a good feeling. Of course, there were always fears, like, if you see the face of God you're going to die, or the story about the man who tried to save the Ark of the Covenant and touched it, and died on the spot. We always had those fears as kids. But the sense of God was loving and great, really wonderful. Especially Jesus, the incarnation. What he did. I became an altar boy because I loved the ritual, the chance to be close to that special moment when God came down to the altar.

For me, Holy Week was always a very powerful time, even more dramatic than Christmas. The rituals were dramatic. The liturgies were beautiful. The Stations of the Cross were very dramatic. This colored my whole sense of God. I preferred Christmas, as I guess everyone does, because you get gifts, and it's more fun. It's a happy time. But in Holy Week, you have to go through Spy Wednesday, Holy Thursday, Good Friday, and Holy Saturday to reach Easter Sunday. The names alone are dramatic. It's called Passion Week. It's very terrifying. It's a scary time. But it's exhilarating, too, and very beautiful.

A young priest in our parish, Father Principe, was a strong influence on me. Not that everything he liked I liked. For example, he was into the serious films, Fred Zinnemann films and that sort of thing.

I remember the first time Father Principe came to make a speech when I was in sixth grade. I was after one of the Academy Award presentations. He said, "Were all of you kids watching the Academy Awards last night?" We said, "Yes, Father." He then made the analogy between the statuette and a false God—greed, money, and fame!

Of course, he was young, he was only about twenty-five. But he was right about the greed, this concept of me, me, me, and getting up there and getting that award, and feeling, "Now I'm better than . . . " I'll always remember that. "Look at that!" he said. "It looks like the idol Moloch!" Remember Cecil B. De Mille's *Samson and Delilah?*

MARTIN SCORSESE IN 1954, AT AGE ELEVEN, AFTER
HIS CONFIRMATION AT OLD ST. PATRICK'S.

I remember talking to him about Hitchcock's *I Confess.* He was a young
priest, and had to deal with celibacy. "Listen," he said. "This film is just
outrageous." He said you can't have a premise of a film where a man
becomes a priest because he is, in a sense, jilted in a love affair by Anne
Baxter. It's crazy. He said, "The priesthood is demanding. If that's the
reason you go in, you'll never make it. You'll never stay. A few months,
maybe a year, but after a year . . . " And that's, you know, that's the truth.

And I'll never forget the day I saw *Pal Joey.* I was at the Capitol Theatre
with Joe Moralli. We came back on Mulberry Street and said, "Father,
we've seen the greatest picture with Frank Sinatra. He plays this dancer
and he's such a bum, and has all these girls, but he's such a wonderful

character." He said, "What is it with you boys? What's the matter with you? A beautiful day like today, and you're in the movie theater again? You should play basketball!"

I talked to him about a lot of things. Especially after I decided to be a priest. I was very taken by religion. I was also taken by the great story of Jesus and his love. That to me is the most important part of it. The theatricality that went with it was extraordinary, of course, but to me, it was about this incredible character, and about those events.

However, to take a religion like that seriously, and then hit those streets that are full of lawlessness, is another story. You want to know how to combine it and try to put the two together. It's impossible. And this is really just a microcosm of the world, isn't it?

I remember talking to Father Maserone. He was a sweet priest, an older one, and I asked him one time—I suppose I was a college student—about the contradictions in our neighborhood. He said, "You know, I find it difficult. I find it very difficult. I walk past the social club, and they tip their hat to me, and I know. I know what they do. They show me respect and yet I can't reach them, I can't talk to them, I can't do anything. What effect am I having?" he said.

I was quite serious about the priesthood and I went to the minor seminary of the Archdiocese of New York for a year. I planned to enter an order of priests after I graduated from Cardinal Hayes High School.

I grew up with a lot of tough guys. They took care of me, and later, after they died, I found out that they were monsters—bloodsuckers, horrible! But they were very sweet to me. I don't go down to the old neighborhood to see them anymore. I was raised with them, the gangsters and the priests. That's it. Nothing in between. I wanted to be a cleric. I guess the passion I had for religion wound up mixed with film, and now, as an artist, in a way, I'm both gangster and priest.

MR. SCORSESE: Now about Marty. Let me tell you. Marty kept a lot in, this kid. He had it in his mind, everything that he wanted to do.

MRS. SCORSESE: Then he realized that he wanted to become a priest. So I said all right. When he said he wants to become a priest, I said to Charlie, "He's going to Cathedral College. I don't know how it's going to turn out." But after the year was up, they threw him out.

MR. SCORSESE: Don't say they threw him out. It was just he didn't know his Latin.

FATHER FRANK PRINCIPE: In those days you identified yourself by your parish. It wasn't, "I'm from the Lower East Side," but, "I'm from St. Pat's." It was a way of life. The boys of St. Pat's wanted me to talk to them about religion. Not all the time, but they wanted the opportunity. Now, I wasn't any Bing Crosby, but I tried to be around in the schoolyard and sometimes a group would go to supper in Chinatown. They wanted to talk and talk, and I mean speculation, not just morality. For example, the Catholic Worker house, was near us on Chrystie Street. Remember, the Bowery was only one block away. The boys would see these guys stumbling through the neighborhood, urinating in doorways. So they'd come to me, ask about Dorothy Day, "Why is she feeding them? Is she nuts?" And I'd say, "Well, if she's nuts, the Gospel's nuts."

The children of people who were mobsters also came to the parish school. They must have wanted their children to learn right from wrong, or why did they send them?

Marty Scorsese was very intelligent and intense, and with a very, very good sense of humor. He was incarnational in his approach to religion; he was able to find God in things. To him, as to most Italians, religion is incarnational, earthy. The worst sins are not the sins of the flesh but rather *superba*, or pride. The sins of the flesh are signs of human weakness. But pride, putting man in God's place, that was very serious because it's a direct rejection of God.

I used to ask the boys to consider the fundamental questions: Why am I here? How ought I to act? What can I hope for? I would tell them they had to become aware of these questions, to face them. Of course, the kids accepted the Real Presence as a mystery, a truth too deep to understand. I used to tell them there is a difference between a problem and a mystery. With a mystery the answer does not exhaust the question. Two plus two is a problem. Four is the answer. But, love, compassion, beauty, those are mysteries. In the same way, you can't turn mysteries of faith into problems. You can't turn people into problems. Christianity is full of paradoxes, apparent contradictions. I have found the answers in my faith, in Catholicism. Maybe they wouldn't, I wasn't going to force them. *But they had to ask the questions.*

FATHER FRANK PRINCIPE, PRIEST AT OLD ST. PATRICK'S DURING
SCORSESE'S YOUTH, WITH THE DIRECTOR IN ROME IN 1978.

MRS. SCORSESE: His Latin was very hard for him.

MR. SCORSESE: Very hard. Today, they're teaching a lot of English, not too much Latin, to become a priest.

MRS. SCORSESE: Marty liked it, but boys, you know, they fool around, and then the tests came out . . . Marty said he'd go back after high school. So then I said to Charlie, "Is he really serious? He really wants to be a priest?" And he said, "Yeah."

MR. SCORSESE: They claimed a priest on my mother's side, way, way back.

MRS. SCORSESE: On my mother-in-law's side none of them went to church. In *your* family nobody went to church. Heathens!

MR. SCORSESE: My mother went to church! I always go back to religion. It's the way I was brought up.

MRS. SCORSESE: When Marty used to go to retreat for three or four days, when he would come back, I'd say to my husband, "I wonder what they do on retreat." He said, "I don't know." I would ask Marty, "Tell me, what do you do on retreat?" and he said, "None of your business." I said, "That's a good answer!" He was an altar boy when he was young. At certain times, it was his turn to serve Mass at five o'clock in the morning, or six o'clock in the morning, poor kid. I used to feel so sorry for him, I'd call him, he'd get up, and I would go back to bed because it was early. I've got a beautiful shot of him at a marriage. When he was twelve years old, standing there with his red robe.

Once he painted two eyes on the wall in his bedroom. They were very spooky! He said to me one night, "I'm going to bed, and tomorrow when you come in my bedroom to call me, you're going to have a surprise." In the morning, when I went in, I saw this pair of eyes painted on the wall, and they were beautiful.

MR. SCORSESE: They were shining in the dark.

MRS. SCORSESE: They were beautiful. I said, "I don't believe this." I called him and said, "Did you do that?" He said, "Yeah. That's the surprise." So when we moved, he said to me, "Ma, I want to take the eyes with me. Could I cut the piece of plaster off?" I said, "Are you crazy? He'll kill us, the landlord!" They're second cousins and they're crazy. He said to me, "Well, I am going to have a photographer come in and take a picture." And he had a great big picture made, just the eyes. He used to say to me, "They watch me while I'm sleeping." I said, "Don't say that," and he said, "Ma, they watch me."

MR. SCORSESE: He was a different kind of kid.

TWO

THE SIXTIES

A S A COLLEGE freshman in 1960, Martin Scorsese could cover the blocks from Elizabeth Street to his classes at New York University's Washington Square campus in less than fifteen minutes. Yet that journey actually completed a voyage of four thousand miles begun by his grandparents in Sicily sixty years before. When his father strummed his guitar in Washington Square Park during the Depression, the university buildings constituted a distant city, an impossible dream. Now his son entered this other world.

Washington Square belongs to a New York older than Elizabeth Street. A triumphal arch commemorating the one-hundredth anniversary of George Washington's inauguration dominates the square and marks the beginning of Fifth Avenue, where stately apartment buildings begin their march uptown. On the north side of the park, period townhouses stand in prim rows. A brass plate designates the residence of the heiress in Henry James's *Washington Square*. Memories of sedate carriages, visiting cards, and literary salons linger here, mixed with images of jazz and Bohemian writers from Greenwich Village's more recent history. But in the early sixties, New York University began imposing new forms. Concrete and steel rose to meet exploding enrollments as the baby boom generation reached college age. Before the decade ended, construction workers building the new N.Y.U. library would jump from their scaffoldings and attack students protesting the war in Vietnam. But in 1960, all was still quiet and serene. Young men with crew cuts wore suits to class. Girls dressed in madras plaid shirtwaists. John Kennedy would soon be president. At N.Y.U., Martin Scorsese joined other children of the working class in entering the American mainstream.

He began as an English major, planning to become a teacher. His parents saw the high N.Y.U. tuition as an investment. Teachers always work. Perhaps someday he might even be a professor—who could tell? Maybe he would even teach at N.Y.U. This would justify all the years of buying him Classic Comic books.

Then one day Martin Scorsese told his parents that he had changed his mind. He was going to major in movies.

MARTIN SCORSESE: So much of what I did at N.Y.U. began with Haig. Haig Manoogian was a person with a lot of passion and he was able to instill that passion in the people who wanted to make films at N.Y.U. He forced you to be dedicated, to the exclusion of practically everything else in life, and I think that was important. In my first year at N.Y.U., I took a history of motion pictures, television, and radio class. It met once a week for four hours on a Thursday, usually, down at 170 Waverly Place. Haig came in and he would just rattle off, talking faster than me—much more energy—and it would be fascinating. There were two hundred kids in the class.

He would rattle off history or show a short film. Before you even got into a production class as a major, you had to go through this. Kids would come in, and think they were going to sit there for four hours and watch movies and take naps. He'd throw them out—literally throw them out.

By the next year, he began a kind of preliminary production class. We played around with a 16-millimeter camera in little groups. Finally, we got to the senior class with maybe forty-six students. That was it. Six films were made, because we'd have six groups. Whoever wrote the script was going to direct. By that time we had gone through a *purging*, you see.

WHAT'S A NICE GIRL LIKE YOU DOING IN A
PLACE LIKE THIS? (1963)

**"I WAS ABLE TO CREATE A VOCABULARY FOR MYSELF WITH CAMERA
MOVEMENT AND CUTTING." —MARTIN SCORSESE**

In his first two student films, Scorsese made artists his subject. His earliest student exercise, *The Art of Flamenco—Inesita,* focused on a dancer. Here he operated the camera and acted as co-director with fellow student Bob Siegal. Scorsese experimented with music and dance, breaking the action into segments in a style later seen in *New York, New York* and in the music video *Bad,* with Michael Jackson.

Scorsese based his first complete film, *What's a Nice Girl Like You Doing in a Place Like This?* on a horror story by Algernon Blackwood. A blocked writer disappears into a painting that fascinates him. The theme of artistic obsession would appear again in *Life Lessons,* his segment of *New York Stories,* in 1989.

MARTIN SCORSESE: The first film I made at New York University was called *What's a Nice Girl Like You Doing in a Place Like This?* It was a nine-minute film, 16 millimeter, black and white. I had made two 8-millimeter films before that, but they were with my friends, shot on the streets on the Lower East Side. I borrowed a friend's 8-millimeter camera. *What's a Nice Girl Like You Doing in a Place Like This?* is kind of a takeoff on the history of movies. At N.Y.U. the French New Wave, the Italian New Wave, some new British films, and the New York underground of Shirley Clark, John Cassavetes, and Jonas Mekas were all combined to give us a sense of freedom and enthusiasm. You were able to try new things with film, new things with editing. We were excited by Godard, Truffaut, and Antonioni, who didn't seem to use any cuts at all in *L'Avventura.*

We were open to so many different ways of making movies that we broke all the rules. That doesn't mean that we did films without learning the rules first. We knew the concept of master and medium shot and close-up and tracking and panning, but I was able to draw on many new films and create a vocabulary for myself with camera movement and cutting. And

What's a Nice Girl Like You reflects that sort of freedom—kind of young, kind of silly, but . . .

I decided that there would be not one match cut. Each cut would be a surprise. I'd cut to a shot that's moving, or to a still or an animated shot, stop-motion photography. In spite of these unusual techniques, I meant it as a homage to old movies.

As Haig said, kids would come up to him and say, "Gee, I can be a director. I want to be a director. All I need is a good script." And he'd tell them, "What do you mean you need a good script? If you're going to be a director, write it yourself. There is no such thing as waiting for a good script. Write it yourself." That's the way I learned it, and so that's what I did. I wrote the stuff, precut it, shot it, and then cut it myself.

Haig had a great passion for what he was doing. We didn't always agree on films. I loved *The Third Man*. He said it was just a good thriller and I never could get him to be as enthusiastic as I was about Hitchcock. But the arguments were great, the energy! He was an inspiration. That was the main thing. That was the key. He gave *me* a great gift. He made me see the value of *my* experience, especially when he encouraged me to do *It's Not Just You, Murray!*

IT'S NOT JUST YOU, MURRAY! (1964)

"IT REALLY SHOWS PRETTY MUCH WHAT ITALIAN-AMERICANS LIVED LIKE IN THE EARLY SIXTIES." —MARTIN SCORSESE

With Manoogian's encouragement, Scorsese began to listen to neighborhood stories for his next project. Scorsese needed only fifteen minutes screen time to tell the tale of Murray, a small-time gangster with a big ambition: "I always wanted to live good." It is not a linear journey. In the very first frame, Scorsese breaks conventional rules of storytelling. Murray looks straight into the camera and winks. Then he becomes the director. He gestures to the cameraman, asking him to pan down. "See this tie?" he says. "Twenty dollars." Then he points the camera down to the ground: "See these shoes? Fifty dollars." Then up: "See this suit? Five hundred dollars." He brings the cameraman down to his white Cadillac, and the camera moves into the back seat, but at that moment Murray says, "Hey wait a minute. I forgot something. Cut the whole thing, will ya? Cut the camera. Cut. Cut what I'm doing." Now he's back at his desk. He laughs, "I forgot to introduce myself. I'm Murray. And the reason I'm here is to tell you how I got here. I'm very rich, very influential, very well-liked. I got lots of friends." Murray tells us that he owes the sweet life, the good living, to his pal, his buddy Joe. Both the good life and Joe depend on racketeering.

Murray comes straight from Elizabeth Street. Scorsese was ready now to begin drawing on the stories and myths of his neighborhood, a process that would provide the context for such films as *Mean Streets, Raging Bull*, and *GoodFellas*. He had always enjoyed the fact that so many Sicilian gangsters acquired the nickname "Murray." Murray is meant to be a comic portrait of an ineffective Mafioso who constantly deludes himself. Though his idolized partner Joe betrays Murray at every turn, he can do no wrong as far as Murray is concerned. Joe gives Murray something no one else can give: "psychology." Even his mother cannot offer that. "The only psychology-type advice my mother gave me was, 'Murray eat first.'" But Joe is quick-witted. He can gloss over any reality. Murray lets him explain away every double-cross. When the police bust their bootlegging operation, Joe escapes; Murray takes the rap. But to Murray, "This is merely a misunderstanding in which I was, ah, misunderstood." After all, Joe does visit him in prison, along with his mother, who feeds him spaghetti through the chicken wire bars.

Scorsese satirizes Murray, but allows him a reality that is endearing. When Murray takes over the filming, using overheard jargon he gets slightly wrong ("Cut, cut the camera, what am I doing?"), it is impossible not to smile at his efforts. Even his rambling, nonsequitur philosophy ("In this life, you need help in order to obtain for yourself the best possible life for yourself") has a naive charm. But the satire is more biting. When Murray says, "I could go on like this for days. It doesn't matter. What matters is this. I always want to live good. How do you live good? Going places, meeting people." Scorsese juxtaposes images that puncture his character's delusions. "Going places" for Murray means riding on a tug through New York Harbor in a yachting cap; "meeting people" means being lost in a crush of gangsters in sunglasses.

Murray's convoluted speech echoes real conversations heard around the neighborhood. His illogical logic will reappear in *Mean Streets*, when Johnny Boy (Robert De Niro) explains to Charlie (Harvey Keitel) how he balances his debts in the inimitable "Joey Clams" speech; and in *Raging Bull*, when Joey La Motta (Joe Pesci) explains to Jake (Robert De Niro) that he must fight because "if you win you win and if you lose you win." This nonlinear thinking and supreme self-confidence combine to create language that can rationalize anything, and appears in its most extreme form in *GoodFellas*. Scorsese plays the division of words from deeds, appearance from reality, for laughs in *Murray*, but it is just this ability to compartmentalize his life that will allow wiseguy Henry Hill in *GoodFellas* to see the killing of his best friend as a matter of business. Code phrases such as "do the right thing," "show respect," and "matter of honor" carry multilayered messages.

In a series of scenes that recall Warner Brothers gangster films of the thirties and forties, Scorsese pokes fun at this split between reality and rationalization. Murray, in the ponderous tones of a creaky documentary, describes the great effect he and Joe have had on all segments of life, while Scorsese reveals how it really is. "Sports were affected by us," Murray says. Scorsese shows an athlete being bribed. "Private grants in foreign aid," Murray says, and we see robed men unloading rifles. "Hotels and motels were affected by us," Murray boasts, and the camera pans over fleabags with prostitutes standing in front of them.

In his presentation of Murray's career as a Broadway producer, Scorsese echoes the style of the great backstage musicals like *Bandwagon*, but the titles on marquees along the Great White Way deflate Murray's importance: "Love Is Like a Gazelle." "Hello Harriet, Goodbye Sam." "Tomatoes Are Too Cheap." Obligatory chorus girls appear, in four-foot feather headdresses. They circle the screen in a kaleidoscope effect worthy of Busby Berkeley, but their song is off-key and they do not tap together.

Murray's testimony in a U.S. Senate racketeering committee hearing has a newsreel-like authenticity until he touches the microphone, asking, "Is this thing on?" Then he says earnestly, "I refuse to answer on the grounds that I might incriminal myself . . . I mean that I might be discriminated . . . "

Only when Murray finally faces the duplicity at the core of his relationship with Joe does the glib philosophy stop. "Cut the sound. Cut the sound. You there with the glasses, cut the sound!" In his confrontation with Joe, Murray's face reveals his pain. He listens to Joe try to con him once again. But habit triumphs—Murray still needs to believe Joe. When

Murray speaks, his voice sounds false. Yes, he and Joe had a misunderstanding, but Joe explained everything to Murray. After all, Murray's wife is still his wife—they live together, they go to parties. And his kids? Well, even if they're not his kids technically, they're cute kids, they live in his house. "So," as Joe says, "I won't win any father of the year awards. Still we are very happy. Modesty forbids my disclosing my true worth . . . "

And so Murray ends where he began: with a new white Cadillac. It cost ten thousand dollars, and becomes the centerpiece for the finale. The characters from Murray's life dance around the car as circus music plays. Scorsese begins with Warner Brothers and ends with Fellini.

The only person in Murray's life who does not indulge in double talk is his mother. Murray's mother, played by Catherine Scorsese, appears in key scenes: the introduction of the young Murray, the prison cell visit, the confrontation with Joe, and the circus ring finale. But she does not speak. Her one line, "Murray, eat first," is delivered in her son's voice as part of his self-rationalization. But she is always there, silent and carrying a plate of spaghetti. "Eat first" is closer to Scorsese's artistic premise than is Joe's psychology. The food is real. It can be transformed.

MARTIN SCORSESE: My second film at New York University, called *It's Not Just You, Murray!*, was a combination of two things: obviously, a homage to the Warner Brothers gangster films in the late thirties and early forties, primarily *Roaring Twenties* by Raoul Walsh, and also *Public Enemy* and a lot of my old friends and relatives down on the Lower East Side. It was actually shot in my grandmother's apartment, in the apartment where I grew up, and in my uncle's apartment. I shot it in the cellars on the Lower East Side. It shows how Italian-Americans lived in the early sixties. The texture of the walls, the basements, are rather important to me. So much so that when I did *Mean Streets* in 1972, though I shot most of it in Los Angeles, I spent five days in New York, mainly to get the halls correct. Because the halls in L.A. weren't the same. I couldn't fake them.

MARDIK MARTIN: I came to N.Y.U. in 1959 as a "foreign student." I'm Armenian and grew up in Baghdad. When the Iraqi revolution came in the early sixties, my father lost everything. Then they took him away

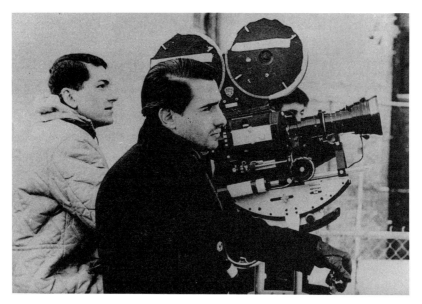

MARTIN SCORSESE, WITH RICHARD COLL, FILMING *IT'S NOT JUST YOU, MURRAY!*
ON THE STREETS OF NEW YORK DURING HIS N.Y.U. STUDENT YEARS.

somewhere and he died of a heart attack from fright. I was left in New York with no money and no right to work. If I went back I would be killed. The only person I told this to was Marty. Of all the students at N.Y.U., Marty Scorsese was the only one who became friends with me. I couldn't speak English well and was a foreigner. Don't forget, this was 1959; it's a lot different now, but those were the Eisenhower years.

I've never forgotten it. We became friends almost immediately. We met in class, we were talking about Dudley Do-Right, Rocky and Bullwinkle. We appreciated Abbott and Costello. I was pretty knowledgeable and he was, too—esoteric knowledge, you know, not anything that was "in." We did films together as students, projects like *Murray*. I helped with *The Big Shave*, and the movie that was to become *Who's That Knocking*, his master's project. To me it meant a lot, because here was an American who treated me like a normal person.

Marty had all these great stories about the guys in his neighborhood. They were wonderful images, but structuring them was difficult for him. I was good at organizing—you know, beginning, middle, and end—and so we would work together. First on *It's Not Just You, Murray!* in 1964. During that period, I became very close to his family. I was there all the time. His mother called me her third son. I think Marty inherited his talent from his mother. She's so full of life, that wonderful overflowing, abundant Italian life. She was so good to us. Always cooking. I remember her that day in Staten Island in the final scene of *It's Not Just You, Murray!* It was freezing and she did take after take.

MRS. SCORSESE: Now, don't forget, I started to work with him when he was in college. Especially when we made the movie in the swamp. When we made that, I had to get up at five o'clock in the morning and make spaghetti. For *It's Not Just You, Murray!* Charlie was in bed. And it was so cold and he said to me, "You know, Katie, you and your son are both crazy."

MR. SCORSESE: I always told her that.

MRS. SCORSESE: So I said, "Well, who's gonna help them? Somebody's got to help them."

MR. SCORSESE: I never denied them help. I gave them money.

MRS. SCORSESE: But what I went through! Well, anyway, when we got home that night I was exhausted. But every picture, he put me in it. But that morning it was so bitter cold. We started out with seven cars, and two cars broke down on the way. That's how Frankie was in that picture, too. And the poor girls were freezing, it was so cold up there. Their legs were out.

MR. SCORSESE: And no matter what Marty wanted, I gave it to him. Because I knew that he was good in what he was doing. This kid used to come home and study and study and study and study. He used to go out only maybe once a week, twice a week.

MRS. SCORSESE: He *never* went out.

MR. SCORSESE: I used to hear that typewriter until three o'clock in the morning. I used to have it in my brain . . .

Twenty-five years after he completed *Murray*, Martin Scorsese was direct-ing a group of actors assembled as extras for *New York Stories: Life Lessons*. Among them he spotted Murray, Ira Rubin, now known as Alex Robeson. Scorsese had not seen him since those student days. He gave him a small speaking part. Nick Nolte, Rosanna Arquette, and Peter Gabriel shared the scene, but for Scorsese the focus was Murray, who had been his first star.

ALEX ROBESON (A.K.A. IRA RUBIN): There was an audition at N.Y.U. for a couple of films. And I remember one film was about a witch and a frog. I was supposed to be a frog, and I was hopping all around the place, leaping on tables and jumping off. The people decided to go with another frog, but they recommended me to Marty. I auditioned for him and got the part of Murray in *It's Not Just You, Murray!*

This was the first film that I had ever done and I didn't know what I was doing. As a matter of fact, at the time, I thought that if you spoke slowly you could always speed it up on the film. My nose had been broken at one point and when I smiled, the nose would turn more, so I was always trying to be photographed so that my nose wouldn't turn into a banana.

I had done some work with a toupee but I was really bald, and if you photographed me from above I looked like a martian. So there were all these things to think about.

My acting teacher came to see *Murray*—Madame Bulgakova, of the Moscow Art Theater. She came over with Stanislavski. I loved her! She had great charm, and she had red hair, and she was in her seventies. Her spine was absolutely straight, and she always wore white gloves. She was my first real teacher. I was very critical of myself and she really didn't have anything nice to say to me and I thought, "Oh my God, Madame Bul-gakova didn't like it." The character of Murray is self-conscious about what he's doing, not at ease. I wasn't sure whether I looked like *I* was ill-at-ease or if she understood that that was how the character was supposed to act.

Over the years I've done a lot of theater, a lot of tours, commercials, extra work, but I never spoke to Marty since *It's Not Just You, Murray!* And now I'm doing this show with him, many years later. It's funny—I was volunteering at God's Love We Deliver where we prepare meals for AIDS patients and this nun, Sister Bianca, said she would pray for me. The next day I got the call to do this movie. The first day that I came to the set Marty walked over to me and shook my hand. Then I saw his father. He stopped me, "Don't you say hello?" I said that I didn't think he'd remember me. "Remember? I got the film at home, I watch it all the time."

WHO'S THAT KNOCKING AT MY DOOR? (1964-1969)

"THEY WERE REAL—BASED ON REAL INCIDENTS. THE DAILY LIFE OF THE NEIGHBORHOOD." —MARTIN SCORSESE

It's Not Just You, Murray! won an award from the Producers Guild as the best student film of 1964. Part of the prize was a six-month internship at Paramount Studios and a weekly salary of $125. Scorsese was packed and ready to leave for Hollywood when a letter came. The Paramount management had changed. The internship was abolished. Scorsese's roller-coaster relationship with Hollywood had begun.

He entered the masters program at N.Y.U. and started a project that would become his first feature film. The picture was first called *Bring on the Dancing Girls*. Its title became *I Call First*, then *J.R.*, and finally *Who's That Knocking at My Door?* Scorsese meant the picture to be part of a trilogy about a group of young Italian-American men on the Lower East Side. The first in the series, *Jerusalem, Jerusalem*, exists only as a treatment. *Who's That Knocking* and *Mean Streets* followed. The treatment's title comes from a New Testament quotation: Christ weeps over the city that would reject him, "Jerusalem, Jerusalem—how I would have gathered you to me as a mother hen gathers her chicks."

Jerusalem, Jerusalem follows the boys from the neighborhood to a Jesuit retreat house in the country. Though it was never produced, the story marks the first appearance of J.R./Charlie, Scorsese's alter ego in the series. This part of the trilogy concentrates on his inner life.

Much of the action in *Jerusalem, Jerusalem* flows from the sermons given by the retreat master, Father McMann. He is a heartier, more American version of Father McNamee in Joyce's *A Portrait of the Artist as a Young Man*. But even though this priest plays basketball with the boys, he still follows the spiritual exercises of St. Ignatius Loyola as did Joyce's priest, and gives graphic descriptions of death and the pains of hell. During these sermons, J.R. imagines scenes from his own experience juxtaposed with episodes from the Gospels: For example, the wedding feast at Cana becomes a marriage celebrated in a tenement.

Father McMann leads the boys through the outdoor Stations of the Cross, a series of tableaux that depict the passion—the events leading up to the crucifixion. J.R.'s imagination produces a parallel scenario. Jesus becomes a contemporary young criminal. He is arrested, beaten by the police, and led through the streets of New York past jeering crowds. The Empire State Building looms prominently in the background, an image repeated in *Who's That Knocking* and *Mean Streets.* The close-ups show the young man's bloody wounds. At the fifth station, "Jesus meets His mother," J.R. imagines a modern *Mater Dolorosa* comforting her tortured son.

J.R. sees Christ's life reenacted in his own neighborhood. He believes that in some way, Jesus could be anyone. This double vision reflects Scorsese's understanding of both Jesus and the inhabitants of those "mean streets." In contemplating religious mysteries, Scorsese had discovered his own soul and found a new way to view the storms of ordinary life. Now he sought to forge, in the smithy of that soul, images which would stir others to consciousness.

In *Jerusalem, Jerusalem,* J.R. obliquely confronts his adolescent sexuality, but it is in the next film that Scorsese confronts the spirit-flesh dichotomy directly. In *Who's That Knocking at My Door?* we meet an older J.R., played by Harvey Keitel. He is out of high school, but still living in a world bounded by Elizabeth, Mott, and Mulberry Streets. Though he and his friends make occasional forays to Times Square movie theaters, they remain defined by their neighborhood. At first, J.R. seems to be just another of the young men who hang out on street corners boasting about scoring, both sexually and through petty crimes. But he is different.

J.R. begins to discover his separate identity when he meets a character referred to in the movie simply as "the girl." Zina Bethune plays this educated blonde, who shows J.R. a world beyond the narrow confines of the Lower East Side. He, in turn, falls in love. With the girl he talks and listens to music. When he explains his devotion to John Wayne movies, especially *The Searchers,* she understands. Instead of the sexual groping he has known with other girls, J.R. experiences both passion and tenderness for the girl. Their sexual exploration takes place in J.R.'s parents' bedroom, where religious statues and vigil lights adorn the bureau. These objects reinforce J.R.'s determination to not "go all the way." He respects the girl and wants to marry her. But then one night the girl tells him a story. She is not a virgin. A flashback shows her raped by a brutish date who drove her into the country to take advantage of her. J.R. is shattered. In his world there are only two kinds of girls: the ones you marry, and the broads whom you party with, share with your friends, and then discard. The girl suddenly becomes a broad. What was she doing in a parked car to begin with? What did she expect?

J.R.'s Catholicism complicates his dilemma. To his friends, the church is like pasta—just a part of their heritage. But J.R. has absorbed an inner morality. He is drawn to spiritual things, yet for him goodness also means sexual purity, and the girl is fallen in his eyes. Still, forgiveness of sin forms the core of his faith—and didn't Jesus refuse to condemn the woman found in adultery? After a prolonged struggle, J.R. decides to forgive the girl and marry her. But she refuses him. She will not allow him to categorize her as a fallen woman, lucky to be lifted from the dirt. Though J.R. tries, forgiveness is as far as he can go beyond the macho ethic of his neighborhood, and for her this is not enough. He may forgive, but he will never forget. The movie ends with a tour de force sequence filmed in Old St. Patrick's church. Shots of statues of the saints move at odd angles as "Who's That Knocking at My Door?" by the Genies blares on the sound track. J.R. kisses the feet of Jesus on a crucifix. Blood flows from the wound.

The picture debuted at the Chicago Film Festival in 1967. The audience received it enthusiastically. Critic Roger Ebert called it "a new American classic," but no distributor would take it on until Scorsese added a nude scene so it could at least play in marginal theatres.

It had taken five years to go from the idea of *Who's That Knocking* to its actual completion. During that time mores changed. Many critics found a movie that rested on a girl's virginity old-fashioned and puzzling. (It would take the woman's movement to point out ways in which the old male double standard remained. In a sense the girl's refusal to sacrifice self-respect for love reflected a choice most feminists would approve.) By the time the film was released, inner-city riots, assassinations, Vietnam, and the civil rights and anti-war movements had cracked open old certainties.

The kind of Catholicism that paralyzed J.R. was also being challenged. In the reforming church of Pope John XXIII, the identification of sex with sin was changing. But for many Catholics like J.R., guilt remained. J.R.'s love does not cast out fear. He is attracted to the Jesus who proclaimed love as the highest law and welcomed prostitutes into the Kingdom of God, but he can not give himself that kind of break. For J.R., the flesh and the spirit are at war.

In *Who's That Knocking*, Scorsese began to chart the battle so central to his artistic vision. His passion attracted others to join him in that struggle. For actor Harvey Keitel and editor Thelma Schoonmaker, *Who's That Knocking* marked the beginning of three decades of collaboration.

HARVEY KEITEL: I responded to an ad in either *Show Business* or *Back Stage*. I went down to N.Y.U. and auditioned for this role in *Who's That Knocking at My Door?* I was there with a bunch of other actors. I got past the first audition, then I had a call back, and it was me and one other actor. Another student, Bill Minkin, was playing the role opposite the actors auditioning. And I got the part. And that's how Marty and I met.

I had been taking acting classes for a couple of years, and I had done a couple of things at the Cafe La MaMa and Off-Off Broadway. I had been away in summer stock, as an apprentice, doing everything from acting to cleaning toilets—in other words, I hadn't gotten paid. Acting was remote to me and to my upbringing, my environment in Brooklyn. It was something I came to very slowly, and very painstakingly, with great uncertainty and fear.

I always knew *Who's That Knocking* would get done because Marty had that passion. We made the film for an entire winter on weekends, because we had to earn money weekdays to buy food and pay the rent. After I saw the first rushes, the scene inside the church, where the song "Who's That Knocking at My Door?" is played, I knew that I was with somebody special.

Marty and I had a very similar sense of humor, and we seemed to possess a similar common denominator, a need for something—a certain truth, a need to express what we saw. I had a sense of his intensity, and I think we saw each other as being brothers of a kind, belonging to some secret society which I haven't got a name for.

We spoke about everything—as we still do. Our emotional needs, environment, parents, brothers, goals—these elements you can only get by sharing experience. And we were close to each other in experience, in dreams. Maybe in nightmares also. I'm sure we've had the same waking nightmares. We were struggling to reach another place.

THELMA SCHOONMAKER: I went to Columbia University for a year of graduate work in primitive art, and then I saw an ad in the *New York Times*. First and last time it ever happened! Someone wanted to train an assistant film editor. I got the job and worked for a terrible old hack who was butchering the great foreign films for late night television. Fellini, Antonioni, Truffaut, Godard—he was just taking their films and shortening them, so they would fit exactly between 2:00 A.M. and 4:00 A.M. This was before anyone considered these people "great artists."

They would say, "*Rocco and His Brothers* is twenty minutes too long," so we would just take out two reels. I couldn't believe it. I learned to cut negatives, and I learned enough to realize that maybe it was something I wanted to do. I had been reading about this New York University summer course, and I went down and took it. And there I met everyone that I've ever worked with. It was real fate. I couldn't have gone at a better time.

Scorsese was there, Michael Wadleigh was there, Jim McBride, Lew Teague, John Binder, who writes scripts—it was an extraordinarily talented group of people. Marty stood out among them all; you could feel that this was someone who was going to be a director. Some of them talked about being cameramen, some of them about being writers, some of them wanted to be directors. But there was something about Marty, he was so obsessed with becoming a director, and it just stood out.

Marty wasn't on my team, but Haig Manoogian asked me to help Marty cut his negative. My memory of this—and it may be clouded, I don't know—is that Marty had been up for days, and was sleeping with his eyes open, sitting in a chair against the wall. I would go over to him and say, "We have to lose six frames here, do you want to do them at the tail or the head?" He would decide and I would make the correction. That was my first encounter with him. Later, all of us just began working together making documentaries in the streets, mainly for PBS. But by this point Marty had already shot part of *Who's That Knocking*, in 35 millimeter, and didn't have enough money to finish it, so we all volunteered our efforts to help him finish it in 16 millimeter, and then blow it up to 35. I remember one time we were shooting on top of a roof downtown. We—the camera-man, soundman, assistants—were linked together by all the various cables. We were pulling back for the shot, walking backwards, Marty directing with his usual intensity. Suddenly someone noticed we'd come to the edge of the roof! I was happy to get back to the editing room after that! I helped him edit *Who's That Knocking*, and that was our first collaboration.

Marty has a very strong editing sense. He creates a great deal of what goes in his movies in the editing room, so we work very, very closely together. He's involved in *every* decision. Some directors don't work that way, but Marty does.

I had seen a spark in his student films. Of course, they were smaller, and *Who's That Knocking* had problems, but the brilliance in certain scenes was stunning. For example, the scene when they pass the gun around was cut to Ray Barretto's "Watusi." The use of music, the imagery, the powerful combination of music and image, which he's continued to excel in, were fantastic.

My memory of the film is of working terrible hours. We worked until two, three in the morning, on Eighty-sixth Street on the Upper West Side. I thought nothing of walking home at the most incredible hours. Marty was still getting up late and coming in late, and wanting to work very late—much later than I wanted to work, of course. He was so driven—incredibly driven—that sometimes he could be really irritating about wanting to work longer hours. He just wanted to *get* there, he wanted to get to the place where he could make the films he wanted to make. He had much more drive and focus than any of the other people I met at N.Y.U. Marty was *burning up* with wanting to get there.

HAIG MANOOGIAN: Marty had proved to be so good that I felt I didn't have to pay any more attention to him as a student. He felt bad about this. He wanted to know when the hell I was going to talk to him about his movie [*I Call First*, which later became *Who's That Knocking*]. I was talking to everybody else about all these other movies. So we went to the blackboard, and we outlined his film very quickly, and we said, "Look, it's okay." I felt he could carry on by himself.

I really didn't do any work on it, and when it was finished it looked awful, and it was on my conscience. I felt that there was a possibility of a good movie there, but it hadn't been worked up.

HAIG MANOOGIAN ON THE EIGHTH FLOOR OF THE
OLD N.Y.U. FILM DEPARTMENT.

It ran about fifty-eight minutes. We screened it at the film festival at
N.Y.U., and it bombed badly. It really *was* bad, but it had some terrific
things in it, and most of the things that were terrific had to do with the
natural scenes—the way of life of these young hoods. They weren't really
hoods, they were guys who hung around. You see them all the time, down
around Elizabeth Street. Guys who hang out on the corner watching the
girls go by, that kind of thing, and their parties and their morals, their
sense of values, their standards, the way they looked at life. These scenes
were absolutely tremendous.

We had no story; it was undeveloped. Marty also had a couple of real
bad actors. The thing just didn't work. So two years later, after he had left,
it still bothered me. I had a little bit of money, a very small amount of
money, and there was another student here at the time who was an older
individual, a lawyer. When he came to register, he said, "A lot of my clients
are film producers and I thought that since I'm handling their contracts, I
ought to know something about film." His name was Joe Weill and we
became good friends. Well, Joe and Marty and I got together, and the idea
was that I had the money, Joe would be the businessman, and Marty would
make the movie, and we would all work together as kind of a trio.

We decided to take all the scenes that were good in *I Call First*, then
rewrite the entire film. Marty sat down and spent six months rewriting the
original film. It was very interesting, because in the writing and through

the entire editing, he interwove the new scenes with the old ones. The only actor who came back from the original was Harvey Keitel. Nobody caught this, nobody saw this. It was never picked up, and don't forget, this was three years later. Harvey Keitel was three years older. Then we got Zina Bethune to play the girl; she wasn't in the original. So Harvey and Zina replayed the twosome.

Dick Cole was no longer available so Mike Wadleigh was brought in as a cameraman, and Mike Wadleigh was the guy who ultimately directed *Woodstock*. And then we got Thelma Schoonmaker to work with Marty on the editing, and she was great. She and Marty had a marvelous rapport. Marty and I used to come down once every week or two to take a look at it, and she'd show us exactly what we wanted to see. So we would ask, "All right, T, what do you think?" and we'd get her opinion, and boy, she had an opinion. Through that system, we developed the picture.

We knew that there were no real "names" in this film. So the only thing that we could do was try to get into a European festival. We had missed I don't know how many of them, but Venice was a possibility. So we sent the print over and we never heard a word. Then someone here at school asked, "Don't you have a picture called *I Call First*?" and I said, "Yeah." He said, "Well, I saw that sitting in the Rome airport." I immediately called Joe, and Joe bought a ticket and flew to Rome. He was furious.

Sure enough, he saw it there. The cans were there at the Rome airport. Joe took the film to Venice and it was too late to enter, but they finally said that they would look at it, and allowed him to sit in at the judges' meeting.

There were five men at the screening, and four of them could not understand a word of English. One man translated while the picture was being shown, in very broken English that was difficult to understand, and in Italian. When the picture was over, there was absolutely no reaction whatsoever. Joe said they just sat there until the chap who spoke English asked how old the man who made it was. Joe said he was twenty-five, and that was the one big thing about the picture that impressed them more than anything else. The jury said that they would let him know. So with that Joe left the print, flew back, and the film was never shown.

We tried to hit the New York Film Festival, but it was too late. We heard of the Chicago Film Festival, and the head of it, Mike Kutza, was in New York, and he had heard about the picture. We met up at Rizzoli's and I screened it for him. He flipped. He loved it, and he said, "Well, we'll run this in Chicago. There's no question about it." So we ran it in Chicago, and it won Best Student Film.

The next morning we read Roger Ebert's review, and he was raving about the thing, so we got ecstatic. "Jesus, we've got a smash hit." Boy oh boy, we had visions. The afternoon paper was not quite so enthusiastic.

We had some limited success. Some reviewers, one girl in Philadelphia flipped over it. But the New York reviews were so-so. We didn't have that kind of polish and professionalism, and there was a mixture of scenes shot in 35 millimeter with scenes shot in 16 millimeter and blown up to 35 millimeter. At that time, Marty was experimenting, and sometimes he did a little too much. He had not yet reached the point where he had fused technique with his ideas.

It ended up that I ran into an old army buddy of mine at a screening. He said we could get the picture in theaters if we added a nude scene. His company distributed porno films. First I said no, but finally Harvey Keitel flew over to Amsterdam where Marty was working doing commercials, I think, and they shot the scenes where J.R. fantasizes having sex.

There's a funny story that Marty tells. Right after *Who's That Knocking* he had written a thing called *Season of the Witch*, which was supposed to be the new one that we were going to do. But I had read it and it was a variation of *Knocking*. I don't know what I said, except that it was something to the effect of, "No more pictures about Italians." And Marty tells it that way after *Mean Streets* came out, because *Mean Streets* came from *Season of the Witch*. He told everyone in L.A. that there's a professor back in New York who says, "Audiences don't want any more Italian movies." Well, that's the end of the story.

■   ■   ■

Scorsese's friendship with Jay Cocks, then film critic for *Time* magazine, began in 1968 when he returned from Europe to teach at N.Y.U. He also met Jay Cocks's wife, Verna Bloom, an actress whose award-winning performances in *Medium Cool* and *The Hired Hand* made her the most professionally accomplished of this young group.

JAY COCKS: We've been friends for twenty years, and it's been two decades of watching movies together. Marty had a girlfriend some years ago, and they broke up, and people would say, "Why did they split up?" and I would say, "Well, she didn't like movies!" And they would laugh because they thought I was being a wise guy. And I'd say, "No, you've got to understand, this is very serious." Movies are the keystone of Marty's life, and if you can't share them with him in some way, then you can't share the most important thing in his life.

I remember most vividly seeing *The Wild Bunch* with Marty in a screening room. Several other people were there, Rex Reed and Judith Crist were there making—literally—retching noises, or very vocal noises of disapproval. Marty and I just looked at each other, and simultaneously tuned out what was going on around us. We didn't have to say, "My God, this is incredible." We could sense each other's responses. It's a communal thing, it's the sharing. That makes a solidarity. There's been a lot of life in twenty years, but movies are what keeps the friendship together and makes it grow.

WOODSTOCK (1969)

"I'M OF THE GENERATION THAT BELIEVED YOU COULD ENJOY IT." —MARTIN SCORSESE

In August of 1969, half a million people traveled to Bethel, New York for three days of "peace and music." A band of N.Y.U. alumni and film students were determined to document what became a gigantic, nonstop happening.

Martin Scorsese was there, cueing cameramen who couldn't hear him. No one slept or ate much. It was hard to find a bathroom. But Woodstock became a cry against repression, against war, against racism, against the forces that had beaten demonstrators on the streets of Chicago during the Democratic convention the preceding year.

The festival—and the movie that recorded it—became a history of rock 'n' roll, from John Lee Hooker through The Band. Scorsese worked under Michael Wadleigh as an assistant director, and under the supervision of Thelma Schoonmaker as an editor. It was Scorsese who suggested printing on the screen the lyrics of the song sung by Country Joe McDonald, partly because the soundtrack was obscured. A bouncing ball followed the words inviting audiences to sing along, and they did, in theaters throughout the country. One audience of draftees near a New York army base sang at the top of their lungs, "One, two, three, what are we fightin' for? Don't ask me, I don't give a damn; next stop is Vietnam . . . " days before they were to depart for the combat zone. The people at Woodstock sang it in protest, the draftees in desperation.

MARTIN SCORSESE: In *Woodstock* we had very often no idea who was going to appear or what they were going to play. We had no idea who would be standing where or when. We barely knew what group was coming up next on the stage. It was a three-day and three-night concert. We had figured that the music would start around eight o'clock at night and end about three in the morning and that would be it. Everyone would go to sleep and get back up. But no. It was a disaster. The music went on from three in the afternoon on Friday nonstop until Monday morning. So cameras were breaking and people were frenzied.

Thelma was an assistant director on that, too. She was up there by the lighting board just yelling at them all the time to give us some light because you couldn't get any exposure. If you look at the film you see a purple light on the stage. But it was so much fun. We had a ball. We had a good time. I'm of the generation that believed you can enjoy it.

THELMA SCHOONMAKER: Our next big thing was *Woodstock*, and it was just a nightmare! The film magazines kept jamming because of the humidity, the whole thing was an incredible nightmare. We were desperately *shooting, shooting*—and the music never stopped. It went on and on and on. We couldn't find any place to sleep, and there was nothing to eat. It was just hell. And Marty, of course, was very amusing talking about it. He said he brought his cufflinks. He brought his cufflinks to Woodstock because he thought it was maybe going to be that kind of thing!

THE BIG SHAVE (1967)

STREET SCENES (1970)

"CONSCIOUSLY IT WAS AN ANGRY OUTCRY AGAINST THE WAR. BUT SOMETHING ELSE WAS GOING ON INSIDE ME. IT WAS A VERY BAD PERIOD." —MARTIN SCORSESE

During the last years of the 1960s, the Vietnam war dominated the national scene and was the focus of energy on the university campuses. In 1967, Martin Scorsese planned to make a short film for a week-long demonstration called "The Angry Arts Against the War." Instead, he submitted the script for the film, *The Big Shave*, to the Palais des Beaux Arts in Brussels, curated by Jacques Ledoux. Scorsese received a grant—ten rolls of Agfa film—which he used to shoot the movie. In it a young man shaves in front of a mirror, cutting his own face until he is a mass of blood. (Many of Scorsese's characters confront themselves in mirrors. Murray did, and so would Travis Bickle and Jake La Motta.) On the sound track, Bunny Berigan plays "I Can't Get Started With You." *The Big Shave* appeared in Ledoux's Festival of Experimental Cinema in 1968, and won Le Prix de L'Age d'Or. Though Scorsese intended it as an expression of anger against the war, later he hinted that it also reflected something of his own emotions.

In May of 1970, at Kent State University in Ohio, state troopers fired on students demonstrating against the escalation of the war through the bombing of Cambodia. Four of the students died. Campuses across the country erupted in protest. Scorsese and his N.Y.U. students formed the New York Cinetracts Collective. They sat in at the film school and demanded equipment in order to document the protests and demonstrations. They envisioned a network uniting campuses across the country through film.

A series of spontaneous student protests began. At N.Y.U., construction workers building the new library came down from the girders and attacked the marchers. Cinetracts was there. Later that week Scorsese and the film students joined the caravan of cars converging on Washington for one of the period's largest anti-war protests. The documentary *Street Scenes* captured the euphoria, the despair, and the fears of those days of protest and hope. When the film was shown at the New York Film Festival, the N.Y.U. filmmakers wore black arm bands.

During that same summer of 1970, Scorsese was appointed to select programs for Lincoln Center's "Movies in the Park" series. Giant portable movie screens rose up in Central Park, Prospect Park, and Riverside Park as part of the city's attempt to diffuse the anger on the streets. Authorities feared the riots that had gone on in other cities during past long, hot summers.

The audiences stretched out on the grass to watch the works by students, experimental filmmakers, and animators that flickered by under the stars. One night, at the other end of Central Park, The Band, on their own after years with Bob Dylan, played "I Shall Be Released." Somehow it seemed that the energy of protest and experimentation that drove the city during those years had reached a zenith. "I see my light come shinin'," The Band sang, "from the west unto the east. Any day now, any way now, I shall be released."

HARVEY KEITEL: In 1970 we did *Street Scenes*. I was upset about Kent State and didn't know what to do, and wanted to participate in something. I called Marty, and he said, "We're taking over the film department, and we're going to make short films and send them around to the universities. Come on down." We were there for a few days. Then we went to Washington, and the result of that trip was *Street Scenes*. I'm in it, as a matter of fact, in a scene in the hotel room, and in some other scene. If you know to look for me, you'll see me there, when we're down by the buses, demonstrating. I see the movie we did as more than entertainment. I resolved then to try to choose roles that have social meaning.

· · ·

Among Scorsese's students at N.Y.U. were directors-to-be Jonathan Kaplan and Oliver Stone. For Stone it was his experience at N.Y.U. that brought him home from Vietnam. He spoke about in a Showtime *Firstworks* program.

OLIVER STONE: I had just come out of Vietnam, and I had a lot of personal problems in dealing with reintegrating into society after leaving that very hostile area of the world. Being able to go to N.Y.U. on the G.I. Bill, and then accidentally running into a teacher like Scorsese in Film-making 101, is about as lucky as you can get. And not only was he a great teacher, he was inspirational. He loved movies, and that's what he con-veyed to us—his love for movies.

It was exactly what I needed at the time, somebody who believed in something, who had a soul for something. Because I believed in nothing at that point, I was burned out. And I was very alienated from the American experience, and I didn't believe anybody who had anything to do with government, I didn't believe family, I didn't believe any of the old values I had been raised with. I think through Marty, and through Haig Manoogian, too, I was able to find a set of values.

I had done three or four short films. They were terrible. They just had no meaning to them; they were silly exercises in trying to be a Keystone Cop or something. Shot in lofts on the Lower East Side with the typical villain and heroine—one's idea of movies rather than one's idea of life. That's the problem, because people always have an idea of movies, and then they do movies of other people's movies.

Marty gave me some criticism once, he just said, "You've got to do something you really feel, something that's personal to you." So I went home and I did this story about what it was like for me to come back to New York City and be alone, and I think some truth got out in the movie. It was a very crude picture, very crude sound. I had a French sound track, with readings from Celine's *Journey to the End of Night.* I had some Russian music—Borodin's "In the Steppes of Central Asia"—on the sound track, and mixed it crudely. But it had some heart, some feeling.

MARTIN SCORSESE: Oliver Stone had just come back from Vietnam. He came to a campus that was rebelling. The campus was Greenwich Vil-lage. He was very quiet. But we could sense that there was something brew-ing in him. He made this beautiful little three-minute exercise about a Vietnam vet back in New York. I remember helping him shape it on the Movieola [editing table]: cuts to music, that sort of thing. Jonathan Kaplan was another student of mine. But Jonathan didn't come to class all the time. Oliver did. Jonathan came to class at the beginning, then went off and shot his film and came back with a rough cut of a film called *Stanley Stanley.* It was good so I didn't complain. But Oliver was always there.

CHARLES MILNE: I was a student at N.Y.U. when Marty was teaching. I knew him through Jonathan Kaplan. I remember I shot some footage he liked and we screened it and talked about it. I'm a musician and music was something we all had in common then. I think Haig got great vicarious satisfaction from Marty's success, especially since Haig had helped finance *Who's That Knocking.* It was really touching. Haig, I think, wondered if he himself could have had a career in the industry.

At N.Y.U. we try to be involved with Hollywood, but keep our New York identity and our connection to international film. We have screenings of our student films in L.A. and the industry comes. But the idea of making films in New York, where there's more of a family feeling, is good.

Among our graduates are directors like Marty, Oliver Stone, Jonathan Kaplan, Marty Brest, but also New York–based filmmakers such as Jim Jarmusch and Spike Lee. Marty comes back to give classes. He inspires the students.

. . .

Each fall the Italian government sponsored a film festival in Sorrento, the International Incontri del Cinema, held so that the directors and stars of a selected nation's film industry could meet their Italian counterparts. In the fall of 1970, the guest country was the United States, and Scorsese acted as a film programmer. He brought to the festival student productions and experimental and animated films done by independent movie-makers working outside the Hollywood system, some of which had been shown at Lincoln Center's "Movies in the Park." Because I worked as assistant film programmer on both projects, I went to Sorrento, and so witnessed what became a pivotal experience for Scorsese's career.

Under the chairmanship of King Vidor, a number of legendary American directors, including George Stevens, Elia Kazan, and Sam Peckinpah, gathered in Sorrento along with younger directors such as Paul Williams, Francis Coppola, and Martin Scorsese. Paul Williams's *The Revolutionary* and Martin Scorsese's *Who's That Knocking at My Door?* were both being shown. Francis Coppola's latest film, *Finian's Rainbow,* was not on the program. Rather, he was there as an honored guest. "I'm used to being the youngest one at gatherings like this," Coppola said. But here's Marty, only twenty-seven, and they're not even showing a movie of mine. Have I become an old man of film already?"

FRANCIS FORD COPPOLA AND MARTIN SCORSESE AT THE SORRENTO FILM
FESTIVAL IN 1970.

Coppola spent one afternoon combing the streets of Sorrento looking for a stationery store. He was then designing scenes for a script he kept in a three-hole binder. But hours of concentrated effort had frayed the holes, and some of the pages were falling out. He found the store, and tried to explain in not-so-fluent Italian and many gestures the concept of "hole reinforcers." The Sorrento stationer, who finally understood the pantomime and came up with them, deserves some credit for the launching of *The Godfather* and ensuring that Francis Coppola did not become an elder statesman before his time.

The festival seemed divided between masters of the past and the New American Cinema, which Scorsese and the experimental filmmakers represented. At home, the generations were at war. That year, *Time* magazine's "Man of the Year" was "The Under 30 Generation." Anyone older was not to be trusted. Students revolted against the politics and culture of their elders. But over the long, slow, al fresco lunches hosted by a festival director, Mario Longardi, such divisions dissolved.

Grape arbors shaded the tables laden with heavy, shiny-crusted bread, platters of spaghetti *alle vongole* and scampi, huge rounds of fragrant cheese, and slices of red *cocomero*. Here, directors young and old, masters and apprentices, American and Italian, shared their love of movies.

But even here, politics did not go away. The mainstream Hollywood films screened at the festival reflected the times. *Getting Straight* (*America, America, Dove Va?*) starred Elliot Gould as a graduate student caught up in campus anti-war demonstrations. *Soldier Blue*, a nontraditional western that exposed the brutality of the American army to the Indians, was meant to be a comment on the Vietnam war. *The Revolutionary* focused on a student anarchist played by Jon Voight. *Years of Lightning, Day of Drums* was about Robert Kennedy's assassination. And *Who's That Knocking at My Door?* raised questions about how the old values and morals worked in the modern world.

The festival's main feature attraction was *Tora! Tora! Tora!*, the story of the Japanese attack on Pearl Harbor, a section of which was directed by Akira Kurosawa. The Japanese fighter pilots who had bombed Pearl Harbor appeared at a press conference. Now advocates of pacifism, they nonetheless did seem to enjoy repeating their battle cry, "Tora! Tora! Tora!"

There were glamorous parties and gala screenings. But the best moments of the festival were late at night, over grapa and espresso in the little cafes of Sorrento. Italy herself sparked, in both Coppola and Scorsese, memories of their families and growing up in the mix of Italian and American culture. Central to that experience was growing up Catholic. *Who's That Knocking* put sex and guilt on the table. While there were the usual funny stories about what Sister So-and-so said in third grade, there was also serious talk probing what faith meant in a world grown so complex.

Two young Italian publicists, Claudio Argento and Adriano Pintaldi, and a journalist, Antonio Troisio, joined in these late night discussions, as did Paris producer Claude Nedjar, novelist Hans Koningsberger, and directors Sam Peckinpah and Paul Williams.

MARTIN SCORSESE: Sorrento was the place where I got to know everybody and meet everybody that would be helpful to me in my future, for my work. I also happened to meet all the older directors that I adored and admired, American and Italian. Most of them are now gone, but I still have a relation with some of the Italian directors.

In some way Italy is my homeland. I mean, America is, but the subculture is Italian. But southern Italian. Not Neapolitan, more southern than that. It's Sicilian—very different. So Sorrento was very interesting to me. But I saw that my real culture comes from the south, even further south.

I had been in Italy two years earlier, but only to northern Italy, Venice and Milan. It was my first time in southern Italy, and I've never been back there, except for Sicily for two days.

I am very close to Italian sensibilities, I think. Italian movies have been really instrumental in shaping my work—they just have been. I saw Italian movies in my neighborhood in 1948 and 1949. On TV there were the British films, the Italian films, and the American films, and that was it. All three combined together, and that's pretty much what my work is like.

. . .

When Scorsese left Sorrento he did not return to New York. His time of apprenticeship was over. That fall he moved to Hollywood.

SCORSESE, WITH MARY PAT KELLY, AT THE SORRENTO FILM FESTIVAL.

THREE

BURNING BRIGHT

S CORSESE HAD trouble adjusting to Hollywood. He drove his 1965 white Corvette only on surface streets to avoid the freeways. When he visited Michael and Julia Phillips at their beach house in Malibu, he sat on the sand dressed in his street clothes, down to socks and shoes.

He attended innumerable matinees of old movies in the cheap, dirty theaters on Hollywood Boulevard, where the condition of the prints left him heartbroken. He combed Larry Edmond's book shop for old stills and copies of scripts. The posters and memorabilia spoke of the Hollywood he loved, a place that existed now only in imagination.

MARTIN SCORSESE: After N.Y.U. I sort of made a "living" as an editor in Hollywood. I had a nickname, "The Butcher." I just worked on other people's footage. It was wonderful! I did anything to get those editing jobs, especially editing documentaries. A person talking can be the most incredible thing. It's fantastic!

Brian De Palma and George Lucas and I were all at the same lot at Warner Brothers. I was editing *Medicine Ball Caravan* and I wasn't very happy about that but it was important for me to be there in Hollywood after *Who's That Knocking*. This was 1971. *Who's That Knocking* had not broken through or won awards, so I had to go and work where I could.

I was editing *Elvis on Tour,* and I was trying to get *Mean Streets* going.

Warner Brothers had *THX*, George Lucas's first movie, and they were thinking of dumping it. Francis Coppola had the power to protect it or not. George was concerned. The studio thought it was a bomb. They didn't know what to do with it. And, Brian DePalma had gotten to direct Orson Welles in *Get to Know Your Rabbit*, but he was taken off the picture and Tommy Smothers finished it. So you had some very depressed people hanging around together.

I was living in an old Hollywood Hills house and it was really depressing. I didn't like it. It reminded me of *What Ever Happened to Baby Jane?* So I actually slept on the set of *Minnie and Moskowitz*, a movie that John Cassavetes was doing, until I found a new apartment. My asthma started acting up and I went into the hospital for the first time. I'd been taking cortisone for a year, on and off. But then it became steady, which is really dangerous. I think it had a lot to do with being on my own, and learning that I had to live alone, had to face a career and work it out.

By September, when I was working as a sound effects cutter on *Minnie and Moskowitz*, someone came in from Herb Schechter's office—at the time he was at the William Morris agency—for *Boxcar Bertha*. I had met Roger Corman the first month I got to Hollywood, in January 1971, but I heard nothing from him for months. He'd wanted me to do a sequel to *Bloody Mama*, but then he offered me *Boxcar Bertha*. I worked hard preparing *Boxcar Bertha*, laying out every shot, five hundred shots in drawings, but Roger Corman said, "Let me see what your planning is like." He went through the first ten pages, then flipped the rest and said, "You're fine because you've got to shoot this picture in twenty-four days, and you've got all the shots. If you're this well planned, you're going to be okay."

BOXCAR BERTHA (1972)

"I THOUGHT, 'GOOD, I'LL DO THIS CRUCIFIXION SCENE AND GET IT OUT OF MY SYSTEM.'" —MARTIN SCORSESE

"Boxcar Bertha," a character based on a woman who rode the rails during the Depression, was played by a young actress, Barbara Hershey. She is in love with a union organizer, portrayed by David Carradine. The railroad hires goons to execute him. The script, written by Joyce H. Corrington

BARBARA HERSHEY (CENTER) IN *BOXCAR BERTHA.*

and John William Corrington, calls for death by crucifixion. Scorsese, steeped in religious images, welcomed the opportunity to get it out of his system.

BARBARA HERSHEY: My view of *Boxcar Bertha* is very colored. I feel like I was not as awake then as I am now as a human being. If I was doing *Boxcar Bertha* now, I would have gotten much more out of it. But it was the most fun I'd ever had on a movie. We covered eight years of a story in four weeks of shooting, and that could have been a nightmare, but in this case, it was a delight.

We managed to improvise. I remember Marty designing a shot in the reflection of a car. I'd never been with a director who thought like that. It's certainly an AIP [American International Pictures] Roger Corman movie, embarrassingly so in some ways to me, but at the core of it are the wonderful characters that Marty helped us create—characters that bump into each other and don't understand what's happening to them. It was a tough movie; they were tough guys, the AIP crew.

Marty had a fragility to him and a vulnerability, but he was able to deal with those people and the situation and make us feel good.

As I got to know him a little bit, I saw that he was very interested in religion. I'd read *The Last Temptation of Christ* myself when I was nineteen. I had always been fascinated by the Christ story, but I never really got it until that book. When you read it, you can't tell the difference between the dream at the end and reality. His last temptation seems to be really happening. One day I was talking to Marty on the set of *Boxcar Bertha*, and I said, "You know, there's this book you should read." Now *I* don't remember saying this, but he assures me I did, and it does sound like something I'd say. I told him, "You should make it into a film, and if you do, I should play Mary Magdalene."

MARTIN SCORSESE: When I made films at New York University, you had to wait on line for the equipment. You couldn't have a camera because so-and-so was using it that weekend. When you got the equipment was when you shot—there was no schedule.

But when I got to Los Angeles, and was able to work for Roger Corman on *Boxcar Bertha*, I had to shoot the film in twenty-four days. I did what I had done at the university. I drew all my shots, so that I was not caught short on the set, at least for ideas and angles. I drew them based on scenes in my head, and also, mainly, according to the actual locations in Arkansas. I remember Paul Rapp was an associate producer for Roger, and he taught me a great deal on *Boxcar Bertha* about the fastest way to shoot, even if it meant breaking up the scene. If you shoot a master, then do a medium shot of one person talking, a medium of the other person talking, close-up, close-up, usually you relight for each shot. We'd do a whole sequence lit one way and then relight it and do it over again. It was murder for continuity and also for the actors, but it got us finished on schedule.

Roger Corman was, first of all, a gentleman, very open to letting you express yourself on film as long as it worked within the structure of what he needed. And that was an "exploitation" film. Roger, for example, would look at the script. Then he'd tell us to make sure there's a touch of nudity or a promise of a touch of nudity every fifteen pages. And violence—there had to be a certain amount of violence in it. Once we knew that and once we dealt with that form, we could move the camera, we could use certain actors, we could cut a certain way, as long as it worked.

．　．　．

Boxcar Bertha opened on a double bill with *1000 Convicts and a Woman.* The *New York Times* critic liked the character studies and admired such old film touches as the iris shots that frame each cast member in the credits. "*Boxcar Bertha,*" wrote the critic, "showed imagination beyond what one would expect from a film showing in a theatre on Forty-second Street."

MARTIN SCORSESE: After he saw a rough cut of *Boxcar Bertha,* John Cassavetes told me it was nice for what it was, but warned me not to get hooked up in it again. What he said was, "You just spent a year of your life making a piece of shit. You're better than that stuff, you don't do that again." He asked me if I didn't have something I really wanted to do. I told him I had this script called *Season of the Witch,* but that it needed work, rewriting. He said, "So do it."

MEAN STREETS (1973)

"WE WORKED OUT OF MY MOTHER'S KITCHEN."
—MARTIN SCORSESE

Scorsese began to concentrate on finding financial backing for *Season of the Witch,* a continuation of lives of the characters in *Who's That Knocking.* Under the new title *Mean Streets,* he sent it to Roger Corman. Corman agreed to make the movie provided all the characters were black. Scorsese was so anxious he actually considered this. But then Verna Bloom arranged a meeting for him with Jonathan Taplin, a road manager for The Band, who had access to financing.

Taplin liked the script as it was. He could raise the money if Roger Corman promised in writing to distribute the film. Scorsese asked for $300,000, doubting he'd get it, but after a number of attempts the money was raised. Scorsese decided to use the same crew as he had on *Boxcar Bertha.*

He returned to the old neighborhood during the Feast of San Gennaro with a six-day shooting schedule for New York exteriors, as well as the interiors he felt could only be found in the city. Tourists crowded Mulberry Street, waiting on line at food and game booths. In the decade since Murray and Joe, J.R. and his friends had hung out here, the old neighborhood had changed. "Little Italy" had become a contrived medley of restaurants and cafes that catered to tourists. Real neighborhood life retreated into social clubs and secret places, like the walled compound of Old St. Patrick's or the graveyard of St. Michael's Russian Catholic church.

Scorsese opens *Mean Streets* where *Who's That Knocking* ended, in the church so central to his childhood. Charlie (Harvey Keitel) holds his finger in the flame of a vigil light. He reminds himself that the fires of hell burn with infinitely greater intensity. Charlie fears hell; he wants to be cleansed of his sins. He confesses them, but the "Our Fathers" and "Hail Marys" he receives as penance seem insufficient to save a soul exposed to the temptations of the street. Charlie asks for a sign, a means of expiation powerful enough to purge his guilt. Johnny Boy (Robert De Niro), the neighborhood wild man, becomes that penance. Charlie's concentration on saving Johnny Boy allows him to ignore the paradoxes in his own life. Charlie wants to be a saint, but his girlfriend Teresa (Amy Robinson) reminds him that sainthood and his job as an errand boy for his uncle, a powerful neighborhood Mafioso, seem mutually exclusive: "St. Francis was not a numbers runner."

Charlie wants to be Johnny Boy's messiah, but he neglects his own salvation. A product of parochial education and a reader of Dreiser and Blake, Charlie exchanges New Testament lines with his friends while he ignores the barely repressed violence around him. "Art thou the King of the Jews?" asks Tony, the bar owner (David Proval), when Charlie enters. "Do you say this of yourself or have others told you?" Charlie replies. When Tony shows Charlie the tiger he keeps caged in the bar's back room, he responds with lines from Blake's poem: "Tyger, tyger, burning bright, in the forests of the night."

Ambivalence marks his relationship with his girlfriend Teresa. She wants them to leave their world. He has promised that they will move uptown when his position as a minor gangster is secure, but he becomes further enmeshed in the neighborhood. Sex and love remain as separate for Charlie as they were for J.R. in *Who's That Knocking*. Charlie, in bed with Teresa, tells her he wouldn't be there if he really loved her. The split between the woman you love and the broad you bang remains.

Charlie's crisis arises when Johnny Boy can't repay Michael, the loan shark (Richard Romanus), and refuses to cooperate with Charlie's efforts to negotiate a settlement. Instead, Johnny Boy delivers such a barrage of insults that Michael decides to kill him. This ends the peace Charlie had maintained with the neighborhood. The anger and readiness for battle that lies beneath the surface of the neighborhood courses through Johnny Boy. In a scene based on an actual incident, the word "mook," whose meaning no one understands, incites a poolroom battle. Charlie settles the fight but Johnny Boy shatters the truce. "How can you be friends with someone who called you a mook?" When Charlie makes a last ditch attempt at diplomacy, Johnny Boy tells Michael the truth. "If you're stupid enough to lend me money," he says to the loan shark, "you don't deserve to get paid."

Charlie suggests that Johnny Boy unload trucks to earn the money he owes. Johnny Boy points out that Charlie would never do such work. Charlie likes work that goes with the monogrammed shirts his mother irons for him. He prefers the illusory gentility of polite sit-down meetings and respect for the Don to facing the real violence of his world. Charlie acknowledges God's supremacy: "You can't fuck with The Infinite." He believes he can remain moral within an amoral world, but Johnny Boy knows that only an appeal to Charlie's uncle can save the situation. Charlie refuses; his uncle disapproves of Johnny Boy.

There is nothing left to do but run. The getaway scene crystallizes the difference between Charlie and Johnny Boy. Charlie squirms in the driver's seat, eager to escape. Johnny Boy refuses to rush; he dances around the car, twisting through fluid jive steps to the song "Mickey's Monkey." Johnny Boy forces the audience to experience him as Charlie does. He is exasperating and wild, but so alive; he expresses the side of Charlie that Charlie himself refuses to acknowledge.

Michael pursues them, and a gunman (played by Martin Scorsese) shoots up their car. Johnny Boy and Charlie survive, dazed and bloody. In the final frame, Charlie kneels in the street, no longer able to ignore the violence and compromises of his own life.

Scorsese spoke about *Mean Streets*, soon after it was completed, to a group of students at the Center for Advanced Film and Television Studies of the American Film Institute in Los Angeles. Some of Scorsese's remarks on the film come from that conversation.

MARTIN SCORSESE: The first version of the script of *Mean Streets* was steeped very much in the religious conflict. See, the whole idea was to make a story of a modern saint, a saint in his own society, but his society happens to be gangsters. It should be interesting to see how a guy does the right thing—that's the old phrase they use, "the right thing"—in that world. Somebody does something wrong, you've got to break his head or shoot him. It's as simple as that. Charlie became a character who refused to acknowledge that and eventually did the worst thing he could do, which was to put everything off, put all the confrontations off, until everything explodes. It's the worst thing you can do. It's the same way in the movie business. You've got to go into the room with the producer first thing and

MARTIN SCORSESE DIRECTS HARVEY KEITEL (CHARLIE) IN A SCENE
FROM *MEAN STREETS*, INSIDE OLD ST. PATRICK'S CATHEDRAL.

say, "Hey, I think this thing stinks. I won't do it." That's what you've got to do. Otherwise you can put it off and put it off until, finally, they cut your picture down or whatever—they fire you or you walk off and it's a disaster. It's a matter of knowing where your head is at right away. But this character wants to avoid unpleasantness at all costs. You notice he's always separating people when they fight. "Come on, we're all friends," he says. The voice-over was the whole business of his own relationship with God, his own way of looking at things. And also his guilt. There's a scene in the film you understand if you're really Catholic and you look at it closely. He would go to confession but he wanted to deal with things in his own way so he would never really feel forgiven. There's an old heretical sect that felt they were not worthy of anything. They would go to confession but would not go to communion because they felt they were not worthy. That's where he says, "I'm not worthy to drink your blood or to eat your flesh." It's a whole guilt thing. No matter where he goes, he's lost.

MARDIK MARTIN: Marty and I used to drive around in my Valiant and write. *Mean Streets*, interestingly enough, was written in that car. We would park wherever we could find a spot, mostly in Manhattan, in the neighborhood. At the time, *The Godfather* was a book. To us, it was bullshit. It didn't seem to be about the gangsters we knew, the petty ones you see around. We wanted to tell the story about real gangsters. Marty could relate to a gangster as well as to a man like me.

Marty is sensitive and loyal, and he'll back you in ways you never forget. He isn't a tough guy. When he was scared he used humor to get what he wanted. The tough guys he grew up with were physical. In order to compete with them—which he couldn't do because of his asthma and because he wasn't big—he decided to be mentally alert. He was very funny; even if the joke was bad, he would laugh. He ingratiated himself. He knew how to make you feel good. He was very popular because of his intelligence. Instead of being a physical person, he was a mental person.

ROBERT DE NIRO: I met Marty at Jay Cocks's house about 1972. I had seen *Who's That Knocking*, and I liked it. I told Marty it was really good. We knew each other when we were kids, a little bit. I didn't *really* know him—well, I'd see him around. We remembered each other.

Sometimes, when we were kids, we'd meet at the dances at a place on Fourteenth Street. We shot the dance scene in *Raging Bull* in that place.

Then it was a Latin-American sort of club, a dance hall, but when we were kids, it was just an Italian-American dance place. I saw Marty around there. We knew each other. Friends of his, from his group, sometimes would change over into our group. We had like a crossover of friends.

I had ideas about being an actor when I was ten or eleven, but no real interest. At about sixteen, I started becoming interested. Marty and I didn't talk about it, but we had a mutual friend who Marty had directed. When I saw *Who's That Knocking*, I said, "He did this about the neighborhood, and he really understands it." It was very, very good.

Marty was starting to work on *Mean Streets*, and we got together and talked about it. He offered me four parts—not Charlie, that was Harvey's part, but four others. I didn't know which one to do. I was kicking them around and talking with Marty and trying to decide. I saw interesting aspects in each one. Then I ran into Harvey on the street. He was going to play Charlie. I told him I thought maybe at this stage of my career, I should hold out for something else. I felt the logical part for me was Harvey's part, but he already had it. But I wanted to work with Marty.

SCORSESE TALKS WITH ROBERT DE NIRO (JOHNNY BOY) AND HARVEY KEITEL
IN HIS MOTHER'S KITCHEN DURING FILMING OF *MEAN STREETS*.

HARVEY KEITEL: Perhaps I got the part of Charlie because Marty sensed that I came from a similar background. I was then just emerging from Brighton Beach, in Brooklyn. I was studying acting. I was new, I was raw, I hadn't much experience. *Who's That Knocking* was my first film, and *Mean Streets* was my first commercial film. I don't think it was my expertise at acting that landed me that work, but the experience Marty saw in me. Our neighborhoods said to a young man, "You have a place and you will not go beyond this place because you do not belong anywhere beyond this place." Marty and I rebelled against it.

RICHARD ROMANUS: I met Marty in 1972 through Jon Voight. Marty approached Jon about playing Charlie in *Mean Streets*, with Harvey as Johnny Boy. But Jon passed on it and he suggested me. In the meantime, Robert De Niro came on the scene.

Jon brought Marty down to a class that we were in together in Los Angeles, along with Teri Garr and David Proval, who played the bar owner in *Mean Streets*. We were a group of peers, twelve of us. Every week one person would become the moderator. The week Marty came, Jon was the moderator.

Marty invited David Proval and me to dinner afterward and offered us parts. We said sure—we didn't know who he was, who anybody was. It was just a gig. They were paying the minimum, and they had no distributor for the movie, so it didn't seem like much.

ROBERT DE NIRO: One day Harvey said, "I can see you doing Johnny Boy." I hadn't thought of playing him at all. I had picked a role, and it wasn't Johnny Boy. I said, "I'm going to do *this* one." But Harvey somehow made me see it in another way. I couldn't see Johnny Boy at first, but in a way it was a good thing. When you play a role you don't see yourself doing at first, you can get things from yourself that you ordinarily wouldn't get. I didn't see myself as Johnny Boy as written, but we improvised in rehearsal and the part evolved. We would find a structure for the improvisations and figure out how to pace it. It's not just freewheeling, it has to have a structure. Then we'd tape what we'd do. It had to build. Working this way takes a lot of personal stuff.

RICHARD ROMANUS: Bobby De Niro was from that neighborhood, and Harvey Keitel was from Brooklyn, and David Proval, who played the bar owner, was from a similar neighborhood. But I grew up on the edge of a forest in the Green Mountain State. I mean, I used to play in a forest. I lived in a town of six thousand people, so I had no idea who these people were or what notes they played to get where they were at the opening of the movie.

I had to try to get the accent down and mimic these guys as much as I could without seeming to be acting. I chose to be laid-back with my character, because Bobby and Harvey had such bristling energy. They had an energy I hadn't seen before. David Proval and I decided that since Harvey and Bobby had such energy, we should take the low energy road, so that we could be a contrast to them. Otherwise we'd be four guys walking around with toothpicks, saying, "Hey, whaddya doin, ba boom ba boom ba boom." It would be a little monotonous, we thought.

MARTIN SCORSESE: Paul Rapp, who had worked for Roger Corman for years, budgeted the picture, and he called me up one day and said, "In order to shoot this picture for $300,000, you're going to have to shoot it in Los Angeles." I said, "I can't shoot this picture in Los Angeles." He said, "Then don't make the picture." I said, "Well, what do you mean, shoot in Los Angeles? What are we going to do?" He said, "Go to New York, shoot some background stuff for four days, and then come back here and we'll do all the interiors here. We can't crash the cars in New York. We can't pay the Teamsters so we'll have to find a place here at night." I said, "Okay, I can write it into the script that they go to Brooklyn." Which is what they end up doing, they go to Brooklyn.

I shot the car crash in downtown L.A. at night. All the other exteriors are New York. Even the beach is New York because the water looks different at Staten Island than it does in L.A. It's true. We shot that in New York and all the interiors are L.A. except the hallways. The hallway stuff is very important because we couldn't find a hallway to double. We shot these literally where the film takes place. In fact, we were working out of the lady's house who was the mother of the boy Robert De Niro was portraying. We worked out of her house and we worked out of my mother's kitchen.

RICHARD ROMANUS: I remember shooting the first scene very clearly. I say that I think we've stolen camera lenses, but they're 'Jap adapters'—much less valuable. When I say "Jap adapters" I have a sour look. But I had that look because I thought I'd said that line badly. So it was a real thought in a real moment. As an actor you incorporate it into the scene. It came out well. The fact that I was from another neighborhood was never in the movie, but it was the only direction Marty gave me. That, and, "Slur your words."

MARTIN SCORSESE: The festival stuff was shot in October before we even started doing preproduction. At one point, Jon Voight was going to be in the picture. The night in New York that we discovered he wasn't going to be in it, I went right back to Harvey Keitel and Harvey did it that day. The stuff you see of Harvey walking through the feast was done right at the spur of the moment, when I said that he was going to be the lead. I got him a coat down at Barney's and we went. That was that. But there were a lot of crazy things like that on the picture.

HARVEY KEITEL: Mine was a gut, root, raw experience of trying to express myself, and express the character of Charlie in *Mean Streets*, and trying to discover what it meant to express yourself in a character. I was learning my technique, learning how to apply it. Marty and I always discussed a scene, and usually he trusted me to do what I had in my mind to do.

RICHARD ROMANUS: Harvey was great to work with. Jack Nicholson once told me, "Harvey Keitel is the greatest actor I ever worked with." I can't disagree. I think he's a hell of an actor, Harvey—extremely under-rated. He's totally organic, fast on his feet. He's not intellectual. He's not the kind of guy you can sit down and discuss the part with. But between action and cut, he's like a broken field runner. He's fast, he's very in-stinctive. And very solid—boy, you couldn't trip him up if you wanted to. He's a wonderful actor.

I was there for the rehearsal that led to Bobby and Harvey's scene—the "Joey Clams, Joey Scala" scene. They would run a part of it and say, "Oh, that's good." Somebody was there writing it down. When Bobby did the scene, I think he was throwing some lines, mixing it up a little bit, but basically it was scripted. I think they do that in order to keep themselves fresh.

Marty and I had a scene together. He's the shooter who fires at Charlie and Johnny Boy. Marty was a little nervous as an actor, but one had the sense that he adored actors. He was a pleasure to work with because he was such a great audience and a great editor. Based on his reaction, you knew how you were doing. He never said a lot to me. Once he said, "I don't quite believe that. Do it again." That was the only time he ever spoke to me as a director. The other times he was simply a wonderful audience.

The scene where I had the cake all over me was a sort of mistake. At the end of the take, I just sat there and I yelled for Marty. He came over and he looked at me and started to laugh. He set up a dolly track and told me to just sit there. He did a slow dolly across me. He was very open to collaborating.

Most directors want you to do what they want you to do. That's one of the reasons I loved Marty. He allowed you to flesh out the character. Even if you were in the middle of a scene and something came up that was organic, he wouldn't dismiss it. He would respond to it, and he would probably include it. To me, that is his great gift. He's an actor's director.

Working with Bobby De Niro was interesting. It was my first movie, and to watch Bobby take charge of his work was a great lesson for me. By taking charge I mean saying, "Whoa, whoa . . . I want another take. I want to do this again." He put the responsibility for his performance on his own shoulders. So he wasn't able at the end of it all to point to somebody and say, "I would have been better but for him."

In the scene when Bobby insults me—tells me I was stupid to lend Johnny Boy money—I started to laugh. Bobby got angry. He thought I should be angry, which I was, but by laughing I was saving face. He thought I should be fuming, but he had no control over my reactions.

If you're working correctly, no one has control over anyone's reactions. Sometimes the reaction you get from your acting partner is not the one you want. Then you simply have to react off that. But in this scene, I laughed organically. I thought Bobby was very funny when he was doing that stuff. And he looked ridiculous.

There's a reel missing from that movie; reel six or seven was lost. Right after the scene where we "sell" firecrackers to some kids, David Proval and I picked up Harvey Keitel outside the bar. We went to Forty-second Street and watched a movie and laughed like hell. But they lost the reel and it never ended up in the movie.

When we were shooting that reel, I was sitting in the car with David

Proval outside the bar. Marty came over and said, "Listen, there's been a bomb threat. They plan to blow up the bar here in about twelve minutes. But if we hurry, we think we can make the shot. Do you mind?" We said, "Well, I guess not. Let's just hurry." So we all scrambled, and it didn't go off. It wasn't a direction from Marty to get a response; he was quite nervous about it.

MARTIN SCORSESE: We only shot six days in New York. We kept stretching it to get more of the New York feeling. That also limited our shooting because the best I could do was put the people in the middle of the buildings and let the buildings do all the talking—atmosphere-wise, you know. When De Niro's shooting his gun off the roof, the roof is New York because you see the Empire State Building, but the window is Los Angeles. When David Carradine gets shot in the bar, the guy falling in the street is actually in New York—that was a double, we shot that first. We blocked out his face just right so that he falls and hits the car, that sort of thing. The rest of the scene was shot in Los Angeles. The guys who were the doubles were all old friends of ours. That guy's name was Larry the Box; he was a safecracker.

I kept adding scenes. I added the back room scene, the long improvisation. I added a scene in front of the gun shop in New York. I added the scene where they steal the bread in front of his uncle's shop. All that stuff. I added a lot of stuff like that. I kept pushing the limits of the budget and drove everybody crazy. But that was the only thing we could do because the more we got down there, the more fun we had and the more we realized the atmosphere we wanted to get. A lot of my old friends are in the film, a lot of guys who are now just hanging around are in the picture as extras. We had to finish and that was that. It was done in twenty-seven days.

RICHARD ROMANUS: Marty wore white gloves during the shoot to keep himself from biting his nails. Every time you saw him, he had these little white editor's gloves. And he drank San Pellegrino. I never knew anybody who drank bottled water before. That's how much of a backwoods kid I was. To me, he was a sort of character.

MICHAEL POWELL: I've always liked *Mean Streets*, one of the great films. I just think it's wonderful, that complete identification of that world, taking part in it. You never feel that anything is staged or done for theatrical effect. Scorsese just honestly stays there inexorably. It's full of that.

The English distributor of the film was frightened by it, like the way my film *Peeping Tom* frightened them. They didn't want to have anything to do with it. I think they sold it off to choppers or something. Warner Brothers never even asked anybody else what they thought. They just acted on what they saw, and it frightened them to death. That often happens to a good film. That was the attitude of the Rank Organization toward *The Red Shoes* in the beginning. At the time he made *Mean Streets*, Marty was not known and they could get away with anything.

MARTIN SCORSESE: The picture opened at the New York Film Festival and was very successful in New York. Because the picture got great reviews and did such good business in New York the first couple of weeks, our producer wanted to open the film in twenty-five cities—just like *The Last Picture Show* and *Five Easy Pieces*. He went to Bert Schneider and talked to him and he said, "Do it, because there's nothing opening in October except *The Way We Were*, and that isn't going to make a cent." Famous last words.

We thought the New York Film Festival meant something in L.A. But nobody even knew about the picture. We had big full-page ads, but the ads were not good. We had no idea how to sell the picture. How are you going to sell it? As *The Gang That Couldn't Shoot Straight*? This was our first concept—guys running around with shorts on with guns and hats, because Johnny Boy takes off his pants at one point. It would have looked like a comedy. In fact, it is funny, but it wasn't meant to be. We'd been advised to let it play in New York. That was probably right—we should have let it play in New York for a few months.

But next thing I know, we opened in L.A., got nice reviews, did two weeks' business, and that was that. Every other city, the same thing. Warner was our distributor and *The Exorcist* was coming in. That was a $14 million picture, and Warner's whole life depended on *The Exorcist* at that time because they were a little shaky about *Mame*. Naturally, they're not going to worry about a picture they paid $750,000 for, and they didn't make anyway. They're not going to pay a lot on prints and advertising for that, and why should they? As they say, "Why throw good money after bad?"

RICHARD ROMANUS: I never thought *Mean Streets* was going to be released. I was sure it wouldn't be. It was the strangest movie I'd ever read. The screenplay was different from the film. Usually you read a script and there are great parts, and some not-so-great parts. When you see the movie, you hope that the great parts are still there. That's not usually the case, but it was with *Mean Streets*. It was mind-blowing, the energy it had. People walked out saying, "It's just great." Film-makers flocked to it. The attention it got from the younger filmmakers was astonishing. People still mention it to me all the time. They quote lines from it. Spike Lee, in the *Los Angeles Times*, said that the two movies that continue to inspire him are *Pixote* and *Mean Streets*. Both have that same sort of rough documentary quality, and both are really creative, with great energy.

We were doing some final sound work one day. We were talking about how sensational the reaction had been from people who'd seen part of the movie, and Harvey said to Marty, "Oh, this is nothing. You'll make much better movies." And I said, "The truth is, you never know. You may spend the rest of your life trying to top this one."

MARTIN SCORSESE: It did well in New York. In the neighborhood, now, west side and east side, if there's any trouble they always say, "Well, it's *Mean Streets* time, gentlemen." It's really made its imprint there.

ALICE DOESN'T LIVE HERE ANYMORE (1974)

"FOR ME *ALICE* WAS LIKE A NEW YORKER'S VIEW OF THE WEST." —MARTIN SCORSESE

Martin Scorsese opened his first real Hollywood movie with a tribute to films of the past. The prologue to *Alice Doesn't Live Here Anymore* is filled with red sky, fog, and other images from 1940s movies. The farmyard is reminiscent of *The Wizard of Oz*, and the wooden house recalls *East of Eden*. As star-struck young Alice acts out her fantasy of becoming a singer like Alice Faye, Scorsese pays homage to the lighting style created by veteran cameraman William Cameron Menzies for the spectacular skies in *Duel in the Sun* and *Gone With the Wind*. This opening scene cost $85,000, two-and-a-half times the entire budget for *Who's That Knocking*.

For both Alice and Scorsese, imagination and movie images merge in the prologue. But Alice has put her dreams away and settled into a suburban life. The death of her truck driver husband pushes her out onto the road.

The action of the movie accelerates as Alice (Ellen Burstyn), her son Tommy (Alfred Lutter), and their station wagon zoom onto the highway looking for adventure. As mother and son hurtle forward, Tommy tells the same joke over and over. Alice just doesn't get it. Revealing characters obliquely is pure Scorsese.

Outside her safe but stifling world, Alice discovers that there's danger. A tentative love affair with a seemingly charming cowboy (Harvey Keitel) explodes. He beats his wife in front of Alice and Tommy, and they run. Alice leaves her hard-won singing job behind her. Survival now seems victory enough.

Alice takes a job in Mel's Diner as a waitress, joining foul-mouthed Flo (Diane Ladd) and spaced-out Vera (Valerie Curtin). At first her dreams seem defeated. But through her friendship with the other women, a stronger Alice emerges. When David (Kris Kristofferson), a local rancher, offers marriage and a settled life, she hesitates. In the documentary-like scene in David's kitchen which grew from an improvisation between the actors, Alice reveals to David the essence of her need to perform. When Alice reenacts the vaudeville routine she and her brother performed as children, she becomes so achingly present that David must accept her dreams. They will go together to Monterey, where she has a chance to pursue her singing career.

As the movie winds to a close, Alice, David, and Tommy are on the road heading for the world of the prologue, where fantasies become real.

MICHAEL POWELL: The first film I saw of Marty's was *Alice Doesn't Live Here Anymore.* I thought it was wonderful. Harvey banging about was really good. He's a noisy actor, so when he gets the right part, it's terrific.

The first thing I noticed about Marty's films was the impeccable casting. Very imaginative—people that really existed. That's very important in directing. The director can't do much with somebody who doesn't want to help. Sometimes in a missionary enterprise, we directors say, "I don't

ELLYN BURSTYN (ALICE HYATT) AND HARVEY KEITEL (BEN) IN
ALICE DOESN'T LIVE HERE ANYMORE.

understand why that actor I like so much hasn't done better. Maybe I should work with him and find out." But that hardly ever works.

Is Marty lucky about getting the right actors? Some directors plug through all the plays, looking, looking. They're not sure what they're looking for. Marty seems to have actors fall into—I can't call it a net, that would be rude—into his orbit. He never gives you the impression that *he* goes to all the plays. He acts like a magnet. I don't think it's only luck.

He attracts people by principles, ideals. Actors, particularly the good ones, sense that working with Marty is quite different.

Way back, twenty, thirty years ago, we [Emeric Pressburger and Michael Powell] were making films with principle. We had that kind of reputation. People don't exactly come to you, but they put themselves in your way. It takes maybe twenty years to establish yourself as anything out of the ordinary. Before then, it's all a scramble. Trying to get financing for an idea, accepting work you don't want for the money or because you convince yourself you can do something with it.

Marty seldom gets caught that way. He's very cunning. Marty—the fox.

ELLEN BURSTYN: I was shooting *The Exorcist* at Warner Brothers. As they were looking at the dailies, they wanted to do another picture with me, and they started sending me scripts that I wasn't very interested in. The scripts were full of stereotypes—the woman as victim, the woman as helper—so my agent started looking for scripts for me to bring to Warner, and he found *Alice Doesn't Live Here Anymore* by Bob Getchell. I said to my agent, "I like it, but I think it needs . . . " Well, most scripts need to be polished but this one needed to be "roughed up." It was good, but it seemed as if it were written for Doris Day and Rock Hudson.

Warner Brothers liked it and asked who I wanted to direct it. I called Francis Coppola and I told him I was looking for a director who was new, exciting, and unknown, and did he know one? He said to look at a film called *Mean Streets*, which wasn't released yet.

I was so impressed. Remember that Bobby De Niro and Harvey Keitel were unknown artists at the time. The scenes between them had such an astounding quality of reality, which is what I felt we needed, and I thought, "This is the perfect guy"—only I wondered what he knew about women, and how he'd respond to me, and what I wanted to do with this script.

He came up to Warner Brothers. He was very nervous. Marty always is, though this may have been the first time he'd ever been called by a major studio to come for an interview to direct a feature.

We met in John Calley's office—he was one of the heads of Warner Brothers at the time. It was a big, fancy office, the kind of thing that makes Marty quake like an aspen tree. I was very impressed with him. He was high-strung, like a young racehorse. We talked for a few minutes. I told him how much I liked *Mean Streets*. Then I asked, "What do you know about women?" And he said, "Nothing. But I'd like to learn." I thought that was a wonderful answer.

He worked the way I wanted to work and needed to work—which is to say, he trusted the actors. We put the script through a process of improvisation, taping our sessions, then rewriting, then editing the improvs. It was methodical and loose at the same time, which is what I needed.

Of all of the directors I've worked with, Marty is best at providing the atmosphere where actors can do their best work. He's open-ended. He'll say, "Okay, we know what this scene is about. Now what is it gonna be?" And the actors will start improvising. All of the actors in that picture were good at improvising; some wonderful actors aren't. Of course, we had seven members of the Actors Studio, who were trained to improvise. Some scenes were done as written, like Harvey's scene when he comes to the motel. Harvey was so real that it terrified me. But it was a very creative atmosphere.

There is a scene with Kris and me in the kitchen that is an example of Marty's way of allowing the actors to contribute their own content. The scene has an air of reality most directors can't attain.

The scene in the car with Tommy repeating the joke over and over got in because Marty rode out to the set on the bus with Alfred. Alfred told him that story. "Shoot the dog, shoot the dog . . . " Marty never got the story, but Alfred kept telling it over and over. Marty just wanted to think about the shooting for the day, but he couldn't shut the kid up, so that went right into the movie.

What I wanted to do in *Alice*—and what nobody was doing at the time— was to tell a story from a woman's point of view. One example comes to mind. At the moment when Alice becomes sexually attracted to Kris's character, I asked Marty to have him be working, to have him do something with his body. That's what was beautiful to me, seeing a man's body with the strength and earthiness and muscularity at work. That was the kind of thing Marty was open to and excited about, because they were things that came from a woman that hadn't been done before.

The relationship between the mother and son was the crux of the film, as Bob Getchell wrote it. The way we worked we used a lot of things that came out of my life with my own son. My son was exactly the same age as Tommy at the time, and was on the set with his tutor.

When Marty and I worked on the script and handed the rewrites to John Calley, Alice didn't end up with David. She didn't get married. John said, "We love the whole thing except for the ending. She has to end up with the guy. We just did a movie with an unhappy ending and it didn't sell." I said, "Only if she ends up with a man is it a happy ending?"

Marty and I were disgusted. The end they wanted was a *movie* ending, not a *real* ending—which was why Marty had everybody in the restaurant applaud, because that was *his* way of acknowledging that this was the *movie* ending. But then Kris Kristofferson made the contribution that saved us all. We were all very disgruntled, because she was giving up her dream of singing to live on Kris's farm. Then Kris came up with the idea of his character saying, "Hey, come on. You want to go to Monterey? I'll take you to Monterey, let's go!" He sprung that on me in an improvisation during rehearsal. I said, "You will?" And I just fell in love and was disarmed. It got me off the hook. It resolved everything. I think at that moment Marty applauded, then everybody applauded.

Marty accepted my Academy Award. I was doing *Same Time Next Year* on Broadway. The producers would have let me off to go to California, but it didn't feel fair to me. People were waiting so long to see it, they had tickets for months. Not to have them see the person they were expecting because I was off getting an award wasn't the tradition I was brought up with. I asked Marty if he would accept if I won, but we were both unsure of what to say. I always felt of two minds about the awards. The nominations are great, but then to pick *one* winner and to make losers of four people who had been winners seemed rude. I didn't know what to say, so I told Marty, "Thank everybody in the cast and crew and thank yourself." And he did.

When you're doing something, you don't always appreciate it for what it turns out to represent in your life. That time with Marty was probably the most creative experience I've ever had with a director. I really treasured that time and what I was able to give and inspire.

MARTIN SCORSESE: For me, *Alice* was like a New Yorker's view of the West. When I was little, I remember being very, very obsessed with Westerns. I guess because of the scenery and the horses and the animals. I like that. Of course, I was totally allergic to animals. I couldn't touch any animals, I couldn't have any animals. So the more I couldn't, the more I saw these beautiful Westerns in Cinecolor and Truecolor. And then, of course, the great Westerns, too, with beautiful Technicolor. But a lot of the B Westerns I saw I liked—*Northwest Stampede*, pictures like that. There were strange pictures made. For some reason there were many movies about horses made in the thirties and forties and early fifties—*Bluegrass in Kentucky*, pictures like that. And I liked them, I guess because of the outdoors and the sense of western life. Of course, where I lived was exactly the opposite.

The experiment in *Alice* was to try to get what seems like a nice little Hollywood picture and suddenly work against that expectation. I think the picture was not conventional because we did so much experimenting in the film with the acting and the ideas. I wanted to take movies from the past that have influenced people, to take the clichés and try to understand them.

I worked with a lot of women on the picture. Marcia Lucas was the editor, and of course Ellen. Jodie Foster played the young girl. I was interested in what these women were thinking about. The relationship between mother and son was, of course, central. Ellen's son was there on the set and so was my daughter. She was twelve. So both Ellen and I had those relationships to draw on.

We played with scenes and found what was important to the plot and story, and to identify the cliché and have fun with it—to try to explore ideas which really have no answer. In it, I had a scene with two people sitting there not talking. What am I going to do, move the camera? I just found it wasn't necessary. I could fool around with it, it doesn't mean anything. I would think in terms of Alice, the character. She comes in looking for a job and her son is worried about going to school. How should I handle that? Should I be nice? This is reality. It's a display of how people act. It's also like a case history. The camera is a witness.

FOUR

VAGABOND SHOES

TAXI DRIVER (1976)

**"IF THINGS GET HEATED ENOUGH YOU KNOW THERE'S GOING
TO BE VIOLENCE, SO THE THING TO DO IS TO STAY INSIDE."
—MARTIN SCORSESE**

MARTIN SCORSESE returned to New York to start making *Taxi
Driver* in 1974. On a hazy night in June, Scorsese took to the streets.
It was—even by New York standards—unbearably hot, humid, and fetid.
As the scene begins, a yellow checker cab emerges from the mysterious
steam that continually escapes from the innards of New York City. Travis
Bickle (Robert De Niro) is driving the taxi. Screenwriter Paul Schrader,
quoting Thomas Wolfe, described him as "God's lonely man." *Taxi Driver*
is his story.

Martin Scorsese had planned this picture for three years. Though he
was finally working for a studio, Columbia, the budget was low. The tight
shooting schedule was often interrupted by afternoon thunderstorms that
would break over the city, scattering cast and crew without cooling the
atmosphere. The oppressive weather fit Travis Bickle's story. He prowled
the stifling streets enclosed in his cab, wishing for a deluge that could
clean away the human garbage on streets the way the rain sluices trash
into the gutters. He could not ignore the world of pimps and prostitutes

and drug dealers as do most others in the city. He despised Forty-second Street, but he was bound to it.

Alienated from his own humanity, enclosed in his taxicab, Travis finds no common purpose with anyone else. Two women represent the extremes of his world: Iris (Jodie Foster), a fourteen-year-old prostitute, and Betsy (Cybill Shepherd), who works in the election campaign of a liberal candidate named Palantine. Betsy is a goddess who could make an ugly world beautiful.

Travis attempts to be normal. He actually finagles a date with Betsy, but when he brings her to a sleazy porno movie house, the only place he goes for entertainment, she quite naturally bolts. Travis seeks to regain her through an apocalyptic act. He shaves his hair into a Mohawk, dons commando fatigues, and appears at a political rally for Palantine, armed with automatic weapons. His plan to assassinate Palantine is foiled by Secret Service men. Instead Travis, the avenger, must descend into hell to save Iris. In a climactic shootout, he splatters the blood of her pimp (Harvey Keitel) and one of her customers on the walls of Iris's tenement bedroom, where vigil lights burn. Police cars arrive in an eerie silence and the bodies are carried out. Travis becomes a tabloid hero. He has saved Iris, and she is back with her family. Then Travis resumes his old life. The movie ends when Betsy sees Travis in the taxi line in front of the Plaza Hotel. Each pretends nothing has happened. The city can absorb such violence.

Taxi Driver won the Palme d'Or at the 1976 Cannes Film Festival. This brought Scorsese new attention, and extended his reputation beyond admiring critics and the devotees of the earlier films. *Taxi Driver* also became part of the twisted fantasy life of John Hinckley, who was obsessed with Jodie Foster. In 1981, five years after the release of *Taxi Driver*, he attempted to assassinate President Ronald Reagan. In his mind, Foster and the film were part of the inspiration for his act. *Taxi Driver* had asked audiences to look at violence in our society. Some refused to look beyond the movie.

PAUL SCHRADER: The script of *Taxi Driver* is the genuine thing. It came from the gut, and while it banged around town everyone who read it realized it was authentic, the real item. After a number of years enough people said somebody should make it so that finally someone *did*.

In 1973 I had been through a particularly rough time, living more or less in my car in Los Angeles, riding around all night, drinking heavily, going to porno movies because they were open all night, and crashing some place during the day. Then, finally, I went to the emergency room in serious pain, and it turned out I had an ulcer. While I was in the hospital, talking to the nurse, I realized I hadn't spoken to anyone in two or three weeks. It really hit me, an image that I was like a taxi driver, floating around in this metal coffin in the city, seemingly in the middle of people, but *absolutely, totally alone.*

The taxicab was a metaphor for loneliness, and once I had that, it was just a matter of creating a plot: the girl he wants but can't have, and the one he can have but doesn't want. He tries to kill the surrogate father of the first and fails, so he kills the surrogate father of the other. I think it took ten days, it may have been twelve—I just wrote continuously. I was staying at an old girlfriend's house, where the heat and gas were all turned off, and I just wrote. When I stopped, I slept on the couch, then I woke up and I went back to typing. As you get older it takes more work. Hovering in the back of my mind is a fondness for those days when it was so painful it just had to come out.

I didn't really write it the way people write scripts today—you know, with a market in mind. I wrote it because it was something that I wanted to write and it was the first thing I wrote. It jumped out of my head.

Right after writing it, I left town for about six months. I came back to Los Angeles after I was feeling a little stronger emotionally and decided to go at it again. I was a freelance critic at the time. I had written a review of *Sisters* and interviewed Brian De Palma at his place at the beach. That afternoon, we were playing chess—we were about evenly matched—and somehow the fact that I had written a script came up. So I gave it to him and he liked it a lot and wanted to do it. De Palma showed the script to the producers, Michael and Julia Phillips, who were three houses down the beach, and he showed it to Marty, who was in town after finishing *Mean Streets.* Michael and Julia told me they wanted to do it but that Marty was a better director for it. So Julia and I went and saw a rough cut of *Mean Streets,* and I agreed. In fact, I thought Marty and Bob De Niro would be the ideal combination, so we aligned ourselves—De Niro, the Phillipses and myself—but we were not powerful enough to get the film made. Then there was a hiatus of a couple of years, and in the intervening time, each of us had successes of our own. I sold my script, *The Yakuza*, for a lot of money. Marty did *Alice*, the Phillipses did *The Sting*, and De Niro did *The Godfather, Part II*.

At the time I remember describing *Taxi Driver*'s Travis as sort of a young man who wandered from the snowy waste of the midwest into an over-heated New York cathedral. My own background was anti-Catholic in the style of the Reformation and the Glorious Revolution. The town I was raised in was about one-third Dutch Calvinist and one-third Catholic, and the other third were trying to figure out why they were there, and sort of keeping peace. Well, both cultures, Catholic and Calvinist, are infused with the sense of guilt, redemption by blood, and moral purpose—all acts are moral acts, all acts have consequence. It's impossible to act amorally. There's a kind of divine eye in the sky that ensures your acts are morally judged. So you know once you're raised in that kind of environment, you don't shake that, you shake a lot of things, but the sense of moral responsibility, guilt, and redemption you carry with you forever. So Scorsese and I shared that. I came from essentially a rural, midwestern Protestant and Dutch background, and he is urban and Italian Catholic, so in a way it's a very felicitous joining. The bedrock is the same.

Taxi Driver was as much a product of luck and timing as everything else—three sensibilities together at the right time, doing the right thing. It was still a low-budget, long-shot movie, but that's how it got made. At one point, we could have financed the film with Jeff Bridges, but we elected to hold out and wait until we could finance it with De Niro. It was just a matter of luck and timing. Marty was fully ready to make the film; De Niro was ready to make it. And the nation was ready to see it. You can't plan or scheme for that kind of luck. It just sort of happens—the right film at the right time.

MARTIN SCORSESE: *Taxi Driver* was, I think, the first script I'd worked on that had direct movement from beginning to end. The *Taxi Driver* screenplay seemed very close to me. It was as if I wrote it, that's how strongly I feel about it. Even though the character is from the Midwest, Bob De Niro and I both felt the same way.

Paul wrote *Taxi Driver* out of his own gut and his own heart in two-and-a-half terrible weeks. I felt close to the character by way of Dostoevski. I had always wanted to do a movie of *Notes from the Underground*. I mentioned that to Paul and he said, "Well this is what I have—*Taxi Driver*," and I said, "Great, this is it." Then Paul said, "What about De Niro? He was great in *Mean Streets*." And it turned out that Bob had a feeling for people like Travis.

Taxi Driver was almost like a commission, in a sense. Bob was the actor, I was the director, and Paul wrote the script. The three of us—Schrader, Bob and I—just came together. It was exactly what we wanted, it was one of the strangest things.

Everything was storyboarded. Even the close-ups because we had to shoot so fast. It would have to be, "Get this shot." Then, "Okay, got it." Then, "Go on, okay, next." That's the way it had to go. But we really felt strongly about the picture. It was the only script that really fell into my lap. I don't like to give scripts to people to write and two months later they come back and it's completely finished. There's very little input that can take place at that point. Thematically, you can change things, you can do things, but visualization is hard then. Schrader's scripts afford me the possibility of going back and then revisualizing.

Schrader usually has shorter scenes and has a better concept of the visual. Maybe not the visual that's going to wind up in my movie version of what he's writing, but at least he has a point of view. Other writers usually take a totally literary point of view, mainly dialogue and long descriptions of scenes. Then you've got to really do the whole thing. And very often, you just wind up shooting dialogue on certain pictures. It's not necessarily *bad*. It's just that they take a *literary* approach, and I prefer a *film* approach, and Schrader had a film approach.

ROBERT DE NIRO: I once told Marty we should put together a movie of outtakes. For example, there were outtakes from *Taxi Driver* I would include. When we were shooting that movie there's this terrible bloody scene and, ironically, funny things happened. That whole slaughter scene in the hallway at the end of the movie took us about four or five takes to shoot. Things went wrong technically. There were a lot of special effects and with those things something always goes wrong. You have this sort of very serious, dramatic kind of carnage going on, and all of a sudden, somebody drops something or machinery breaks down. It just blows the whole thing and it turns out to be funny. Oddly enough, in that sort of scene, I guess because it's so gruesome, everybody's ready to laugh. There

MARTIN SCORSESE AND ROBERT DE NIRO (TRAVIS
BICKLE) IN CONFERENCE ON THE SET OF *TAXI DRIVER.*

was a lot of laughing and joking during the shooting between takes. I
remember that. It was a lighter period, even though the material was very
heavy.

MARTIN SCORSESE: I had a basic idea that caused me to be precise.
Whenever I shot Travis Bickle, when he was alone in the car, or whenever
people were talking to him, and that person is in the frame, then the
camera was over their shoulder. He was in everybody else's light, but he
was alone. Nobody was in his frame. As much as possible, I tried to stick
with that. That is a big problem, because Travis is in everybody else's
frame. There would be a certain look in his eyes, a certain close-up of his
face, shot with a certain lens. Subtle—not too wide, not to destroy it, not to
nudge the audience into, "Hey, this guy's a whacko." Not that sort of thing.

But rather to let it sneak up on the audience, like Travis does, and move the camera the way he sees things—all from his point of view. Only one scene is from another point of view: The scene that was improvised was Keitel dancing with Jodie Foster.

I think Bob's range is quite extraordinary. Harry Ufland—who, at the time, was both my agent and Bob's—came by the set one day and Bob had a suit on. He was in between takes, checking out a suit for the wardrobe for *Last Tycoon*. Harry didn't recognize him. For twenty minutes Bob wasn't Travis anymore, he was Monroe Stahr. It's amazing.

HARVEY KEITEL: When we did *Mean Streets* I was living in Greenwich Village, and by *Taxi Driver* I had moved to Hell's Kitchen. I had seen a lot of pimps in my neighborhood. I just put a number of them together, and out came Sport.

There is a great humanity in a pimp. I don't mean humanity in its benevolent sense, I mean humanity in its suffering sense. They come out of a place of great need, usually of poverty, of broken homes, of never having opportunity. What comes out of an environment like that is often a pimp, a thief, a drug addict, a mugger. What the hell does someone like that know about giving love, caring for, supporting, being the most you can be? They're trying to eat, keep the rats out of their food.

I worked with a pimp for a few weeks in creating the role. We wrote nearly all of the dialogue, me and this pimp. I recorded the improvisations we did. He'd play the pimp and I'd play the girl; I'd see the way he'd treat me, then I would play the pimp and *he'd* play the girl. We did that for a few weeks over at the Actors Studio.

PETER BOYLE: We filmed my scene in a place called the Bellmore Cafeteria, which used to be open twenty-fours a day. At one A.M. it's one of the great places to observe human nature. It's also a hangout for cab drivers, and a few months before the film, Marty and Paul Schrader and I went down and talked to several cab drivers at the Bellmore. The scene with the Wizard, my role, and Travis, was in the script, but it was very general. After that trip to the Bellmore, I told Marty that I had some ideas. I wrote down a few notes, and I went to Marty's suite at the St. Regis Hotel. He liked to stay there because it was Orson Welles's favorite hotel. I said, "Here's what I'd like to do," and I did this improvisation. He said, "Do it

HARVEY KEITEL (SPORT) AND JODI FOSTER (IRIS) IN *TAXI DRIVER*.

again," and he pulled out a tape recorder and recorded it. Then he sent the tape over to his secretary, and that was the scene.

I really wanted to communicate the idea that Travis is in such a state that you couldn't communicate with him. No wisdom of any kind could reach him. I didn't know how that was going to happen. When we did it, Bobby looked at me and said,"You know, you're full of shit, Wizard." I was really pleased. That's what I'd been working toward.

I think the essential problem in *Taxi Driver* is a lack of general feeling, and a lack of general release. That's why the guns are always there. When the passenger, played by Marty, sits in the back of the taxi, and talks about what he wants to do with his wife and about the Magnum he wants to use, these are all images of his inability to experience the flow of feeling. Travis creates dead bodies because the feeling is not released, and the blocked energy creates a deadness.

MARTIN SCORSESE: The scene I did in the taxicab was filmed during the last week of shooting. It just worked out that way. All the people that I wanted to see in New York had been used in the film already. George Memmoli, the guy who said "you're a mook" in *Mean Streets*—a very fat guy—was to play that part. George, unfortunately, got into a bad accident some place in the South doing a film called *The Farmer*—ten years later he died from that accident. He just couldn't make it, and there was nobody else around. I didn't trust anybody with it. So I just got in the back of the taxi and played the part myself. I learned a lot from Bob in that scene. I remember saying, "Put down the flag, put down the flag." De Niro said, "No, *make* me put it down." And Bobby wasn't going to put down the flag until he was *convinced* that I meant it. And then I understood. His move had to be a certain way and if he didn't feel it, the move wasn't going to be right. For me, it was a pretty terrifying scene to do.

MICHAEL CHAPMAN: Marty needed a cameraman for *Taxi Driver*. Someone recommended me, and I met him and we talked. We immediately started talking about movies in terms of the classic shots, like, "Remember this from that movie . . . " and it went on from there.

SCORSESE PLAYS A PASSENGER IN TRAVIS BICKLE'S CAB IN *TAXI DRIVER*.

We worked from Marty's storyboards and they are the best. I know because he makes no pretense of their being art. Storyboards can be inhibiting, if they have a very elaborate and overdrawn style. That can force you to try to duplicate the drawing in your shot. But Marty's storyboards are much more liberating. They give the idea of what he wants and they allow that idea to interact with the realities of whether it can, in fact, be done. He gives you the essence of what he needs to say without oppressing you.

It is so hard to talk about cinematography because it is cinematography. There is no separation between the technical part and the images. Much of what passes for art in movies is the correct solution to technical problems, like meter and rhyme in poetry.

Movies that solve mechanical problems very well—often, in Marty's case, complicated technical problems that force you to work harder— seem to me to be better movies emotionally than movies that simply concentrate on dredging up emotions in the actors. When Marty's on, the motions and angles of the camera genuinely have emotional content.

MARTIN SCORSESE: We had a good team. Michael Chapman was a hell of a guy to work with. Michael did *The Last Detail.* I liked it. It had a certain look I liked.

It was the first time in New York I actually shot a film the right way. But once you put a camera in the street, it's not real anymore, I don't care what you say; you pick up things, certain things happen, it's never quite the reality.

For *Taxi Driver* we shot political rallies at Thirty-eighth Street and Seventh Avenue in the garment district in one-hundred degree weather with thousands of people in the street. It was crazy. Every time I turned away to talk to somebody, I couldn't get back to the camera. It was quite an experience.

I was accused, in *Mean Streets,* of just showing the garbage on the streets. When I was shooting *Taxi Driver,* it was filthy because of a garbage strike and everywhere I aimed the camera, there were mounds of garbage. I said, "They are going to kill me! Guys, take away some of the garbage." Here I was trying to control reality, but that *was* the reality. In L.A., with *Mean Streets,* we had to put garbage in the street to make it look like New York.

As for the score, I had become aware of Bernard Herrmann's scores when I was eleven or twelve. I loved them! He had a contract at Fox, and he is known for all those strange films with wonderful scores. Later, when I saw them on television I said, "No wonder I liked them. Bernard Herrmann. Of course." He did the Hitchcock pictures, especially *Marnie* and *Vertigo*; *Psycho* is the traditional one to mention, but the *Marnie* score is even more interesting.

In *Mean Streets*, the score is music I heard on the streets where I lived, in the neighborhood, in the tenements. You often have one song coming from one window, another coming from another—opera, rock 'n' roll, Frank Sinatra. That's the kind of score we had for *Mean Streets*, and the kind of score I wanted to keep. With *Alice Doesn't Live Here Anymore*, it was the same thing, the music you listen to is the music she listened to—Alice Faye, that sort of thing.

But Travis Bickle in *Taxi Driver* didn't listen to anything! The only person who could capture this was Bernard Herrmann. He was very cantankerous about it, and said, "I don't do things about cab drivers!" But after reading the script he agreed. He said, "I like when he poured peach brandy on the cornflakes. I like that. I'll do it."

In terms of the John Hinckley shooting, people ask me how I feel about it. Well, I'm a Catholic. It's easy to make me feel guilty. In fact, I only learned about the connection on Academy Award night, the day after the President was shot. I was washing up and dressing. I'd been nominated for *Raging Bull*, but I knew I wasn't going to get the award. I knew it. I knew I wouldn't get it, but it was okay, I was going to go anyway. There were some pictures on the TV of the president being shot the day before, but I had turned the sound off, so I didn't know any connection to *Taxi Driver* existed.

When I got to the Academy that night, it was myself and Harry Ufland, my wife, and De Niro. We were the first ones let in. I said, "This is great. This is terrific." And then I had to go to the men's room, and suddenly, these three big guys came with me. Three big guys with jackets, with a lot of metal inside. I'm not kidding! I thought they had radios, they had wires and things hanging out of their ears. I said, "Gee, this security is incredible tonight. The security is remarkable." A few years earlier, at the awards, when Jodie Foster and I were nominees, I had received a threatening letter about *Taxi Driver*: "If Jodie Foster wins for what you made her do, you will pay for it with your life." So we got the FBI then, and that night when Billy

Friedkin was directing the awards show, he let me in first. They showed me my FBI person, a woman in a gown, with a gun in her bag. Jodie didn't win so that was that. So now I said, "Well, the security is even better than the last time, this is fantastic!" Now, even in the men's room, they say, "Are you okay?" "Yes," I say. "I'm fine, I'm washing my hands. I'm fine."

When Lillian Gish was onstage to give the award for Best Picture, someone said to me, "Come on, it's going to be the Redford picture [*Ordinary People*]. Let's get out of here." I said, "No, no, no, you can't. Lillian Gish is on the stage. You don't get up and walk out on Lillian Gish." But it was the FBI that wanted me out!

I went backstage with Bob to put some sort of statement together. [De Niro won Best Actor for *Raging Bull*.] They didn't want me moving around. Everybody knew why but me. Bob told me that a connection to *Taxi Driver* had been made in the shooting of the president. I never thought in a million years that there was a connection with the film. It turned out even the limo driver was FBI.

We thought it was rather unfair, in the Hinckley trial, to show the film over and over. The film is a disturbing picture, but we made it as a labor of love. I really thought nobody would see that picture. Only Bob had a sense that the movie might be more successful than we thought. When he put on that Mohawk wig, he realized we had something special.

But showing the movie at the trial was unfair. It's like the end of *Fahrenheit 451*, where the guy is chased, and they just pick up anybody at random so they can tell people at home, "It's okay. We caught him. You can rest." It's okay; he did it because of our picture. Now you can all sleep.

NEW YORK, NEW YORK (1977)

"MARTY SAID HE WANTED TO MAKE *NEW YORK, NEW YORK* BECAUSE THE NEW YORK HE GREW UP IN HAD NOTHING TO DO WITH THE NEW YORK HE LOVED IN THE MOVIES."
—LIZA MINNELLI

On a Hollywood back lot, Martin Scorsese began *New York, New York* with a re-creation of V-J Day, 1945. This day, so important in his parents' stories, came alive. In the jubilant Times Square crowd, one goofy ex-soldier in a

Hawaiian shirt stands out. This is Jimmy Doyle (Robert De Niro). The first image is of his brown and white wing-tip "vagabond shoes."

We follow Jimmy into a crowded ballroom, where for fifteen minutes he tries to get Francine Evans (Liza Minnelli) to dance with him. Jimmy tries every possible approach—direct, coy, humorous, obnoxious—and still Francine refuses him. Every movement, every thrust and parry, is timed to be both comic and touching. The scene encapsulates their relationship, the key to the movie. He is enticing, seductive, funny, and dangerous. She is warmhearted, generous, and sensible. She should say no. She tries but somehow the attraction draws her back. In the background, the band that plays for the dancing couples introduces the other element in the story. Both Francine and Jimmy are musicians. Jimmy wields his saxophone like a weapon in a war waged to create new sounds that will blow away old musical patterns. Francine does not want to challenge audiences. She wishes to exhilarate and entertain within the bounds of tradition.

For six days, a thousand extras and dozens of crew members watched Minnelli, Scorsese, and De Niro invent a relationship between a woman destined to be the top singer of her generation and a cool saxophone player with a new sound in his head who dreams of finding "the major chord." All the lines were improvised. They made it up as they went along.

The participants found that acting without a net both energized and terrified them. Martin Scorsese called this film his "valentine to Holly- wood." He wanted to show big band life after the Second World War using the styles of that period. But as the movie unfolded, contemporary themes kept breaking through and the film became the story of a marriage between two artists. *New York, New York* is *The Red Shoes* with boxing gloves. Love does *not* conquer all. Jimmy writes a bluesy tune and Francine adds the lyrics: Together they create the song "New York, New York" as a tribute to the talent each one recognizes in the other. But their differences are too great; they must part. Near the conclusion of the movie, Jimmy watches Francine in her latest hit movie at Radio City Music Hall. In a mammoth production number reminiscent of *A Star Is Born*, Francine sings of "Happy Endings." As Jimmy watches, it seems this moment is the only happy ending possible for them: a life apart, in which each pursues his or her own artistic career. Francine, though tempted, does not return to Jimmy. Scorsese's "valentine to Hollywood" has a most un-Hollywood ending.

New York, New York is the first of Scorsese's movies to get the real Hollywood publicity treatment. Pre-film hype is high. Minnelli and De Niro appear on the covers of the leading news magazines. The critics are eager to see this first full-blown example of Scorsese's talents, but the movie confuses them. Why is the director of *Taxi Driver* and *Mean Streets* doing a lavish Hollywood musical anyway? When the film comes out, some judge it as too dark for a musical and too musical for a serious drama. Audiences are enthusiastic, but the critical ambivalence has its effect. The movie does not succeed at the box office. Scorsese senses that the Hollywood establishment deems it a failure.

Yet moments in *New York, New York* carry an emotional charge as strong as any Scorsese had created. The amazing first scene is a triumph of acting and editing. The street ballet between a sailor and his girl evokes the simple past portrayed in *On the Town*, while Jimmy Doyle's brooding presence points to a sharper reality. Francine and Jimmy's walk in the snow is as romantic as any classic movie scene of the forties, but seconds later, Jimmy shatters that idyll: He lies down under the tires of a taxi to coerce Francine into immediate marriage. Later, when their marriage is breaking up, Francine and Jimmy fight so fiercely that she goes into labor. At the hospital, the wife and mother, soon-to-be-abandoned, comforts her husband, who can not even look upon the face of his newborn son. She understands that if Jimmy sees the baby, he will not be able to leave—and that Jimmy cannot stay.

The emotions Scorsese captured were so powerful that it would be years before he himself understood what the movie really meant.

MARTIN SCORSESE: Since I was born in 1942, the music I grew up with was big band music—that was the music I first learned. The making of *New York, New York* came out of my having fallen in love with a record my parents had by Django Reinhardt, a great guitarist, and the Hot Club of France, a swing group from the late thirties. Jazz violinist Stephane Grappelli was part of the group. I fell in love with that song " 'Deed I Do," and with "Love Letters." I was also fascinated by this photograph of my uncles in World War II uniforms—a sepia shot of them standing with their feet on the bumper of an old Morton. Those elements helped me make the film.

MR. SCORSESE: I used to take Marty and Frankie to hear the big bands—to the Paramount, to the Capitol.

MRS. SCORSESE: The Strand, the Capitol. You remember, Charlie?

MR. SCORSESE: I took them to see Ted Lewis. I took them to see Louis Prima. I took them to see *every one* of them.

MRS. SCORSESE: I saw Lucille Ball and her husband, Desi Arnaz. I saw the bandleader, what was his name?

MR. SCORSESE: Xavier Cugat?

MRS. SCORSESE: Xavier Cugat, I saw. But that's not him.

MR. SCORSESE: Who?

MRS. SCORSESE: The one that used to sing "Racing with the Moon."

MR. SCORSESE: Vaughn Monroe.

MRS. SCORSESE: Vaughn Monroe. I saw him.

MR. SCORSESE: Paul Whiteman I used to love. I used to love Eddy Duchin. I took the boys.

MARTIN SCORSESE: I read in the *Hollywood Reporter* that someone planned to produce a film on the big band era called *New York, New York*. I called my agent and said, "Hey, can I do that?"

I wanted to make a different kind of film, about a struggling band in the forties trying to make it, one that was totally personal. I thought there was really no difference between a struggling band in the forties and myself, trying to make it in this business with all the pressures. It's also about two creative people who are struggling. They don't know where their next meal is going to come from, and it's worse because they are on the road. The film deals with a relationship, and how it grows, and then gets destroyed, and hopefully in the end is resolved.

I wanted to do it as a real Hollywood film because the Hollywood film is still something I treasure. When I first came to Hollywood I was disappointed to find that the studio system was *over*. In the early 1960s it died. All the great directors were dead or not working. When I went, I said, "I'm going to make a film that is in the old style of Hollywood." The sets would be designed like the musicals beginning in about 1945, and it would look like the films made then. As it built, as it went on in time, it would reflect that type of film made at MGM and Universal, films like *I Love Melvin*.

The film was to be a mix of *The Man I Love*, Raoul Walsh's forties *film noir* with music—*The Man I Love* has all the Gershwin songs—plus a little touch of *Road House*, a Fox picture with Richard Widmark, plus the technicolor films. I wanted to do a valentine to Hollywood. But update it, update it to the point where you have the look and feel of an old Hollywood film that grows in time, and each time, each date, it would look like a film of that period. It would look like a film of 1947, then it would look like a film of 1950. This was done through sets, costumes, hair and makeup.

Everything was exaggerated. Shoulder pads were an inch bigger inside, and the ties were made even wider. Giorgio Armani said that he studied the costumes and decided to make clothes "like *New York, New York*."

We called it *New York, New York*, but my concept of the film could never be shot *in* New York. It had to be shot in the backlots of Hollywood. When I was a kid I'd go to the Sixth Street and Second Avenue Loews—which became the Fillmore East in the sixties. They showed MGM and Columbia films and pictures by Paramount. I would go there and see films that took place in New York, but the streets looked different to me. The curbs were the wrong size. The people looked kind of strange and lifeless, walking around, and very polite. They were like those books in public school, "See Jane run. See Dick."

It had to be shot in color and look like the back lots of Hollywood. It had to have Hollywood extras that looked a certain way and acted a certain way. The extras were there, but the back lots were not, and the sets were not. Even the train station was gone where Fred Astaire sang "I'll Go My Way By Myself" at the beginning of *Bandwagon*, my favorite musical. *Nothing* existed.

I had studied a lot of the older films, including a picture called *My Dream Is Yours*, with Doris Day and Jack Carson, and when Doris Day heard that we were dealing with that, she said, "That's my life story." It was similar to what Francine Evans goes through in *New York, New York*.

The sets were designed by Boris Leven. I wanted Boris because he had done *Giant* and *The Sound of Music.* His first job, I believe, was the icons on *The Scarlet Empress,* a Von Sternberg film. He understood the look of the time. Cinematography was very important. I worked with Laszlo Kovacs. The camera movement usually had to be on a plane, even if it's just tracking shots of people walking. It was cumbersome and took a while to do. I didn't want any *new* look to it. In fact, the ending was reshot by Vilmos Zsigmond. I asked Vilmos not to use any filters, but I think he couldn't help it. There's something beautiful in them, something so fantastic. And if you look at some of the close-ups of Liza Minnelli waiting at the elevator in the final scene, I think you can tell the difference. Maybe it's the lighting—whatever he did, I *noticed.*

I wanted an audience to remember those films as though they were back watching a film literally made at that time. Every cut, every frame was a reference to Vincente Minnelli, a reference to George Cukor, and many of the directors of the period. Of course, the difference was that I wanted to do something that was contemporary.

IRWIN WINKLER: I liked the script of *New York, New York* a great deal. Earl MacRauch wrote the first version. Marty brought Mardik Martin in. When you make a picture, you always assume that the people involved with you have that same enthusiasm for it. But there was a basic unhappiness with some of the fluff in the script, and Marty was going for more reality. Against this background of the forties kind of unreal-fantasyland of shooting on the MGM lot—almost a homage to the old MGM musicals—Marty wanted to tell a very contemporary story about two people in conflict about their careers, and in their own lives. But what happened, at some point, was that the actors and Marty both lost confidence in the script and tried to improve it as they were going along. Now, all the physical problems about making a musical are difficult to begin with. Making any film is complicated, but the problems are compounded when music has to be prerecorded and played back on the set. And if you're improvising and you don't have much preparation, it's even worse.

MARDIK MARTIN: The trouble with *New York, New York* was that in the first eight days, they shot the scene in the beginning where Jimmy tries to pick Francine up, and the improvs worked beautifully. That whole thing could be a twenty-minute movie. Then they went crazy. Then everything got out of hand. Everyone was trying to improve it by improvisation; it doesn't always work.

The picture never had an ending. I came up with a dozen endings and none of them worked. If you have an ending, you can improvise toward that goal. If you don't know where you're going . . . . I mean, there was a resolution to this story, but never a dramatic ending. Even today, you watch it, and something is missing. The production number "Happy Endings" was left out and now it's back in. That ran twelve minutes and was wonderful. I haven't seen that version and so I don't know the difference it might make.

New York, New York was painful for me. I did a lot of work on that film. It was the kind of work that would drive you nuts, writing the night before you shoot, trying to save the picture.

ROBERT DE NIRO: On *New York, New York*, they were having a lot of trouble with the script from the very beginning. A lot of time was spent on the script. Marty, Liza, and I would get together and work on it. We'd all be

LIZA MINNELLI (FRANCINE EVANS) AND ROBERT DE NIRO (JIMMY DOYLE) IN *NEW YORK, NEW YORK*.

trying to rectify things that just were not working. We were trying to shape it, but because of the improvisation we were always trying to build on what had been shot before or to fit a scene in if we shot out of sequence. There was always a shaky structure. I think Marty would agree with me that you have to work those things out before you do it. It has to be in the script before. You don't want to waste time figuring it out, because it's very costly as you're shooting. We had a schedule and we were slowly getting close to the time where we had to finish the film. So we started before we really had the script in shape and did a lot of improvising.

LIZA MINNELLI: In *New York, New York*, all the improvisation came because I had a great director and a great co-star in Bobby De Niro. I had never improvised in my life. They kept encouraging me, saying, "You'll be great, you'll be fine." It even got to the point where we improvised dance numbers. I'd say, "Okay, whaddaya want? You got it!"

In the first scene of *New York, New York*, we did an hour of improvisation and Marty decided that all he was going to do was use the parts I said "No" in. I had said a lot more, but that's what he kept. I think I said "No" twenty-seven times in twenty-seven different ways. That's Marty. The whole movie was improvised. We would get together in a room and Marty would explain the sequence of the film. Then we would improvise on a situation. We started this about a month before the movie was actually filmed. Marty would videotape all that improvisation, take it home, write a scene from that. He would bring the scene back so that we knew exactly where to hit our marks and then he made us improvise on that. It was a structured improvisation.

In a scene where Bobby takes over the band, that improvisation was just fascinating. Neither Marty nor Bobby had been in staged musical numbers, so Marty asked me, "Okay, the band would be where? Here? Okay. And you would be . . . " So we set it up, then he talked to Bobby and me separately so neither knew what the other was thinking about. Then he simply turned us loose.

Marty used to sit underneath the camera and kind of conduct my performances. I wasn't looking at him, but I could sense him, could feel him conducting me. I knew when he wanted me to speed up or to put a lid on it, to calm down.

I think what Marty knows and is able to get across to his actors without ever hitting them over the head with it is that it's not what you say, it's what you don't say on film that's important. That's what's interesting. That's what's mysterious, and he understands mystery.

MARTIN SCORSESE: I had always planned very carefully on the other pictures. In *Boxcar Bertha*, every shot was laid out, five hundred shots all drawn. Then doing *Mean Streets* in twenty-seven days, that was all laid out, every shot. Then *Alice Doesn't Live Here Anymore*, every shot laid on paper because we only had forty days to shoot, though we did improvise the last part of the script. In *Taxi Driver*, every shot was drawn out because of the special effects and the awful nature of what the actors had to do. So by the time we started *New York, New York, Taxi Driver* came out and *Mean Streets* had gotten some nice reviews, and *Alice* had gotten some nice reviews. Ellen won an Academy Award and Bobby had begun to work on *The Godfather, Part II. Taxi Driver* won the grand prize at Cannes. We started to get cocky. So throw away the script! We improvised a lot of it. And so we shot a lot of film.

The big band pieces from the opening on V-J Day night, the dance sequence, went on for about twenty minutes. Jimmy Doyle tries to pick up Francine Evans and she resists him. That's when everything sort of fell to pieces and came together at the same time, that's when we decided to go with our instincts and improvise. It was beautiful. Both Minnelli and De Niro did an extraordinary improvisation that went on for five to six days of shooting—with a thousand people behind them, all the time, dancing.

IRWIN WINKLER: I was nervous! We were going over budget, we didn't know from day to day what would happen. We had big problems. What I tried to do was keep a balance, tried to maintain some semblance of an organization, and also tried to make the best film possible. So on one hand, I was trying to encourage as much as I could as far as getting the script better, and on the other hand, trying to deal with the reality: If you finish shooting at eleven o'clock at night, you can't start the next morning until eleven. You can't have people coming in at seven the next morning; it doesn't work that way. So I was trying to maintain a balance of getting the best film, and also trying to keep some real fiscal responsibility.

One incident stays with me. Marty and I were shooting very, very late one night. We were doing the scene with Bobby and Liza, by now it was eight-thirty, nine o'clock, and we were on the twenty-second take. Everybody was exhausted. And the next day we had to go to an exterior location, and if we didn't start by some reasonable time the next day, we couldn't finish the next day's work, because we'd lose the light. All the problems started multiplying. And I said to Marty, "Listen, you know, at twenty-two takes, how do you feel, don't you think we have it?" He said, "You know, Irwin, on the last take I think I saw a tear coming out of the corner of Liza's eye. I think if I go two more takes, maybe three, I can get the tear. Do you want me to go for the tear, or do you want to stop?" And I said, "Go for the tear."

LIZA MINNELLI: I got my entire performance by looking at Marty's eyes. I think Marty understands the struggle between feelings and thought—that intellect and emotion are always at war in people. He seems to be able to bring that out and express it.

In *New York, New York*, the era, the times, the values were so completely different. As a woman, you didn't think "career." It was still every girl's dream to get married and have children and be a good wife and mother. If, as a woman, you sang, that was okay on the side, but you didn't give up everything or risk losing your child to go on tour with a band. It was out of the question. Francine Evans was a product of those rules. She didn't have the anger or pain in her life or the hurdles to cross. Everything had been easy for her. She always sang well, and got a job here and there, and was working steadily as a jingle singer. She was respected in the business. She was marking time and enjoying her life. All of a sudden, here comes this whirlwind man who knocks the wind out of her and who she is crazy about. She tries to put the sense of values that are all around her into this relationship and, of course, that never works. It should, but it doesn't. Then, once you have that kind of pain and that abandonment that she felt, it just pushes you into fighting a little harder for some attention to be paid, as Willy Loman would say. It was the hurt that made her a star. She put everything she had been through into her songs. Jimmy Doyle loved Francine, but he was a musician, and that was his priority, and he left her.

But I think to be a great star, that isolation, that pain is a necessary part. The funny thing about Marty is the more emotionally painful something is the more humor he finds in it. Human nature *is* truly hilarious when you look at it from a certain point of view. So he has more courage because he has more humor.

ROBERT DE NIRO: There was a scene with Liza where we had a fight in the car. I thought it was funny to be so hopping mad that my head was sort of banging on the ceiling and I'd hit my hand somehow. I didn't get out of control, but I just went a smidgen over, which can happen. Liza got hurt, and I think I hurt my hand, too. But we would try anything. So sometimes you can't predict the outcome.

LIZA MINNELLI: My singing performance was completely different from any I had done before. I studied the way big band singers sang, and even how they held their hands. You never went out as the "star," you went out as part of the arrangement. I went so overboard with it that I almost backed up too much. Marty said, "You can't be like that, you get out there and it's going to be different." But he trusted me musically on everything. I did a lot of the arrangements, laid them out. It was marvelous because I had studied all of this as a kid. Marty guided my performance so that it was tailored to that of a performer in that era. It had to be, otherwise it wouldn't make any sense.

In my own act, when I get out on stage I'm an animal. I feel my job is to entertain and *win* that audience. To be a part of the band would never enter my mind. So it was great fun doing that and doing it with such style.

About a year before we filmed it, Marty came to see me. I was at Lake Tahoe performing at Harrods. At the end of one of my big numbers, people stood and started to take pictures, flashbulbs were going off. He came back and saw me and said, "I want to use that. It's marvelous." Then when I saw how he did it, he had heightened reality because he used the old-fashioned bulbs with the aluminum backing. Not necessarily because that's the kind of camera used then, but it just heightened that scene. He takes reality and pushes it.

The last scene, where I'm singing "New York, New York," is like being part of the sound, an energy. You feel it. Then when you feel the audience send that energy back to you, it's like an explosion.

During the musical numbers at the end, I felt he took the audience to a height. It was, "This woman is going to be all right, she's creating, she's found her thing, she's okay." And it gave you a much better feeling once she pushed that elevator button in the end of the film. That was the most couragous thing she did. She was saying, "I'm not going to walk back into something that I'm so drawn to that it's going to destroy me." If life and talent are God-given gifts and the only thing you really have in your whole life is yourself, then you have to look out for yourself. Those were my thoughts when I pushed the button. That was Francine Evans.

MARTIN SCORSESE: We used the same set for the end of the film that we used for the opening. Jimmy walks away with a cigarette, and Francine is singing "The World Turns Around" as he sits down and she watches him. Then she says, "I'm going to sing *you* a song," and it's "New York, New York."

Originally we'd had a big production number also—the "Happy Endings." But it never made it into the film. Or rather it *was* in until two weeks before I locked it, and then I just dropped it. I shouldn't have pulled it out. It was the first thing we shot. It worked so beautifully. We'd had a ten-day shooting schedule, and ten days shooting is what we took. It was a beautiful sequence. We showed it to anybody who wanted to see something from the film. The studio people loved it. But at the end, the movie was long and there was pressure to cut it. People said, "You are too close to it, you fell in love with that number, you are indulging yourself. Take it out and look at the movie once without it in." So I did that, and I said, "Okay, you're right. Okay, you're right. I'll show you that I'm not indulging myself. It *stays* out. The hell with it!" And I let it go. I was so tired and so out of it and so crazed by that time, my judgment was off.

I had three editors. I was editing day and night, a very bad way to work. We tried to cut the film down, and it didn't want to cut. It didn't want to go down. It was like a monster. It was impossible. We did each scene painstakingly—and they were beautifully constructed scenes. But the problem was the whole. See, we were wise guys, we had won a prize in Cannes, and we didn't need the script. So while each scene might work, the whole suffered. But in spite of everything, I think it's a better picture than the original script. There is no doubt about it. But if I had gone about the reconstruction of that script and that story, and known what I wanted from the beginning, it would have been much stronger.

But if we hadn't gone through that pain we never would have gotten that story—the story of the marriage in the film. In the final analysis, it's a very honest film about marriage and, in some ways, it's a beautiful film. I don't know whether it would have been better if I had planned it out and stuck to what I wanted to do. Because I don't know if the rawness of it, and whatever truth we had created, would have been reached if we hadn't gone through all the pain.

LIZA MINNELLI: Marty absolutely loves what he is doing. And he's a great audience. Everybody wants to please a great audience. And when you watch him in the editing room, you really know that you're watching a master. He can edit faster than any editor I have ever seen. He was wonderful with me because he'd say, "See that take? That's not good. Now this one, that's good." Now he would have *never* said that on the set. He never says it's bad, he just says try it again and give me a variation. He can recognize the truth. He knows how to put what he has in his mind on the screen.

I come by my understanding of being directed honestly from my father and mother. I've been around movies all my life. It never bothered me to be shown how to do something. But I never had to watch what Marty was *doing*. I would watch his eyes and then I knew what to give him.

He was my dad's favorite young director. That is some compliment, because my dad was an incredible man. Marty had this feeling that *New York, New York* was his valentine to Hollywood and then Hollywood rejected it. But I get the most incredible emotion from people on that movie. People love that film.

IRWIN WINKLER: The reaction to *New York, New York* was a surprise. We thought we were making this great film that was also a great musical. The critics were somewhat kinder to us than the audience was. The audience didn't go to see it initially, and it was not a big success by any stretch of the imagination.

I think Marty was as disappointed as I was. We got no nominations for that picture. Could you believe the song "New York, New York" was never nominated for an Academy Award? So I can see how he would see it as a "rejection by Hollywood." But I don't feel that way, we were all working again ten minutes after we finished.

After doing *New York, New York*, two weeks later, Marty was doing *The Last Waltz*, so he wasn't rejected, and then we did *Raging Bull*, which nobody rejected. We did what we wanted! I don't know what it means when anybody says "rejected by Hollywood." I mean, *who* is Hollywood? There's no such person.

MARTIN SCORSESE: Maybe a European director could have gotten away with it, but this was an American film that promised to be a happy musical from the 1940s. It starts out that way, and then it goes another way. I was interested in the jealousies that grow between two artists working together. I think it was a fascinating movie. But it was a heartbreak. It was rereleased in 1981 and got much better reviews, though it was essentially the same picture. There were an additional fifteen minutes or so added. There had been an implication, especially in Europe, that United Artists had originally forced me to cut fifteen minutes from the general release and the European release. But they didn't force me at all. Eric Pleskow said to me, "Look, we haven't been doing very well with it. I'll leave it up to you totally. But if you can cut another twelve minutes out of it on the general release, we'll be able to make some money." Because we had gone way over budget, I felt a responsibility, and I also felt that the people who really wanted, really needed to see the film had already seen it. Unfortunately, the cut without the fifteen minutes was what the Europeans saw.

But I think the reviews were better because by that time the industry had changed. In 1977, a week or so after we first opened, *Star Wars* opened. The whole industry went another way. It became megabucks. I'm not condemning it, and I'm not criticizing it either. *Star Wars* was a wonderful film. It started a whole new way of thinking, and of looking at films. It's just that people became interested in something else entirely, and *New York, New York* looked hopelessly old-fashioned. And, obviously, the picture was too long. I think that people originally simply didn't want to see our film. That was all. The film has a kind of down feeling to it. It had been pummeled by the press and by Hollywood itself. If I'd had better control of myself when I was making the picture, and if I'd had better control of the scripting, it would have been a much more concise film.

Look, I'm a very impressionable person. My picture got bad reviews and it was very badly received in Hollywood. It seemed that as much as they loved me for the other three films, *Mean Streets*, *Alice*, and *Taxi*, I got pounded badly for the fourth one. Sometimes I think the best thing would be to make films here in New York, to not deal with Hollywood, simply try to do the things you really believe in.

Eventually, I understood the picture. Jean-Luc Godard came over for lunch one day and he was talking about how much he liked *New York, New York*. He said it was basically about the impossibility of two creative people in a relationship—the jealousies, the envy, the temperament. I began to realize that it was so close to home that I wasn't able to articulate it while I was making the film.

But I had to go through that. Some people go through it and don't come back. I came back with *Raging Bull,* but it was tough. For a time after *New York, New York* I had really been thinking of going to live in Italy and making documentary pictures on the lives of the saints for the rest of my life. But *The Last Waltz* came along and that helped.

THE LAST WALTZ (1978)

"WE STAYED ON THE STAGE."
—MARTIN SCORSESE

In an atmosphere reminiscent of Woodstock, Martin Scorsese and his cameramen friends gathered to film a concert—only now instead of students, the cameramen were cinematographers of great note: Freddie Schuler, Michael Chapman, Laszlo Kovacs, Vilmos Zsigmond. The Band—Robbie Robertson, Richard Manuel, Rick Danko, Levon Helm, and Garth Hudson—who had backed Bob Dylan for fifteen years and created rock 'n' roll history with albums like *Music from The Big Pink,* were holding their farewell performance at Winterland in San Francisco, on Thanksgiving Day. They invited a few of their friends—including Van Morrison, Joni Mitchell, Neil Young, Neil Diamond, Muddy Waters, Bob Dylan, and Ringo Starr—to join them in this final jam, the "Last Waltz." It was an opportunity to make a memorable concert film.

Scorsese, still revved-up from shooting miles of film on *New York, New York,* supervised the action, a whirling dervish in headphones. On the notebook in front of him were lyrics of all the songs, broken down and matched to camera movements. Order was difficult to maintain in the barrage of sound. He screamed instructions to the various cameras, gesturing to them over the music, but his real focus was on the stage.

MARTIN SCORSESE: The only good thing that happened in the period after *New York, New York* was *The Last Waltz. The Last Waltz* was done

MARTIN SCORSESE DIRECTS ROBBIE ROBERTSON AND THE BAND IN
CONCERT FOR *THE LAST WALTZ.*

right at the end of the shooting of *New York, New York,* which had been
planned for eleven weeks but dragged on to twenty. In the nineteenth
week of shooting, Jonathan Taplin, the producer of *Mean Streets,* called
me. He had been a roadie for *The Band.* And Taplin said there was going to
be this farewell concert, and he's got all these people there—Bob Dylan,
Muddy Waters, Van Morrison, Neil Young, Joni Mitchell, and others—and
I said, "It sounds great." I was in a shooting mode. I was really tuned into
shooting. And I was just shooting everything. I was shooting, shooting,
shooting, and I wanted to *keep* shooting. We had wrapped *New York, New
York* around October, and the concert was going on in November—
Thanksgiving Day.

What I wound up doing was getting in touch with Robbie Robertson. He
just wanted to get the concert on film, and that could be done in 16
millimeter, the way we did *Woodstock.*

Ironically, The Band hadn't wanted the camera crew on the stage at
Woodstock. They were very nervous. The footage that we did with them

was murky, but we loved their music. It was like our culture—you know, like John Ford movies—but it was difficult to get a good cut out of their stuff, so I was skeptical about working on this.

ROBBIE ROBERTSON: When I decided I wanted to do *The Last Waltz*, and I tried to figure out who had the sensitivity, or the knowledge of music, to direct the film, I started to make up my list of the directors. I wrote down Marty's name. I couldn't think of anybody else! I had one man on my list, and a big long piece of paper!

In *Who's That Knocking*, there is a scene where these guys are throwing a gun around, and the song "El Watusi" is playing. Ray Barreto is singing in Spanish. "El Watusi" sounds like it should be an African thing, and these guys are all Italian. Now, none of this makes any sense, but when it's going on it is absolutely brilliant.

So I met with Marty to tell him about this idea under the worst circumstances at the worst time for him. He was doing *New York, New York*; his life was in shambles; everything was wrong. And he still agreed to do it! I thought, "This guy's just crazy. This guy's up my alley. If he's crazy enough to get into this trench, well, he's all right with me."

MARTIN SCORSESE: I figured at least with *The Last Waltz*, we would have control. We talked about the type of shooting we'd do. The idea was, for archival purposes, to record the concert. We would put two cameras on the side behind The Band, and a camera on the lip of the stage. The idea was that it not be a typical concert film. We had decided that if we were going to do that with the cameras, if we had that much control, we should use 35 millimeter instead of 16. I said, "Really, what's the worst that can happen? The worst that can happen is that you wind up with archival footage in 35 millimeter." But the floor was built over an ice rink and the floor bounced when everyone was there jumping up and down. The place would rock—literally. In this case the joint was really jumping, so we had to pour concrete to lock the 35 millimeter cameras into that. Then we had to anchor a big tower for shots of the stage. Bill Graham helped with all this.

I got Boris Leven to come in and design the set. He was at that time of his life where he was able to work on pictures that could cost two dollars and pictures that were costing $20 million. It was insane, because here is this guy who was about seventy years old—rock 'n' roll wasn't his thing—

but he had a great sense of humor, and he walked in with us and looked up and said, "Chandeliers, covered with chandeliers." "Great," we said, "covered with chandeliers." I said, "Absolutely!" And Robbie said, "Yes, yes. Fantastic!" And the kids from Winterland who were in charge of props said, "Excuse me, we only have two chandeliers." He says, "Fine, we'll go with two chandeliers." He put the two over there, bang, without dropping a beat. We got the set from *La Traviata*, from the San Francisco Opera Festival, but the stage was small. We had these big, wooden pillars and chandeliers, so there was very little room on the stage.

The main thing was that I was forced to make a script from what Robbie gave me. He gave me a sheet for each song, which had the title, the vocals, the verses, who would be playing what instrument, who would be the most important person at that place in the song. I designed the lighting with different lighting effects going on and off. Not like the old psychedelic shows but very, very simple, with each color in some weird way meaning something.

Michael Chapman was at the light board. He got upset because I wanted to use violet and yellow for the song "The Weight." He said, "Those two colors are Catholic colors and this is a Protestant song. I'm not going to let you do that." He loved The Band's music so much. He argued with me that since I'm Catholic, I don't understand their music because it was so influenced by gospel music. We had great religious discussions and fights about it. It was great to have that kind of enthusiasm.

ROBBIE ROBERTSON: In writing "The Weight," I'd been influenced by Buñuel, especially the *Nazarin*. It seemed that as much as you try to be righteous, something pulls you the other way. The biggest thing was the religious connotation of the song. I remember there was this huge argument between Marty and Michael Chapman about the mood and the lighting for "The Weight." Marty was insisting that it was a Catholic vision, it had to be. And Michael said, "No, this is a very Protestant story, it's Baptist, Marty." He was explaining to Marty the gospel music connotations.

I liked everything they were saying because I had never thought of any of it, though I was brought up Catholic. I thought it was quite brilliant, the credit they were giving to me. For me it was a combination of Catholicism and gospel music. The story told in the song is about the guilt of relationships, not being able to give what's being asked of you. Someone is stumbling through life, going from one situation to another, with different characters. In going through these catacombs of experience, you're trying to do what's right, but it seems that with all the places you have to go it's just not possible. In the song all this is "the load."

MARTIN SCORSESE: We couldn't have done it without that two-hundred-page script. I had butterflies in my stomach the whole time. With the earphones on I couldn't hear the music or refer to it. So we were constantly screaming. A cameraman would say, "What, what? I can't hear you." I'd yell back, "Camera two close-up on Levon. He's going to sing."

Vilmos Zsigmond ended up on the tower camera. He had just shown up at the concert, and I said, "Get on the camera!" And he said, "I'm so glad that I am able to . . . " And I said, "Yeah, yeah, yeah, just get a wide shot and zoom in on it." We had a two-hundred-page script that we had worked out, and he was up in the tower and he could refer to the script. He could see where I wanted to zoom in and out. The guys down below couldn't resort to the script. They had to use earphones. I was on the side of the stage behind Bobby Byrne, who was a cameramen and the operator for Laszlo Kovacs, and my two-hundred-page script was being jostled around and I was screaming and yelling the number of the camera I wanted to shoot.

I love music films. And in *The Last Waltz*, the main thing to consider was that we were sick and tired of all these shots of the people in the audience in most concert films. So we said we were going to stay on the stage. And we stayed on the stage. You see the intensity of the interrelationship of the performers, and you see how they work as a group. That was the idea. Each song became like a rounded person. It's amazingly physical. You begin to see the interrelationship of all the people, especially in the sequence with Bob Dylan, where they give each other these signals at one point when they're about to go into another song—I think they're getting into "Baby Let Me Follow You Down." They were probably teasing each other, who knows? But it looks great, and you actually can see it go on. What I discovered in *The Last Waltz* was to stay on the stage, stay with the people.

ROBBIE ROBERTSON: I had wanted the people at *The Last Waltz* to represent all the spoke wheels of the music that we played. New Orleans gumbo music, English blues, Chicago blues, gospel music, country music,

Tin Pan Alley—all those things. That's why Neil Diamond was in it. Everybody would say, "Why is Neil Diamond in it?" And I would say, "Tin Pan Alley." Marty understood that.

Our dignity was at stake, so we worked very, very hard. It turned out to be really a spiritual experience. It was like, "My God, these kinds of things don't come along often in anybody's lifetime." And I'm not talking so much for the audience, or for the critics. I'm talking about him and me! That's all! When we finished *The Last Waltz* I didn't care if anybody liked it, or if anybody saw it! I thought, "I know I'll be able to look at this at any time, and I'll be very proud of this work."

MARTIN SCORSESE: It was two years before the film was released in 1978, although we shot it in one night, and then shot those other scenes, which took about five more days in the studio. Then we shot some dialogue, and interview scenes. We wound up with some of the most hilarious interviews and we all looked like—probably what we *were*— strange.

It wasn't really a feature film for me, although it was something very special, something very close to my heart. It was the most perfect thing I had made. With *The Last Waltz* it was really "that's for me." But during the rest of that period I was extremely unhappy.

ROBBIE ROBERTSON: After we did *The Last Waltz*, we both ran into big personal problems in our lives. I keep claiming that we were just misunderstood artists, but I don't know if that really plays. I didn't know what to do with my life. I didn't know where to go. I said to Marty, "I've got to tell you, I'm a little bit lost because I'm on the street!" Marty doesn't like to be alone very much, so he said, "Oh, you got to move in with me, that's all there is to it!" He had me by the shirt. He was saying, "This will be great! You can move in here, you can stay with me." It was a tremendous sense of relief for both of us.

So here we were, slammed together in this house where all we did was listen to music and look at movies. All day, all night. While he'd be working, I'd be in the studio finishing up some recording, and we'd get back to the house about midnight, and then we'd start watching movies. We'd watch one or two movies before dawn. And this went on every night for a long time.

We would look at these Buñuel films and say, "See, somebody else understands." The emphasis for me was on the writing. The big deal for Marty was the guilt in these movies. We would watch things like *Simon of the Desert*, these bizarre, surreal things but very, very Catholic. And they were wonderful to me. It was like, "Look at this man here, he's feeding beggars. Watch. In two minutes, the beggars will be attacking him." That's life. That's what it's really about. So we'd make up the list of movies we wanted to watch. I'd be writing down these things by Kurosawa and Buñuel, all these classics. Marty would be writing down all these horrible B movies that had some point of brilliance to them. "It's coming," he'd say, and when the moment of brilliance would come up, he would explain it to me in the filmmaking sense. I would look at it in a whole other way, and looking at it in this way was amazing. It was so exciting to have your eyes adjusted like that.

After that we traveled around, to festivals all over the world, receiving awards for *The Last Waltz*. We had a tremendous time, but a scary time, too. Because we were living crazy lives, never sleeping, going here and there. But we survived. We came out the other end.

At one time, Marty was kind of teetering on the line about doing *Raging Bull*. He was just run-down, working and crazy, running everywhere in the world. He was living with exhaustion, and he got sick. I remember saying to him, about *Raging Bull*, "Let's get off the fence on this thing. Are you passionate about this? Do you have to do this movie? Because if you don't have to do it, don't do it. And I don't mean obliged have to, I mean *passionately* have to. Can you go on with your life without doing this?"

He was squirming around in some kind of hospital room and his asthma was really bad. He was exhausted. They had been working up to doing this movie, writing scripts and saying, "No this isn't right," and "What about this?" But all that was secondary. The main issue was how passionate he was about doing it. Finally, he got back the anger that always helps him work well by saying, "I can't live without doing this." He came to the conclusion, "Yes, if I don't do this movie, I have no reason to live." It became that clear, that black and white. So I said, "There you go—do it and do it really good."

FIVE

BLOOD ON THE ROPES

RAGING BULL (1980)

"*RAGING BULL* IS ABOUT A MAN WHO LOSES EVERYTHING AND THEN REGAINS IT SPIRITUALLY." —MARTIN SCORSESE

MARTIN SCORSESE entered the old boxing arena through heavy lengths of canvas that masked the entrances to the set, blocking out the harsh California sun. In April 1979, after years of preparation, the shooting of *Raging Bull* had begun.

On the set, the year is 1946 and the place is Madison Square Garden. Jake La Motta (Robert De Niro) battles Sugar Ray Robinson (Johnny Barnes) yet again for the middleweight championship of the world. La Motta cannot touch Robinson for speed or boxing finesse. As he complains to his brother Joey (Joe Pesci), even his hands are too small—they're girl's hands, not the powerful fists of a fighter. In addition, no matter what he does, no matter how good a fighter he becomes, he will never fight heavyweight champion Joe Louis, the greatest of all, because Jake is a middleweight, not in Louis's class. But Jake has one undeniable achievement. He can take a punch. He can stand there, let himself be pummeled by the sophisticated combinations Robinson throws, and not go down. Robinson has a sweet, flowing style that inspires his fans to call

ROBERT DE NIRO AS JAKE LAMOTTA IN HIS ACADEMY AWARD–
WINNING PERFORMANCE FOR *RAGING BULL*.

him "Sugar" Ray. But Jake has raw anger, endurance, and his own epithet: "The Raging Bull."

Scorsese and De Niro are moving a step further. On this, their most ambitious project so far, they have taken apart this man, Jake La Motta, and reconstructed not the fighter of reality, but the figure of a man so unconscious of his own feelings and emotions that he can speak only through violence—a man Scorsese sees as almost another order of being. He cites St. Thomas Aquinas, who said that perhaps animals serve God better than men because they have no choice but to live their natures purely. Jake, for Scorsese, has that primal quality. Yet Jake is conscious of the "bad things" he has done, and sees his defeats as a kind of punishment. His rise to the championship and his relationships with the women in his life seem marked with a gratuitous brutality—for example, he destroys the face of the good-looking fighter whom his wife Vicki has admired. And yet, near the end of the film, in the jail cell in Miami, when Jake has destroyed everything and everyone important to him, he cries out, "I am *not* an animal!" He faces himself and, somehow, redemption begins. The sign of salvation is small—he embraces his brother—but the moment is unforgettable. A man recognizes his own soul.

Scorsese began filming *Raging Bull* in L.A., but finished editing it in New York in November of 1980. Martin Scorsese had moved back to the city he left ten years ago, to an apartment on Fifty-seventh Street. He set up editing space there, and traded L.A.'s horizontal sprawl for the vertical intensity of New York. He was home.

MARTIN SCORSESE: The motives for making a movie are very important—why you make a picture, why you go through the process. It's a terrible journey each time you do it; it's really a hard thing to do. And you have to have clear motives, and they have to be good motives.

Between *New York, New York* and *Raging Bull*, in my personal life and also in my career, I was very disappointed. People loved *Mean Streets, Alice Doesn't Live Here Anymore,* and *Taxi Driver,* and we got wonderful reviews and good box office for both *Alice* and *Taxi Driver*. But nobody liked *New York, New York*. It was as if we did something absolutely dreadful. And I said, "Wait a second. This picture is not dreadful. I mean, there are some problems with it, but . . . " I became very disillusioned with the whole process.

Everything was very destructive, and it was very bad for me. In the fall of 1978 everything clicked together, and I kind of woke up and said, "This is the picture that has to be made, and I'll make it that way. These are the reasons why it has to be made—for me, anyway."

The motive became to achieve an understanding of a self-destructive lifestyle—of a person who was destructive to the people around him and to himself—who finally eased up on himself and on those other people, and somehow made peace with life.

I used *Raging Bull* as a kind of rehabilitation, thinking all the time that it was pretty much my last picture in L.A., or America.

Bob De Niro gave me the book *Raging Bull*, about Jake La Motta, when I was doing *Alice Doesn't Live Here Anymore* and he was doing a couple of other things. He said, "There are some really good scenes and he's an interesting character." And I said, "A boxer? I don't like boxing." The only boxing I was aware of, besides the Friday night fights that my father would watch, would be the films we saw as kids on a Saturday up at Sixth Street and Second Avenue. Any week there had been a championship fight, we saw it. All fifteen rounds, and from one angle, that was it. All these guys were yelling in the audience, even though everybody knew the outcome of the fight—it had happened a week before. It was absolutely boring. We kids just wanted the other feature to come on.

The only logical fight I ever saw was a Buster Keaton film. He's in the ring with this big guy. The guy comes out swinging, Keaton goes to the corner and gets a chair and hits the guy with it. That was the only logical boxing scene I ever witnessed. The idea of, "Let's get two guys into the ring and let them hit each other," was something I didn't—couldn't—grasp.

But I did read the book. According to Peter Savage, the co-author, Jake's whole life was shaped by an early incident. He hit one of his mugging victims, Harry Gordon, in the head, and assumed he had killed him. But later in the book, Jake's at a cocktail party and guess who happens to be there? Harry Gordon! He didn't kill him after all. So Jake had been guilty all his life over something that never happened.

ROBERT DE NIRO: I had liked the book originally because I thought it had some good scenes. A good scene is something that you think has a lot of dramatic possibilities, and irony, and humor, and something that people can relate to, the way Marty and I relate to it. It could be the situation, the character in the moment. All these unexpected things. You just say, "This is a great scene." You've never seen a scene like this. You want to do it. Or you have seen a scene like this, but you've never seen it done as well as it's been done here. You can imagine it being done in a certain way, it could be terrific. But then you have to worry about its being tied into the rest of the film, and/or story; whether it's going to work.

MARDIK MARTIN: *Raging Bull* was Robert De Niro's idea. He read the book and gave it to me. We made a deal and I worked on a number of drafts. Marty didn't exactly want to do it, he wasn't too convinced about it. Jake La Motta was this crude symbol, the bull in the china shop, who was cursed because he was so macho yet very fragile when it came to women.

I wrote a draft of *Raging Bull*, integrating some of the things that Marty was trying to put in about his family, about his grandfather's fig tree in Staten Island and all that. Robert read it, and he said, "What is this? What's going on here?" I was really trying to please Marty. I had another job at the time, also, and I'll never forget Irwin Winkler coming to me and saying, "You're going to go crazy. Let's have someone else do it." I said, "Thank God." I gave all the drafts to Paul Schrader, all my research, everything. I had come to the point where I just couldn't do it because it was too much.

MARTIN SCORSESE: It took Mardik about two years. We just left him alone, and he came back with a chronological story, based somewhat on the book, but also on the recollections of various people. It was like *Rashomon*—everybody had his own version of what the truth was.

At one point we said, "Let's change it, let's make it a play. Let's do it as a play first, and then do it as a movie afterwards." Then we had a better idea. "Let's do it as a play at night, and shoot the movie in the day time." We were out of our minds. Mardik said, "Great idea!" He was crazy too! He stopped writing the script and made a play version. What happened was that at a certain point we felt we had just lost control of everything.

In 1977, De Niro read the script and said, "What's going on? This is not the picture we agreed upon." And I said, "Well, look, I don't know what else it ought to be." I wasn't coming to grips with it, but what I really wasn't coming to grips with was myself.

PAUL SCHRADER: *Raging Bull* was *not* a film that either Marty or I wanted to make. De Niro talked Marty into it and then the two of them talked me into it.

The real Jake La Motta's great gift was an ability to take a beating; he took a beating almost better than anyone else. It's really all he could do. I don't really think Jake was redeemed in life as he was in the film, but when Marty and I addressed this we had to set the real Jake La Motta off to the side.

The biggest change Marty made in my script was that he dropped one of the best soliloquies I ever wrote, a two- or three-page masturbation monologue, which happens when Jake is in his jail cell. It was to be the climax of the film. La Motta is trying to masturbate and talking to himself, conjuring up images of the women he's known. He manages to get an erection and then he remembers how terribly he treated people and can't manage to masturbate. Finally, he blames his hand, and smashes his hand against the cell wall.

Bob and Marty both felt that it was too much. I liked that scene; I was surprised that Bob didn't.

DAVID FIELD: Irwin Winkler set up a meeting at Marty's apartment in the Galleria on Fifty-seventh Street. We had the Schrader script. We didn't have the script we shot. In the Schrader script, Jake's character is darker. The centerpiece was a six- or eight-page scene when Jake is in solitary confinement. He has this endless dialogue with his dick. There's another scene where he douses his erection in a glass of water, but that was what he would do in preparing for each fight, and that seemed right. But that monologue in prison was very dark.

There wasn't any way to fudge that scene. If you had it, you had to just do it. It wasn't like you could frame it discreetly. It was very strong. It was what it was. But I didn't think United Artists, or any major studio, could distribute what had to be an X-rated film. Not so much even because of the X—though the studio, of course, didn't want that—but also because I didn't think anybody would want to see it. I thought Marty's work should be seen by as many people as possible, but I didn't even know if United Artists would make it with that scene in it. I wouldn't vote for it, and I really *wanted* it to be made.

Bobby De Niro and Marty didn't know that the movie was in jeopardy. I did five movies as an executive with Irwin. Whenever I'd have a problem, he'd say, "Well, you tell him." And I'd say, "You're the producer, Irwin." And he'd say, "Yeah, well, executives come and go, but the directors go on. So I'm not going to tell him."

MARTIN SCORSESE: Irwin Winkler told me I'd better have a meeting with the guys from United Artists who were financing this film. "Just say hello and talk about the script and everything." I said, "What is it? What do they want to know? What do we have to talk about?" "Just say hello. It's just a hello meeting. It's just something so that they're part of it." We knew one of them, David Field, and we liked him.

Well, they came into my apartment, and I mentioned that I wanted to do the film in black and white. They said, "Black and white?" And I said yes. The reason was that five boxing films were opening: *Rocky II* or *Rocky III, The Main Event, Matilda, the Boxing Kangaroo,* and two others. They were all in color. I said, "This has got to be different." And besides that, I told them that the color stock fades. I went into the whole business, that I was very upset about the Eastman color stocks fading, the prints fading in five years, the negatives fading in twelve years—things like that. I said, "I just don't want it. I want it to be something very special. On top of that, though, it would also help us with the period look of the film." We had an idea of making the film look like a tabloid, like the *Daily News,* like Weegee photographs. That was the concept, so they talked about that, and said, "Okay, all right." They were listening. Then, evidently, something was mentioned about how can you make a film about this guy who was such a cockroach, and De Niro said, "He's not a cockroach"—very flat. But it wasn't a big confrontation of any kind. In fact, we had a very nice meeting. But it turns out that they were deciding whether they were going to stop the film or they were going to make the film, based on this meeting. I didn't know that. I found that out later.

DAVID FIELD: I don't remember that I ever said the word "cockroach." It's confusing to be a studio executive, when you think of it as shuttle diplomacy between a roomful of money guys and a roomful of creative people. You try to explain one to the other. They heartily distrusted each other. I identified with the filmmakers, but still, I wasn't one. I was associated in the creative people's mind with the money guys, because they paid my salary. You become kind of an odd man out. Even when the filmmaker agrees with you, it was fairly common for them not to tell you to your face. Why would they? You're kind of parachuting behind enemy lines.

I remember authorizing the checks to send Marty and Bobby down to St. Martin. They were there for four to five weeks. They came back with a screenplay that had their initials on it but no names. That's the script we shot.

ROBERT DE NIRO: We worked on the script for almost three weeks, in St. Martin. Marty and I liked parts of Schrader's script but not others. We still had to make it our own. So we revised the script, and went over each scene, sometimes adding dialogue.

Marty and I talked about how people had this kind of hippie attitude towards relationships. Everybody is so accepting. At the time, people were saying, "I don't care what she does," or, "I don't care what he does," and, "If you really love the person, you won't make demands," but to me and to Marty, that attitude was a lot of bullshit. It was ignoring basic emotions. It was saying that you have no right to feel them, and if you do, you're a jerk or you're not hip. It's a lot of bullshit! The fact is, you're *entitled* to have those feelings. Some people may really feel they don't have them, but they're unusual. Other people express them, but in a hostile kind of way. I used to see people smiling and saying hi, like Hare-Krishna types. Smiling at me, but they're really aggressive, and hustling you to give money.

What we wanted with Jake was to have something that was very straight-out. Jake himself is primitive, he can't hide certain feelings. I worked with Jake, the real Jake LaMotta. I would pick his brain. There are a lot of things going on in there. I admired the fact that he was at least willing to question himself and his actions. But what's he going to do? Should he be like a college professor and try to say, "Well, I think the reason that I did that was because . . . " He would talk that way sometimes, but he was more cunning. He'd look at you dead-pan, or he'd laugh about certain things. He would protect himself sometimes, but then he would say, "Aah, I was a son-of-a-bitch." I always thought there was something very decent about him somewhere.

MARTIN SCORSESE: Paul had said, "You guys do your dialogue." He also said, "If you want to compress it, you can combine characters, too."

And this is what we wound up doing down in St. Martin. Schrader had done a great job but we had to make it our own.

The most important thing we found was that Jake had all his news clippings. He had great stuff. The scenes that weren't in Paul's original script came from those. For example, the scene after he throws the fight, in the dressing room, when he's crying— that was from a column we read. The columnist had gotten into the dressing room and said that if this guy was acting, it was the best job he'd ever seen. He wrote, "I never saw a man cry that way, it was really just awful, and I think it was a clean fight." Jake's father was in the room. He said, "That's it. You're not going to fight anymore. Don't fight anymore!" So we gave that line to one of his trainers. And you have to understand that Jake's the only guy who ever admitted that he threw a fight.

I really came to understand Jake's character because of what I learned about myself during the two-and-a-half, three years that followed *New York, New York*. But now I was ready. We had the script. I started to work on storyboards for the nine fight scenes. Each had to be approached differently.

I had been to a fight at Madison Square Garden with Brian De Palma and some other friend. We sat up in the bleachers and from there, I saw the sponge go into the pail. The trainer squeezed it over the fighter's back. It was full of blood. That was pretty interesting.

After Bobby and I came back from St. Martin with the rewrite, I saw my second fight. That time we were in the third row, and I saw blood on the ropes. I used that at the real climactic moment, after the sixth Sugar Ray Robinson fight when Jake is defeated.

I R W I N   W I N K L E R : At one point I had been very discouraged about *Raging Bull*, and I really thought about not doing the film, but Cis Corman urged me to hang in.

When Marty and Bob came back from the Caribbean, they sent me the script and it was sensational. Obviously, neither one of them ever got credit for writing it. But it was *great*. Then I got enthusiastic! I produced the *Rocky* films, and with the strength of those in back of me, I was able to convince United Artists to go ahead without any trouble at all.

C I S   C O R M A N : Irwin Winkler brought me into the group as casting director. I had worked with Irwin on two films, *Up the Sandbox* and *The*

Gambler, and I met Bobby De Niro when I was doing *The Gambler*. Bob wanted that part very badly and I wanted him to have it. But the director ended up casting Jimmy Caan. When Irwin said, "I'd like you to meet Bob De Niro," I was a nervous wreck. Bob is not the most forthcoming person when you first meet him, in fact, he's shyer than I am. But it was okay. Then I had to meet Marty. I'm pretty good at meetings, I can handle myself. But I probably did not understand three-quarters of what he was saying throughout that whole interview, and I wasn't about to say, "Could you explain that to me? Could you repeat that? Could you slow up a little?" And for probably the next three months, I only understood half of what Marty was saying. But somehow or other I just put the pieces together, and figured out by his enthusiasm or his lack of it that I was on the right or wrong track.

It was not easy. I had never met anyone like Marty. There were spurts of things, it was erratic, it was not like dealing with any other director I have known or worked with before. I was uncomfortable and I was so afraid it wasn't going to work out. Marty does not take to people right away. It takes him a long time before he feels he can trust people.

I wasn't sure if I was fitting in—and I *wasn't*. Marty looked at me kind of strangely. In the beginning, I worked much more closely with Bob because the picture wasn't really ready and it wasn't going to be for some time, but Bob was ready to start casting it yesterday. We worked together closely for several months before Marty was ready to start. Marty is asthmatic, he's hyper, he's erratic, and very emotional—*and* he's Italian—so I figured he couldn't be rushed. He'd start when he was ready. But in fact, my greatest experience has been doing *Raging Bull*.

When I read the script, no question, I thought to myself, "Jake La Motta is a terrible, evil man. Why would you want to do a movie about this?" And Bobby said something like, "Well, people sometimes *are* that way."

Since I was a novice around Marty, I didn't understand about what he does with scripts. I had no idea that he was such a genius. Usually I read a script, and that's what you're going to get, okay, we all know that it's going to be the visual, and what they're going to do with the music here and there. But Marty's scripts are blueprints. His genius is his ability to take images from his head, and make them work on film. It's extraordinary.

If you're casting and you call an actor and say, "I'd like to know if you'd be willing to cough in a film for Marty," they say, "Oh! When? When can I come?" I mean, they're out of the door, I don't care who they are.

Marty probably is one of the few people in this business who I have never heard use the word "commercial." And I am in a business where everybody talks about that. But I have never heard Marty say, "I don't think that actor will be commercial enough." Everybody else I work with is definitely very sensitive to the studios; they want their film to be successful at the box office. I think it was Bobby, after I had said something dumb like, "Do you think this film is going to be commercial?" who said, "I never think about that. I only think about what I want to do." Marty's the same way.

He is wonderful to actors. I have to be there, because he could *never* tell an actor, "Well, we have to go now." He would sit with an actor for three hours because he didn't want to hurt the actor's feelings. I'm the one who interrupts and says, "Okay, Marty, that's all. You have no more time. I'm sorry." The onus is on me; I don't want it to be on Marty.

MARTIN SCORSESE: Joe Pesci, who played Jake's brother, is an example of how lucky we were in getting actors. Joe Pesci did a film called *The Debt Collector*, directed by Ralph DeVito. Bob saw part of it on videotape somewhere and said, "This guy is really interesting." We looked at the film. We liked the scene where he was running a crap game. We met him. He had decided to stop his acting career at that point. His attitude was, "I don't need this, I don't need this from you or from anybody." So we sat him down. I said, "All right, just sit down and we'll talk about it. It's not a big deal, we'll talk and see if we can come to terms of any kind. Or even if you just want to read." He said, "I don't want to read for anybody." I said, "Okay, okay," and that kind of thing. And we listened to him and talked and we liked the way he spoke. He had a wonderful way of improvisation.

JOE PESCI: I was worn out trying to be an actor. I had given up. I didn't want to get involved in acting again because I don't like the business of acting. I like acting as an art. See, I was a child actor, I've been in the business since I was four, five years old, on the stage. I hadn't done any films until 1975, and that's the one Bobby and Marty saw me in, *The Debt Collector*.

In the beginning, I really didn't care because the part of Jake's brother was small, and I figured they should give it to a working actor who really wanted it. At the time, I was running a restaurant in the Bronx for some

ROBERT DE NIRO AND JOE PESCI (JOEY LA MOTTA) AT THE
CARMINE STREET POOL IN A SCENE FROM *RAGING BULL*.

friends of mine. I was out of that place in Hollywood where you're at everybody's mercy all the time and you wind up being a sissy. You get to the point out there where you bump into walls and say, "Excuse me," so as not to offend anybody so you can get a job. I wanted to get away from all that and get back into the position where everybody treated you like a man. But when I met Marty and Bob I saw that working with them would be different.

CIS CORMAN: Joe Pesci had seen Cathy Moriarty's picture, in a club. He called and said I should meet this girl because she looked very right for the part of Vickie La Motta. She had never acted. I had seen about a hundred women, I had gone to every Playboy club, I had even investigated Florida, because I figured that's a good source. They came up by the droves. Then Cathy appeared. She was tough, bright, a smart young woman. She had it all, and she even looked like Vickie. The part of Vickie needed a toughness, an edge, and she had to be a beauty.

You see, Vickie La Motta had something special. I mean, this woman was fifteen pounds overweight, but in her tight dungarees and shirts and with all that hair, she had an attitude that was extraordinary. It said, "I'm beautiful, I'm happy, life is joyous, and I've got no sorrows." She walked down the street, and heads would turn. I'm sure Vickie was very bitter in her day. But by the time we met her, this was a Vickie who had come to terms with her life and was very, very happy—or at least she told me that.

When it came to using Cathy I had to work out something with the Screen Actors Guild. I was very honest, I never tried to fool them. When I knew Marty wanted her, I thought, "Oh boy." So I went up to SAG and they told me we couldn't use her. That we'd have to use a professional actress. So what I did was I brought ten pictures of Vickie and ten pictures of Cathy, and I spread them out on the desk. "See?" I said. Then they said yes.

C A T H Y   M O R I A R T Y : I became involved with *Raging Bull* when I met Joe Pesci and he remarked that I looked like Vickie La Motta. He wanted a picture of me for Marty for the film, and I said, "Yeah, yeah, sure," thinking it was one of those modeling jobs where all they really wanted was for you to take your clothes off. But I gave him a picture anyway because I wanted to be an actress and was going to open casting calls every day.

I took my screen test in February. We started with the pool scene, then a fight scene, and then the bathroom scene where Jake breaks down the door. The next day Cis Corman called and said, "Honey, I just wanted to let you know you have the part," and we started filming in April.

It was quite a while before I actually saw a script. I had read a lot of the book *Raging Bull,* and it was more-or-less a story seen through Jake's eyes. I had to play by instinct because I really didn't get to know anything about Vickie. I had never met her. Marty didn't want us to get together. He was afraid she would influence me, and when she came to L.A., he kept me away from the set for a few days. It was difficult to play a woman I had never met, and knew very little about, but even more difficult to play a character seen entirely through Jake's eyes.

There was a scene where Jake brings Vickie to his father's house. Marty had all these little touches, like the crucifix over the bed. Even in the scene where I look at the picture, on the dresser there were rosary beads, a little medal, a crucifix, and a holy water container. It was very important for

Marty to include those things. He knew exactly what he wanted on the set. The scene with the reflection in the mirror where you can see the religious statue in the background was done purposely. This was all very familiar to me, since I'd been raised Catholic and my mother used to help out in the neighborhood convent. We were friendly with the nuns.

MARTIN SCORSESE: I remember the first day of shooting *Raging Bull*. Paul Schrader sent me a telegram saying, "I did it my way, Jake did it his way, you do it your way." That gave me a certain kind of freedom, then, to move.

In *Raging Bull*, all the fight scenes are done in drawings. It's very much like staging a dance to music. Instead of a verse with maybe twelve bars of music, it's four bars of punches. Because it's all *choreography*. With the fight scenes, you knew one thing—it could only be what it was, nothing extra. You just lay it out. For example, fifteen punches this way, then a tracking shot, then move in on the last punch. He goes out of the frame—bang, cut to the next shot. This gives a dynamic to the cutting. If you did anything else somebody was going to get hurt. And nobody did get hurt.

MICHAEL CHAPMAN: It was always only one camera: Each shot was drawn out in great detail, almost like Arthur Murray, those weird dance steps they used to draw on the floor. We did that.

Marty has a very visual imagination, which he allows free rein. He's truer to his emotions and instincts than most people are. It's not just that the camera moves, it's the emotion that it shows. That was his focus during all the days of complicated and arduous shooting.

MARTIN SCORSESE: The fight scenes would take some really critical physical stamina on the part of Bob and everybody else involved, because they had to be shot over and over again. It would take patience, too, because very often you have maybe two or three shots a day, and that's *it*.

I wanted to do the ring scenes as if the viewers were the fighter and their impressions were the fighter's—of what he would think or feel, what he would hear. Like being pounded all the time. And again, the very, very important thing about the fight scenes in the movie was that you never see the audience. You don't get a shot of a guy going, "Kill him, kill him!" Or the overweight woman eating as people are beaten and blood is flying. You know that she's sitting there eating a frankfurter and popcorn. None of that. None of that. Stay in the ring.

It was really funny. I was talking to Bob two days in a row, and he said, "What do I do in this shot?" I said, "In this shot, you get hit." And we went on to the next one. I got that one all worked out, and then he said, "What about this one?" I said, "In this one, you get hit!"

I had to shoot the punches in slow motion or you wouldn't see them. Once we got the rhythm of the slow motion itself we'd have to go with it. I decided to do the second Sugar Ray fight with long lenses. Once I planned the action, I knew exactly whether it was a medium close-up or ten punches and a medium close-up. A lot of the Robinson fight was done in the cutting. But most of it was very, very clearly laid out. During this fight, there were some shots of Vickie La Motta watching. At first, she's applauding. I took this from an actual photograph from *Life* magazine. First she's applauding, then she's laughing, then holding her head in her hands, then

CINEMATOGRAPHER MICHAEL CHAPMAN (TOP RIGHT), ROBERT DE NIRO,
JOHNNY BARNES (SUGAR RAY ROBINSON), AND CREW SET UP THE
CAMERA FOR A FIGHT SCENE IN *RAGING BULL*.

she brings her head down, and you'll see that in the montage. It comes right from *Life* magazine.

In the last Sugar Ray fight, the trainer takes the sponge away from Jake's mouth. The pail of water the sponge is dipped into is bloody. The sponge goes up to Jake's back. It's squeezed. Then the blood drips out. First in slow motion, then in normal speed. And now the sponge is on his stomach. And then a shot of the sponge after it got rubbed on the back. We decided to open the sequence with that image from the pail to his back, and then we added other shots. We move into his face. The trainer was putting vaseline onto Jake's face, but it looked like some sort of blessing almost. It looked as if this guy was anointed to be sacrificed, so I thought that was very interesting. We also used an actual kinescope of the real fight that night. We used the announcer's voice. Sometimes, in certain theaters, it's hard to understand what the guy is saying, but it's fantastic. "No man could take this punishment," he says. That's really the announcer's voice from the actual sound track of the fight, so we used that voice.

In the last round, there's a fast move-in on Jake, then a shot on Robinson. Sugar Ray gets Jake on the ropes and he beats him and slips back and we cut across the axis here. The action crosses the camera axis. The montage sequence took forty-four shots. This is the last flurry that Jake actually did. He let all this energy out with that one. At the beginning of the last round, the announcer says, "Round thirteen—the 'hard luck' number." We took that from the kinescope. Again, I wanted to give the impression of the fighter in the ring, what he would experience, what he would feel. What he was going to hear.

Of course, the actual fight footage itself had only one angle. It's really devastating to see this guy standing on his feet being pummeled for twenty seconds—a twenty-second beating. It was bloody and messy and that's when the announcer said, "No man can endure this punishment." So, I actually had the real print of the fight and basically did a montage and did drawings based on that.

The drawing says, "Left hook, right." As far as the actual punches in the fight, I didn't make that up. Jimmy Nickerson made that up with Jake La Motta and with Bobby in the gym on Fourteenth Street. I went there one day and watched the fights. I made a videotape from that one angle, the same one I talked about in the big fights on the Loews screen I saw when I was a kid. I played that tape over and over again, and imagined the cuts inside that one angle. It was just like watching a dance videotape. I did the same thing with the *Bad* video with Michael Jackson. I had a videotape VHS of the dancing, then stopped at every three bars and came up with different ideas for different shots. You can't do it without choreography. You cannot do it. Say the fourth left hook doesn't look right in one frame. Tough. There can only be four left hooks in that shot, because if you suddenly do *five*, someone is going to get hurt!

ROBERT DE NIRO: In the fight scene, the punches were all choreographed. Your opponent has to move his head when you hit him, and the camera has to be at an angle so it looks like a hit. You lay in the sound later. When I was alone, dancing around the ring, like in the opening scene, there's no problem. I do whatever I want. Sort of warming up and shadowboxing, and so on. But with another person, you have to rehearse so that nobody gets hurt accidentally. It's pretty specific. Once you do it, it's like learning lines—you know them, and then you just do them. It's part of the rehearsing, the practicing.

MARTIN SCORSESE: De Niro came up with a brilliant idea. He had a punching bag put in the ring. He'd be up there punching and when he'd jump to the spot where we were shooting, he was already worked up.

In the fight between Jake and Dauthuille, we followed the storyboards exactly. It was almost like it was precut. We had the punches laid out. Then I used a shot that was taken from the newspaper when he kissed the ground. He really did that. Jake kissed his gloves and kissed the ground. For that I also did one of the biggest shots in the whole picture—a tracking shot. It went all the way up and over a thousand people. But we cut it from the picture. That day we did two shots in one day: We did a Steadicam shot where he comes out of the basement into the Olympia Stadium. There are over two thousand people in the crowd. That shot we kept. But then in the afternoon we did another shot, and we realized that it went all the way up and it went around, people were cheering—it was boring. So we didn't use it.

I used a lot of tracking in that fight. I had to cover Don Dunphy, the announcer, at one point. His dialogue was rewritten a thousand times. We shot more than we needed, so we always had extra footage. We used an extra piece for when Jake, who's been playing possum, turns on him and surprises him.

I used a very interesting close-up in the scene. Jake comes up and the backgrounds change. In order to get that kind of shot, the camera and the fighters were on a lazy Susan kind of a thing, and we were swinging it around. It took take after take—day after day—to get what we needed. There was one shot that we had to have. The punch had to come into the lens and then we would cut to the mouthpiece flying out. It had to be that shot, it couldn't be any other shot. We kept reshooting until we got that.

There were times when we'd change screen direction because something would happen. A punch would look better from the other way or we would be in a situation where he had been left to right on one side, and had to continue that way. Sometimes I had just drawn it the wrong way. But when the crews started discussing "crossing the camera line," I'd usually just sit down for a while. "Don't worry," I'd say to myself, "they'll come up with that in a minute, don't worry about it. That's what they're paid for." Really, as much talk as there is about crossing the camera line, in a way you get the same thing, only a mirror-image flip.

There were times when we would change speed right in the middle of a sequence. In the second Sugar Ray fight, where Jake knocks Sugar Ray down, there is a medium shot of Bob as he walks past Sugar Ray and he looks at him. The referee is telling him to go to the corner. Bob pulls up his trunks. At that point, we overcranked, so that it was normal, twenty-four frames; and then we went to forty-eight within the shot so it became slow motion; then back to twenty-four as he came around to his corner, the neutral corner, to wait. Then bang, cut, and he came back in fighting. That we did on the set.

We had to really go at extremely high speeds to get the punches. The rushes were hilarious. The rushes were hours of a guy standing there like this, bleeding. Close-up. Then suddenly, *bam*—eight frames, that's it. When it comes up, people say, "Oh, Peckinpah's stuff; it's like Peckinpah's style." But really it's just that the punches wouldn't register unless you shot at high speed. You would not be able to see them.

With the amount of camera movements and editing pyrotechnics in the fight scenes, I felt that in the dramatic scenes I had to hold back. So the camera moves were simpler. We knew that basically if Bob was going to move in or sit down in a certain way, we knew where to set the camera. I had drawings of the dramatic scenes, too. But, very often, after the actors worked in rehearsal, in the actual location I'd simply rearrange the shots. I might realize that I had too many shots listed, or that camera movement wasn't necessary.

JOE PESCI: I hate long dialogue. I like dialogue that's sharp and witty and Marty likes it too. We improvise and then we keep cutting it down to the point of one liners, two liners. But once we've got the line, he wants it to stay that way. He's very structured. A lot of people think he just lets you run off at the mouth. It's not true. I told him the other day that he's the best acting coach I ever had.

Marty would have us bring our own experiences into the film. The scene in *Raging Bull* with my kids in the kitchen, just before Jake beats me up, was an example. My father was very particular about the way we ate. Even to this day, I love eating with my hands. But my father used to smack me and say to me, "If you put your hands in that plate one more time, I'm gonna stab you with this fork." When we were doing this scene in *Raging Bull* where we were eating at the table, and I was talking to my little girl and the baby was crying—it was total madness—and Robert was walking in to beat me up, I saw this little kid, who was playing my son, put his hand on the plate, and just at that time I couldn't resist saying, "If you put your hand on that plate one more fucking time . . . "

MRS. SCORSESE: Remember Joey La Motta's wedding? Marty based the scene on our wedding reception. We were married on June 10th. And it was so hot that day. We lived on the fourth floor. We were always out on the roof. It used to be beautiful on the roof. Well we were dying from the heat. I was so hot that when they threw the confetti paper at me, it melted on the wedding gown. That's how hot it was. So we brought the whole party out of the apartment up to the roof. That's why Joey's wedding is on the roof.

MR. SCORSESE: Marty was sick the day on *Raging Bull* for the wedding scene, and he said to me, "Go up there and direct it. Tell them what to do up there on the roof." So when I went up there, I saw candelabras, and sliced bread on one side, cold cuts on the other side. I said, "What are these candelabras doing here?" I said, "First, we didn't have candelabras. Secondly, we had rolls made up with ham, cheese, things like that, Swiss cheese—not *sliced bread*."

Anyway, they took everything off. They took the candelabras off, they went and got rolls—everything. And he had the beer and the soda on the roof, and there was a little confetti on top, which was all right, and cookies. See, at the wedding reception, someone from one end of the roof would holler out, "Hey, Charlie, you want a ham sandwich?" I'd say, "Yeah," and he would throw it over.

Bobby acted exactly like Jake La Motta. Jake La Motta was a rough guy. He was really rough. He'd go in there, take a beating, and he'd kill you, he'd maul you, he'd murder you. That's exactly the way Jake was in real life. Bobby studied the way he spoke, the way he walked—everything. Bobby is what you'd call a real perfectionist. He wants to do things, he's got to do them *the right way*.

CATHY MORIARTY: Some of the scenes with Bobby actually made me nervous. He would come up with things out of nowhere. Like, in the scene where Vickie's making the bed and Jake's being nice to her, and the next thing I know Bobby grabs me by the hair. It was strange, since I didn't expect it.

I remember the hotel scene where I order a cheeseburger and Bobby slaps me. I didn't know it was coming. I began concentrating so much on not getting hit or learning how to go with punches that I thought, "I'm never going to be able to say my lines." I would actually get bruised during those scenes, doing it that many times. I never did learn how to go with the punches.

I remember the scene where Bobby and I are in the bedroom and he gets up for the ice water, and I'm standing in the doorway. The Madonna statue is almost right next to me. That particular scene was my first love scene, and I was absolutely petrified. I remember the script said one thing and during the shooting it changed. I was upset and nervous, but they made me feel very comfortable. I felt as though someone was watching over me and I felt okay. Bobby and Marty were wonderful to me that day.

JOE PESCI: Bob and I work great together, but it seems as if he has his own little technique at times. If it's a scene where I have to be aggravated, he will aggravate me by doing little annoying things, probably not even aware that he's doing it. Like he would start a scene, then stop, start the scene, then stop. "Was my hand in this?" he'd ask the script girl. "Do I have the sandwich in my left hand or my right hand?" Then he'd start again. "Joey, okay, okay, I'm sorry. Was I bending down or was I up?" And finally, I'd blow up! "Come on, let's do the scene already!" See, by this time I'm hot, I'm ready to go.

In the kitchen scene where Joey's holding the baby and he says, "Will you look at this? If you win, you win; if you lose, you win." A lot of people like that scene. I think we did about thirteen takes. We couldn't get anywhere with it. It was just not clicking. I remember I was really frightened that I wasn't going to be able to do that scene and Marty took me to the side and he said, "I know what it is. You don't know what you're talking about. You know your lines, but you don't know what you're talking about—you're just saying the lines. You don't really know, you don't understand it. You have to convince *him*!" I went back in and on the next take we nailed it. See, I hadn't committed to making Jake understand. This time I began, "What's your problem? The weight?" And then I said my lines. I made him understand.

There's a scene where I suggest Bobby should take his wife out, and we should go to a nice place. My line, "Don't say anything to my wife because I'm not taking her," came from an improvisation. We cut it down and used it.

MARTIN SCORSESE: Bob was playing Jake La Motta as if he were a stone wall. Every cut to Bob was so strong, even just a medium shot. The camera was rock-steady and he would walk across the room. It was just his bulk. Even before he gained the weight to play the older Jake, even in the early part, when he is in fighting shape, his presence alone took you across the room.

While we were shooting the fight scenes, I kept telling the guys who had to invent rigs to get the cameras flying the way I wanted, "Don't worry, guys. In the dramatic scenes, the camera doesn't move, it just pans." Then every time they had to do some complicated move in the dramatic scenes, the guys would wave to me and say, "Sure, the camera doesn't move!" But if you look at the Copacabana scenes where Jake is looking, you see a bend of movement. That gives a nice quality to the film. I like to experiment with slow-motion not just in action scenes, but in simple scenes like drinking a glass of water.

In the scene where Jake and Joey are trying to fix the television set, Vickie comes in and goes upstairs—and we pan back to the stairs. The pans were anxiety-producing, because you knew, from Jake's attitude, that something terrible was going to happen. It was the beginning of the sequence where Jake says to his brother, "You fucked my wife," and repeats it over and over again. Then Jake goes upstairs and knocks his wife around, and beats up his brother. But before that, from early on in the scene, you know it's going to end in violence.

ROBERT DE NIRO: The scene with Jake La Motta fixing the TV is an example of a great scene. The domestic situation, fixing a TV, talking about something that has nothing to do with anything, and then finally just going right to the point: "Did you fuck my wife?" We came up with the scene right on the set. We said, "How about fixing a TV?" Some stupid, little, domestic sort of thing, where there's an incident waiting to happen. It can erupt from the most mundane kind of thing that just triggers something off and then that's it. Everybody's off and running. Some little pedestrian thing, and all of a sudden it creates a drama. It just unleashes something that's always been there. It's just below the surface, you're living with it, and all of a sudden this jealousy Jake had with his brother comes up.

He has strong feelings about his brother and his wife that are close to the surface. So if he gets angry about something or he's not in a good mood or whatever, or something's picking at him, rubbing him the wrong way, then whatever his brother says or does sets him off. Jake beats up his brother because he thinks he's been with his wife. And he happens to be right. And that's the whole thing in the TV scene about what's right, what's true and what we think is true, or perceive to be true. Maybe it's better not to know. On the surface nobody has really seen anything or alluded to anything or shown anything that might have happened. But Jake's jealous of Joe and Vickie. Even though he hasn't seen anything, he knows something. It's like a sixth sense. A woman may ask her husband when he comes home late, "Where were you?" She knows something's up. She can't prove it, and maybe she doesn't want to know. But Jake wants to know. Here's Joe and here's Vickie, maybe there's something. Jake's not sure. He's jealous on principle. So what does it mean? Does he have the right to pursue it? Maybe a person who is more middle-class, a refined type, someone not like

Jake, would just let it go and not make a big deal about it. But Jake goes after his brother, and he's right, the brother *was* with Vickie.

JOE PESCI: Bobby said that? He's wrong. Never. Jake La Motta's wife Vickie did *not* have an affair with my character, his brother Joey. That's Bobby's paranoia as Jake. No way, no way. Joey would not touch his brother's wife.

CATHY MORIARTY: Vickie *never* did fool around with anybody else, especially Joey, it was all in Jake's mind. I remember during one scene saying, "I don't care." And then there's the scene where I'm packing to leave him the first time and I end up hugging him. I dropped the things on the floor. I had this whole entire speech I could have said, and I just never said anything. We let it end like that. That was exactly what Marty wanted.

Jake and Vickie found a little peace when they first moved to Florida. But then there was the scene of the interview by the pool. The reporter

SCORSESE DIRECTS CATHY MORIARTY (VICKIE LA MOTTA) IN *RAGING BULL*.

asks me a question and Jake cuts me off—with his cigar in hand. He only wanted attention for Vickie if it focused on him. No one was ever allowed to speak with her. She was just to be looked at. She was his possession. I could relate to this from my own life. I've known men like that. Vickie married him at fifteen, and by thirty she had grown as a person. But Jake would never let her grow.

He never thought she would leave him. Even in the end, she didn't really want to leave him. But it got to the point where he started drinking bad and she became afraid for her children.

The thing that always bothered me was that you seldom saw Vickie laugh or even smile in the movie. Which is a contradiction to how she really felt. She told me at times she was very happy being with him. The miniature golf scene and a few scenes in the beginning were really the only times you see her smile.

MARTIN SCORSESE: We spent ten weeks instead of the scheduled five weeks for the fight scenes. Then we did ten weeks of dramatic scenes. Afterwards, Bobby started gaining the weight.

In the first ten weeks of the dramatic scenes De Niro is thin. Then in the pool scene and some others he is getting a little heavier.

We took a hiatus. Bob went to Europe and ate his way through Italy and France. "It's very hard," he said, "You think the more you eat, the more you're going to gain weight. It's very hard. But, you've got to do it three times a day. You've got to get up and eat. Eat that breakfast, eat those pancakes, eat lunch, eat dinner, even if you're not hungry. It's murder."

Around October or November, we did a scene with Bob at an intermediate weight. He is interviewed by a reporter, and says he's not going to fight any more. That was the day of one of the earthquakes in L.A. We were looking through the lens, and all of a sudden, everything moved. I said, "Who pushed the camera?" It was absolutely terrifying. It's one of the main reasons I moved out of there. The big one in 1970 hit one week after I moved there. That should have told me!

Bob went back to Europe and continued eating. We met again at the end of December and he was the full weight. I shot the Miami scenes in San Pedro, California. We decided to do it in San Pedro because the Navy shipyards are there, and they have a lot of old Art Deco bars. After all a palm tree is a palm tree, and these guys hang out in bars anyway. I had a fake palm tree put outside the window. That's Florida. We wound up doing ten days shooting, although we had planned for two-and-a-half weeks. But Bobby's weight was so extreme that his breathing was like mine when I'm having an asthma attack. With the bulk he put on he wasn't doing forty takes, it was three or four takes. The body dictated. He just became that person.

ROBERT DE NIRO: As far as my gaining the weight, the external speaks for itself. But the internal changes, how you feel and how it makes you behave—for me to play the character, it was the best thing I could have done. Just by having the weight on, it really made me feel a certain way, and behave a certain way.

The scene near the end when Jake is in jail, we felt that we did it a better way than Paul had it. We went onto this set that we had. The walls were made of rubber so I wouldn't kill myself pounding them. We didn't do too many takes, as far as I remember. We just did it.

I think of Jake as someone just battering along, doing all the wrong things, getting banged around. He made the wrong choices about things, sometimes for the right reasons, sometimes, maybe, just because he didn't want to be told what to do.

In the end, there was a lot of remorse with Jake, I think—with his brother, his wife. He sort of takes it, and he's sort of stoic. He takes the punishment. He created it, so he has to live with it.

JOE PESCI: The last scene, Joey and Jake hadn't seen each other in a long time. Neither had Bob and I. I had gone on this crash diet to make myself look really skinny and older because the last scene is years later. Marty was running back and forth between my trailer and Bob's and he didn't let us talk together. He was very conscious of keeping us apart. He said, "Let's see what happens on the set. Let's do it, let's do it. Just say what you feel."

The last scene was a chance to be dramatic. I mean, every actor in Hollywood would love to be opposite Robert De Niro in a Martin Scorsese film, and at the end cry in each other's arms and beat each other up and go for this big dramatic ending. It's the kind of part every actor goes for. They can't wait for a scene like that to come—to die in someone's arms or cry in their arms.

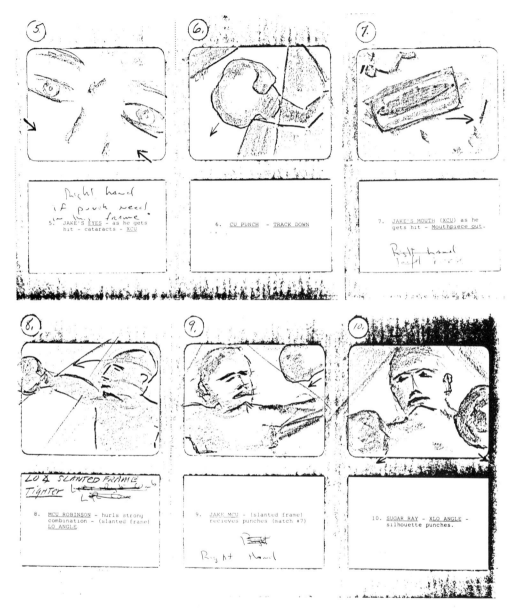

A STORYBOARD FOR A SCENE IN *RAGING BULL*.

11. HI ANGLE DOWN - shock effect angle.

12. XCU JAKE'S FACE - first special effect - BLOOD shoots from MOUTH

13. HI ANGLE DOWN - FIGHTER

14. XCU FACE - PROFILE - second special effect BLOOD shoots from NOSE.

15. MED SHOT SUGAR RAY - punching - same.

16. XCU FACE - Profile opposite of #13.

But Bobby told Marty to tell me, "Don't go for it. Don't fall in that trap. If we don't feel it, let's not do it." The way the scene was written he was to hug me when I didn't want to be hugged. I'm carrying coffee in my hand. It was supposed to spill and I am supposed to get pissed off. I push him off me and I want to hit him, and he drops his hands. He was *supposed* to say, "Go ahead, Joey. Hit me. I deserve it. Hit me. I deserve it," and I start beating him up. Then I was supposed to stop and look at him, and we cry in each other's arms: "My brother. My older brother." However, the scene didn't go that way.

Bob was like a bear when he grabbed me. I couldn't get out of his embrace. He was so big and he just held me and the coffee never fell, so I had no reason to be mad at him except like, "Come on, I don't want to do this." I remember I was going to cry, but if you see the film and really look at it and listen to my voice, you'll see I was going to cry but I stopped. I just choked and went, "Yeah, yeah, I know." Somehow it was okay because they were brothers. We did that on the first take. We got a bunch of other takes after that and we never got near it again. Marty used that first take.

THELMA SCHOONMAKER: *Raging Bull* was my first feature! When I came to work with Marty, I said, "You know, I've never cut a feature film before." And he said, "Don't worry, we'll do it together, it'll be okay." It was my assistant, Sonya Polonsky, who taught me how to organize an editing room for a theatrical film. Marty had called me several times for other movies but I hadn't gotten into the union when I was younger. Now they said I would have to work as an assistant for eight years before I could be an editor. I said no. But on *Raging Bull* Marty, through Irwin Winkler, used lawyers and standby editors and I got into the union.

We were working all night. I'm not a night person. I've never adjusted to working all night. But in that solitude we found an incredible ability to concentrate. It was enjoyable working on it, even though a lot of people consider it a very brutal film. Working on *Raging Bull* was one of our best times. We edited in Marty's apartment. The tininess of the room, the quality of the work, and Marty in his kimono, watching film after film on video while we were working, made it very special. He was studying Michael Powell's films and he would stop and say, "Look at this, look at this great shot. Oh, look at how they did this. Look at the camera angle, look at this." He would always find something unique in it, maybe only one shot, or one cut, but something to admire. Michael Powell would come to the editing room, but being a studio man, he couldn't believe we had so little space.

Marty was watching Michael Powell's *Tales of Hoffmann* all during *Raging Bull* because of the movement in it. He said that Michael Powell taught him so much about physical and facial movement. He was watching it over and over again. He would stop, run it back and forth, and back and forth. He borrowed a 16-millimeter print from the museum several times. One time he wanted it and couldn't get it. They kept telling him, "The film is out. The film is out." And I remember, once, he said, "Who *is* this? Who keeps borrowing this film besides us? I want to know who it is." And you know, it was the director George Romero, who is one of the biggest fans in the world of *Tales of Hoffmann*.

Painters go to museums to look at other painters' works because they learn, or they are inspired. The difference between Marty and other directors is he doesn't imitate what he sees. It goes *into* him and it comes *out* as something entirely different—it's not distraction so much as it is *feeding*. Michael Powell once said, "He breakfasts on images."

Marty's such an *auteur*. Every frame of *Raging Bull* has his stamp on it. He's not afraid to listen, or to use other people's ideas. Any director deserves to go his own way with the footage first. He's been thinking about it a lot longer than I have, sleeping and waking in the middle of the night, worrying about it, and I always think he should be given his shot. Even the times when I didn't think a sequence was going to work, I always put it together the way Marty wanted first, because he's the first person to see if it *doesn't* work.

MARTIN SCORSESE: I had started working with Thelma during the shooting. We watched the rushes together and took notes. We talked about each scene. I'd say, "I like this take. We'll use it. Forget the others."

The editing is really rewriting. That's why I always have a hand in it. The cutting in *Raging Bull* took a little too long. Just getting all the sound tracks okay, so that people basically understand what language they're speaking, took ten weeks.

THELMA SCHOONMAKER: The construction of the sound, and the mix, was very difficult. Frank Warner, our sound editor, helped us to build all these layers. It was sort of like tapestry, on which Marty kept laying down little, tiny details. I remember Irwin Winkler taking us outside and saying, "You can't mix this film *inch by inch.*" And Marty said, "That's the way it's going to be done." And it *was.*

MARTIN SCORSESE: None of the sound was preplanned, but I knew I wanted it to be from Jake's standpoint. What does a punch sound like in his ears? How would he hear the crowd? I figured, okay, it was going to take about seven weeks to mix the picture, but it took *sixteen more weeks!* It was day and night, in California, day and night. We got in at 9:00 A.M. and worked until 10:30 or 11:00 P.M., got something to eat and then kept at it up until about 2:00 A.M.

I remember taking about half a day on the ripping of a shirt. I'd bring people in from the hallway and say, "What does that sound like to you?" They'd say, "It sounds fine." But it didn't sound like a rip to me. I'd say, "What is that to you?" "Oh, a guy flew off a chair and people are hitting him." "Did you hear a shirt rip?" They'd say no. I'd say, "See? He didn't hear the shirt rip."

I said, "It's got to be done frame by frame. Why do we have to stop *now?* We've waited so long to do the film. It took so long to shoot it. Bobby gained the weight. It took so much time to cut it. Now we're going to rush it in the mixing?" Bobby was so good, we had gotten to such a good point in our collaboration, that I wanted it to be right.

During the six months it took to finish, Irwin Winkler would come up and say, "I've got to show them something. I keep going to the backers for more money, and they haven't seen anything." I started to get very tense, but that didn't mean that the vision of the film changed. At one point, Irwin came in, extremely upset. He was worried about the opening date. We reversed the roles! Now, I told Irwin to be calm, be very calm. I said, "What's the worst that can happen? It doesn't open." He said, "Right. That's terrible." I said, "It isn't worth getting a heart attack about."

IRWIN WINKLER: It took a long time to shoot the film and the editing was even longer. Marty was going through a period of editing all night. I remember I flew in from L.A. to New York, and we were all kind of depressed because the cut really didn't work. We were all nervous about it. There was stuff in the script, but we looked at the rough cut and the continuity wasn't as successful as we wanted it to be. It had to do with the ending. I went back to California, and Marty called me and said, "I think I've got it. Why don't you come back." So a couple of days later I came back, and he had taken the last scene and put it in the beginning. And suddenly, the picture was magic!

I screened it for the UA executives. Andy Albeck, who was the CEO at the time, was a very businesslike guy. We showed it to him with great apprehension because nobody had ever seen anything like *Raging Bull.* The screening ended. Andy Albeck walked over to Marty. With a sense of high drama, he said, "Mr. Scorsese, you are a genius."

We were opening on Friday in New York and this was now midnight Sunday night. The lab told me we had to get the picture into the mail by Sunday night, so they can print it on Monday. On Sunday night I said to Marty, "We *have* to finish the film by midnight to get it over to the lab." I said, "That's the deadline. I'm pulling the plug at midnight."

He wasn't very happy with one scene in which a minor character, played by Marty's father, orders a drink at a nightclub. Marty said you couldn't hear the words "Cutty Sark." *I* could hear the line just fine, but he couldn't hear it. At midnight I said, "Marty, that's it. The picture is over. You have to give it up. If you can't hear 'Cutty Sark,' it's just too bad." He looked at me, and he said, "I'm taking my name off the picture."

I said, "People are going to look at this picture one hundred years from now and say that it's a great, great movie. Because you can't hear 'Cutty Sark' which, by the way, everybody else says they can hear, you're taking your name off?" And he says, "Yes, I'm taking my name off the picture." I said, "Okay. If you want to take your name off the picture, it's off, but meanwhile, the picture's going in to the lab." And that was it. Obviously, he was a little emotional at the time. That's when I guess he needed a hard-hearted producer.

MARTIN SCORSESE: When I finally locked the reels, we had two prints made. Irwin Winkler's son took one print to Toronto, and I took the other print to New York. It opened two days later in a theater two blocks away from where I was living.

It wasn't the best way to make a picture, but we didn't want to make any compromises.

The idea had been to make this film as openly honest as possible, with no concessions at all for box office or audience. I said, "That's it. Basically this is the end of my career, this is it, this is the final one." I was very surprised when it was received well.

THELMA SCHOONMAKER: When I won the Academy Award, I felt it was Marty's. He should have won as director. I felt that *my* award was *his* because I know that I won it for the fight sequences, and the fight sequences are as brilliant as they are because of the way Marty thought them out. I helped him put it together, but it was not my editing skill that made that film look so good. In a way it was a tribute to him that the Academy voted for me even though I was just then getting into the union. Certainly De Niro deserved his award, but Marty should have won one as well.

Raging Bull was seamless. It was perfect. We participated to a certain extent, but it felt as if we were being guided through it by this omniscient hand.

SCORSESE AND DE NIRO IN THE RING DURING FILMING OF *RAGING BULL*.

THE KING OF COMEDY (1983)

"WE WERE TRYING TO SEE HOW FAR WE COULD PUSH
THAT CHARACTER." —MARTIN SCORSESE

Scorsese had found a way to understand Jake La Motta. "Jake La Motta," he later said, "was able to ease up on himself and the people around him, and make a kind of peace with life. He was someone who lost everything and then regained it—spiritually. It had taken five years of my own process before I understood *my* take on the picture." But Rupert Pupkin, the would-be "King of Comedy," presented a different kind of challenge.

Pupkin, played by Robert De Niro, is a man obsessed with Jerry Langford, a Johnny Carson-like figure played by Jerry Lewis. Rupert is convinced if he can only perform his standup comedy routine on Jerry's show, the doors of show business will open to him and fame and fortune will follow. After innumerable snubs by the show's staff, Rupert kidnaps Jerry. As ransom, he demands an appearance on the show. The comedian Sandra Bernhard, in her first screen role, plays Rupert's accomplice, Masha, who also wants a personal relationship with Jerry. The movie becomes a complicated look at the ambivalent nature of celebrity worship: Rupert covets fame, but also has hostile feelings toward his hero.

At this stage of his career, De Niro, a most private person, had met his own Ruperts—the single-minded celebrity hounds who somehow felt they had a right to a public person's attention. But Robert De Niro chose to play Rupert Pupkin—in fact, he initiated the project, purchasing the script and bringing it to Scorsese's attention. In direct proportion to De Niro's reluctance to focus on himself is his interest in other people. He could humanize even a Rupert.

Perhaps De Niro's attraction to the character of Rupert reflected his new position as a celebrity. Martin Scorsese, the man behind the camera, was not recognized on the street, accosted for autographs, or besieged by photographers. But with *Raging Bull*, following *Taxi Driver* and *The Godfather II*, De Niro had become a star. De Niro had owned the script for *The King of Comedy*, by Paul Zimmerman, for a number of years. Subsequent events such as the shooting of John Lennon by a fan, Mark Chapman, made it even more important to identify the forces that drive a Rupert

Pupkin. The fixation on stars exploded in the early 1980s. Where before only the supermarket tabloids fed fan hunger, now mainstream publications like *People* and television shows such as *Entertainment Tonight* legitimized the craving for personal information. Scorsese himself began *The King of Comedy* with little direct experience of the kind of extremism displayed by Rupert Pupkin. During the picture's production, however, John Hinckley's obsession with Jodie Foster led to his attempt on Ronald Reagan's life. *The King of Comedy* eerily echoes the extremism of fans determined to play a part in their idols' lives—even if it means appearing as executioners.

Rupert's obsession in *The King of Comedy* matches Jake La Motta's in *Raging Bull.* His skewed view of life recalls Travis Bickle in *Taxi Driver.* While Rupert appears benign—he "just wants to make people laugh"— the barely suppressed rage that drives him is palpable. Shelley Hack, playing a stylish TV production assistant, dismisses Rupert with the glib politeness of a smug insider. This may reflect the industry's view of its audience, but it underestimates the danger of a man who takes his values from television.

In New York, famous people walk on the streets, if only on their way to a cab or limo. Stars can not live hermetically protected lives in New York City as they can in Beverly Hills and L.A. In *The King of Comedy*, an elderly woman spots Jerry on the street, but her rapture quickly descends into invective. When he does not acknowledge her claim as a fan, she screams, "You should get cancer!" This mix of adulation, envy, and anger lies at the heart of *The King of Comedy.*

PAUL ZIMMERMAN: I remember watching a David Suskind show on autograph-hunters in the late sixties or early seventies. I was struck by the personal way they related to the stars. One said, "Barbra is hard to work with." Barbra Streisand had asked this guy not to bother her—but he turned that into "Barbra is hard to work with." He used language to transform experience. That became an important part of Rupert Pupkin's character. He is able to transform experience through language. In one scene, security guards tell him to move along; he'd just be wasting his time waiting for Jerry Langford. Rupert says that it wouldn't be a waste of time, he'd be glad to do it. Rupert turns rejection into an opportunity to do Jerry a personal favor.

I had also read an article in *Esquire* about a man who kept a diary in which he assessed each Johnny Carson show. "Johnny disappointed me tonight," he would write. The talk shows were the biggest shows on television at the time. I started to think about connections between autograph-hunters and assassins. Both stalked the famous—one with a pen and one with a gun. I wrote a treatment and then worked with Milos Forman on a screenplay. We ended up with two versions—one he liked and one I liked. After a few years Milos dropped out of the project and I sent the version I liked to Marty Scorsese. This was about the time of *The Last Waltz*. Marty read it, and liked it, but was already doing a script about a comedian with Jay Cocks.

Later he said that he hadn't really understood the script at first. But he did send it to Bobby De Niro. Bobby loved it. We met. He really understood it. He understood the bravery of Rupert Pupkin, his chutzpah, the simplicity of his motives. Bobby said he liked the single-minded sense of purpose. People speak of De Niro as an instinctive actor, but he also understands these characters on an intellectual level. I think Bobby understood Rupert because he's an obsessive person himself. I knew Bobby when he was just beginning. I was the film critic at *Newsweek* and an advocate of both Marty Scorsese and Bobby. Bobby was always full of dignity and full of ambition. Then and now, he seems to carry a larger world, an imaginative world, along with him. Sometimes when you're with him you feel part of him is living in that greater, instinctive world. Brando had that same quality. Bobby could see Rupert as someone who would rather die than live anonymously.

Eventually Marty decided he wanted to direct *King of Comedy*. He and Bobby took the script, and a novelized version of the story I had written, and went out to Long Island. I didn't know what to expect. But when I read the script they did I literally jumped up and down. I was thrilled. They had synthesized the script and the book. It was great. I felt they had collaborated on the work, not eradicated it—built on what I'd done rather than replaced it.

MARTIN SCORSESE: *King of Comedy* was an uphill battle for me. It was more Bob's project than mine, and I wasn't a big help at the time. The motives for making a film are very important to me. They have to be good motives. Mine weren't very clear when I started out on this picture.

But there were some wonderful things in *King of Comedy*! My mother did an improvisation with De Niro when he's in the basement. He's talking to paper cutouts that represent guests on his imaginary talk show. My mother's yelling down the stairs to him to keep the sound down, and it's the only time I've ever seen him crack up on the set. Well, there was one other time, when a neighbor is yelling at Jake in *Raging Bull*, "You're an animal, you're an animal," and Bob says, "I'm gonna kill you, you'll find your dog's head in the hallway." He was laughing in the shot, because we could hear some guy yelling in the alley. If you watch him, you know he's laughing. It's because of that voice, the one we knew from childhood, from the streets of our neighborhoods.

ROBERT DE NIRO: I liked the script for *King of Comedy*. I liked the character and I thought it was funny. We shot it on the streets in New York City, and it gave us a chance to use things that we both knew happened there. There's a scene in *Raging Bull* where everybody's yelling. I was yelling at my wife, she was yelling at me, people were yelling in the building, in the alley. Those neighborhoods were loud. Someone yelled from the street and I responded, as Jake, and the crew laughed and we kept it. We could use that kind of craziness in *King of Comedy*. One time an old lady, just a regular person, came over. I was sitting down outside of the building waiting for Jerry Lewis to come out. She came over and started talking to me, and kissed me and said something to me. It was very cute and funny. Everybody laughed. We'd use spontaneous things like that.

MARTIN SCORSESE: There was another sequence of comedy when Rupert first meets Rita [Diahnne Abbott], the girl he wants to impress, in a bar. At the bar is a tough guy from Kentucky, played by Dan Johnson. Dan was a Vietnam veteran who cooked for us. He died at the age of thirty-nine, and we dedicated the film to him. Dan was on the other side of the bar when Rupert was talking to Rita. Dan and Bob started sliding beers at each other. It became a very interesting comedic ballet. Then Dan poured a beer down Rupert's pocket. Bob said, "That was unnecessary; you didn't have to do that"—trying to be very cool. But that's all cut out.

PAUL ZIMMERMAN: It was funny, about the scene with Rupert and Rita that was cut out. I had always felt that it was extraneous in the script,

ROBERT DE NIRO (RUPERT PUPKIN) AND SCORSESE ON THE STREETS OF
NEW YORK DURING FILMING OF *THE KING OF COMEDY*.

but it just somehow stayed within it like a foreign body. Cutting it moved things along faster, but you lost a moment when Rupert is seen sympathetically. At first I'd seen Rupert as a kind of Danny Kaye figure, and his story as a fantasy. But Marty and Bobby are realists. They made it much better, much deeper, tougher, more important. The character of Masha is a good example. I'd seen her as a weepy sentimental character, less threatening. Marty gave her that predatory quality, that danger. Sandra Bernhard did an incredible job.

SANDRA BERNHARD: All my friends who had done standup comedy had gone up for the role. I read for Cis Corman. She said, "I think you're pretty good so I want you to meet with Marty and Bobby."

So my first audition was a week later, and I went in and I had no style at all. Now I would never, ever do an audition the way I was dressed then—

jeans and a T-shirt. But not cool jeans—very uncool jeans and an uncool T-shirt. So I read for them and I improvised. My energy at the time was completely insane because I was twenty-five. My whole life was kind of desperate and weird, very similar to the character.

Meeting Jerry Lewis made me much more nervous than meeting with Marty and Bobby, because they're very relaxed, they make everybody feel good. But it turns out Jerry Lewis is just like somebody's dad—like my dad. He's from another generation. He's a comic, but he would never understand the kind of comedy that I do in a million years. I did the scene with him and it actually went very well. Marty told me later that he had thought I really scared Jerry Lewis. I think it was probably the kissing scene, I think that was it.

FREDDIE SCHULER: It was a slow-paced picture. We were shooting in New York and therefore dependent on the environment and the surroundings. Marty has an inner drive, an intensity, perhaps a creative conflict within, but he doesn't have a personality that expresses anger, so that conflict stays within. It becomes a tension that is perhaps necessary in the creative process. John Cassavetes had a similar sense that conflict and tension were part of creating. I worked with him on *Gloria,* and he liked to have almost a sense of panic as part of the atmosphere. Of course Cassavetes, as an actor, was intuitive. Marty plans more.

MARTIN SCORSESE: We got into a rhythm where we'd go through maybe twenty-two takes, sometimes more. I recall doing forty takes on some scenes, but that was due to acting style, especially Bob and Sandra Bernhard. Jerry Lewis finally got into it too and he improvised in the scene when he's trying to talk his way out of the kidnapping. What De Niro and I were trying for was to see how far we could push that character— how far over the top Rupert could go and still remain within a realistic framework. How much could he get away with as an actor playing a character like that.

SANDRA BERNHARD: During the shooting, the whole dynamic between me and De Niro happened naturally. He was such a total geek in that outfit. It was De Niro at his absolute most vulnerable. In a strange way he'd always been protected by his characters, who are usually these kind of shut-off, deep, frustrated, angry people.

But as Rupert, De Niro was out there. He didn't have that helmet on. He didn't have that shield, because somebody that intense and desperate, they don't even think about protecting themselves, because it's not even an issue. With his character and mine, it was like the clash of two cuckoo birds. When we were shooting on the streets, it was incredibly hot, ninety or a hundred degrees. It was July, and just boiling on the street. New York in the summer with all these people around just felt out of control. With Marty, there always seemed to be a sense of total freneticism, which he's controlling in his own way. I think Jerry Lewis found it difficult. I think he was uncomfortable, and felt it was an unprofessional situation. He's directed, himself. I think that he felt it was too freewheeling and too improvisational.

SANDRA BERNHARD (MASHA) AND SCORSESE ON THE SET OF
THE KING OF COMEDY.

MARION BILLINGS OF M/S BILLINGS PUBLICITY, SCORSESE
REPRESENTATIVE FOR TWO DECADES WITH THE DIRECTOR SHOOTING IN
NEW YORK CITY.

King of Comedy made a very interesting statement. It was ahead of itself in exposing what motivates our whole culture. Everyone wants to be near the immortals. Today the immortals are the stars. It's very chilling. The closer I get to greater success, the more I see both sides of it. During *King of Comedy*, I was very much on the other side of it. Now I'm walking a fine line between being a part of the public and a part of stardom. But that's always what my work has been about, anyway. I've always been fascinated by people's drives and needs, and the power they feel they draw from being near celebrities. People get angry because they can't have that kind of rich and famous success and beauty. I think that anger motivates people like Hinckley, and fans in general. It's a real double-edged sword of "I love you, I hate you."

Marty's a pretty self-conscious guy in a lot of ways, so he really empathizes with people's insecurities and fears, rather than playing on them. He's able to create an atmosphere that says "Hey, it's okay. We're all messed up and we're all searching."

I think everything he does is absolutely based in his strong relationship with Catholicism, however it may be affecting him. Whether he's angry with it, or a victim of it, or in love with it—there are all those different elements that come into play with his work.

I think all of us have our base, our bottom line. It could be family, or religion, or whatever. Sometimes it's a positive thing, sometimes it's a really destructive thing, but ultimately it all works if you're a creative person.

PAUL ZIMMERMAN: I had a different ending in mind for the movie. I saw Rupert performing on Jerry Langford's show as the "Kidnapping King of Comedy." You're not sure if it's real or a fantasy. But Marty was uncomfortable with such an ambiguous ending. He called me into his trailer one day to hear Jerry Lewis give his idea for the ending. Marty said to me, "Listen, just listen to it." Now, I thought Lewis was a brilliant choice for Jerry Langford, but as he explained his idea I started to shake my head no. Marty stopped me: "Never shake your head when someone talks to you. If you do that you'll never find out what the person has to say." He was right. I think that's why on the set he'll say after a take, "That's good. Let's do it again." He never says, "That wasn't right," or, "I didn't like it." It's always, "That's good," then "Let's do it again." That's his genius. He gets a hundred percent from everyone. He gives a hundred percent. It's very collaborative, and yet it all looks like Marty. It's not imperious, but everything seems to work toward his vision. It's magic.

DAVID FIELD: I remember one meeting in Marty's loft in TriBeCa during the editing of *The King of Comedy*. I had been in six cities in six days and I thought my heart was going to burst, I was so tired. I was in this exhausted state, which can lead to more interesting awareness at times. And he was pacing, and I guess Thelma was around someplace. I don't remember what we were talking about, what the business was. At some point he started to describe his life as a child in the streets of New York. I grew up in Missouri and Tennessee on farms, so I don't have these city associations. But as he spoke I could feel and smell the streets and I could hear the music. Suddenly I had this clear vision of Marty as a man born without enough skin. Everything came in at him at incredibly full strength, at a level of reality most of us screen out. I wanted to weep for who he was, and the courage it took for him to simply live any given day, given the fact that that's how the universe hit him. And I just thought I was in the presence of this extraordinarily heroic man.

I was at Fox at the time. *The King of Comedy* was a pick-up. We loved Rupert Pupkin, but the preview audience hated him, saw him as this sick terrorist. In Kansas City we got such bad numbers, it became funny.

I remember being at a birthday party for Marty—his fortieth, I think. It was an extraordinary group—directors, stars, his old friends, his mom and dad. I thought the studios should make sure that Marty always had the money to make the movies he wanted to make. He is one of those rare people, and we should just do that. Of course, you say that in a studio meeting, and people reexamine what they think of you as an executive. But I do feel that way about him.

PAUL ZIMMERMAN: I think people knew the movie was funny as they were watching it, but they didn't feel safe enough to laugh. When you laugh, you're defenseless, so you need a context of reassurance. *King of Comedy* had such a climate of danger that people didn't allow themselves to laugh. That confused the studio. They didn't know how to promote it. It broke house records in New York and did well in some other big cities, but never really broke through. I received the British Academy Award for the screenplay. I was very happy with the movie. It was like giving birth. And you know it's your baby, but it looks like Marty.

MARTIN SCORSESE: Marlon Brando was a big fan of *King of Comedy*. After it came out he invited Bob De Niro and me to his island.

I was on edge, I figured we'd get down there for five days and we'd discuss his project. For five days he wasn't there. For five days, we just walked around, and let me tell you, I'm not one of those return-to-paradise people. Forget it. I'm an urban person.

I'm figuring this guy is going to ask me to work with him. He's Marlon Brando. It's not some guy from the streets. This is Brando! At one point he came by and suggested walking around the island. I said, "Yeah, we just did that." He said, "What are you doing now? Reading a book?" I said, "Yeah, we were just reading." He said, "Well, after you read, you can walk around the island the other way." There was nothing to do! There was nothing.

After five days of that, I gave in. I was getting annoyed. And then he started discussing things, and we wound up talking for three weeks. It was the first time in my life that I realized that, in a sense, it is good to relax. But not when you're young. When you're young you should just keep going. Use the energy up when you have it.

SIX

ALMOST THE LAST TEMPTATION

THE LAST TEMPTATION OF CHRIST (1983; CANCELLED)

"I TOLD THEM MAKING THIS MOVIE IS LIKE PRAYING FOR ME."—MARTIN SCORSESE

S CORSESE MAY have had to convince himself to do *The King of Comedy,* but he burned to make *The Last Temptation of Christ.* At age ten he had drawn the storyboards for a movie he wanted to make on the life of Jesus. Thirty years had not dimmed that desire. In Nikos Kazantzakis' novel *The Last Temptation of Christ,* he found his vehicle. Scorsese optioned the rights to the novel, and in 1977 gave it to Paul Schrader. Schrader completed the script in 1982, and in early 1983, Paramount Pictures agreed to finance the movie with Irwin Winkler producing.

In the fall of 1983, Martin Scorsese had lunch with Eleni Kazantzakis at Alexandre's in Beverly Hills. This continental dining room, with its immaculate table linens, heavy silver, and a maître d' who spoke Italian and French, seemed more suited to the Old World sophistication of his guest than the usual L.A. restaurant. The widow of Nikos Kazantzakis, along with Patroclos Stavrou, a dignitary in the Cypriot government and Kazantzakis' literary executor, were in the U.S. to attend ceremonies at several universities in honor of the centenary of Kazantzakis' birth.

Eighty years had not diminished Eleni Kazantzakis' passion for her husband's ideas, nor had it blurred her elegant beauty and intelligence. She told Scorsese that her husband had been a shy man; all his life he had alternated between sorties into an active, public life and retreats into private contemplation. He had spent one six-month period in the very strict monastery on Mount Athos in Macedonia. Although Albert Schweitzer and Thomas Mann put forward his name for the Nobel Prize, Kazantzakis never sought the literary limelight. *Zorba the Greek* received praise and popular acceptance, and his re-telling of Homer's *Odyssey* in his *Odyssey: A Modern Sequel* received scholarly recognition, but later his name became synonymous with controversy because of his struggle to understand and reinterpret Christianity in contemporary terms. In a creative outpouring during the last nine years of his life, he had written eight books. His novel *The Greek Passion* presented the life of a village too honestly for easy acceptance. The Greek Orthodox Church threatened to excommunicate him. But the greatest controversy came after the publication of *The Last Temptation of Christ.*

In the prologue to *The Last Temptation of Christ*, Nikos Kazantzakis explained, "The dual substance of Christ—the yearning, so human, so superhuman, of man to attain to God or, more exactly, to return to God and identify himself with him—has always been a deep inscrutable mystery to me. This nostalgia for God, at once so mysterious and so real, has opened in me large wounds and also large flowing springs. My principal anguish and the source of all my joys and sorrows from my youth onward has been the incessant, merciless battle between the spirit and the flesh." Kazantzakis had even embraced Buddhism in an effort to transcend the conflict altogether. Ultimately, he turned back to Christianity.

"Struggle between the flesh and the spirit, rebellion and resistance, reconciliation and submission, and finally—the supreme purpose of the struggle—union with God; this was the ascent taken by Christ, the ascent which he invites us to take as well, following in his bloody tracks," Kazantzakis wrote.

The Last Temptation of Christ was his response to that invitation. He wrote:

I never followed Christ's bloody journey to Golgotha with such terror, I never relived his Life and Passion with such intensity, such understanding and love, as during those days and nights when I wrote *The Last Temptation of Christ.*

This book was written because I wanted to offer a supreme model to the man who struggles; I wanted to show him that he must not fear pain, temptation or death—because all three can be conquered, all three have already been conquered. Christ suffered pain, and since then pain has been sanctified. Temptation fought until the very last moment to lead him astray and temptation was defeated. Christ died on the cross, and at that instant, death was vanquished forever.

Many found his book an inspiration, but others shouted "Blasphemy!" Kazantzakis portrayed a Christ tempted to leave the cross for the happiness of an earthy life, a Christ drawn by the sexuality of Mary Magdalene and tormented by doubts about his mission. The Greek Orthodox Church's response to Kazantzakis' Christ came most brutally at the author's death in 1957. As his translator, P.A. Bien, recalls, "The Archbishop of Athens refused to allow his body to lie in state in a church, in the normal manner. In Crete, however, he was granted a Christian burial and a colossus, seemingly right out of one of his books, seized the coffin and lowered it singlehandedly into the grave."

Now, in 1983, Scorsese was proposing to bring *The Last Temptation of Christ* into public consciousness again. Other directors had tried and failed to make the movie, but none with Scorsese's determination and passion. Eleni Kazantzakis spoke to Scorsese of her husband's spiritual transformation and tried, perhaps, to alert him to the dangers ahead. Many people see Christ in their own terms and resent any questioning. "Remember," she said "even his own mother misunderstood Jesus' mission at the beginning."

PATROCLOS STAVROU: Scorsese wanted to make the film. His request was passed to Mrs. Eleni Kazantzakis. We were always very cautious about that book. I would say that our lunch was the determining factor— the final yes. I don't remember if there were any contacts before, but we wanted just to see Martin Scorsese. He is not a tall man. He's a man of my own dimensions. So we were speaking eye to eye. And what I saw in him was the eagerness to make the film, a great sense of consciousness and responsibility about the task to be undertaken. I saw also in him a sense of absolute honesty, a very honest approach to the book, to the spirit of the book, and even, I would say, to the deity of Christ as such, as it is described by Kazantzakis. He was very convincing that he meant to do an honest film, a film corresponding as much as possible to the book, and the *spirit* of the author. The film he was intending to do was not just for money or for any other selfish or material purpose. He was convincing. Also, we liked his charismatic approach. He spoke with great openness and sincerity. I would say that we communicated. That was my feeling. That was absolutely the feeling of Eleni Kazantzakis.

"What do you say?" she asked me. "I say yes," she said, "but we must help him as well, if he needs our help." We were so convinced that Scorsese would make an honest work that when we had to make another agreement in the future, we wanted to say that Scorsese would direct the film, and only in the case of the death of Scorsese would someone else make it. We were wondering, well, how could we write in a contract, "if the death of Scorsese . . . " Eleni Kazantzakis didn't wish to speak of the death of such a young man! However, in the subsequent contract, a condition was included that only in case Mr. Martin Scorsese, for any reason, is not able to do the film, would it go to anyone else. This is a proof of the trust he inspired in us!

ELENI KAZANTZAKIS: Scorsese is a deep creature and a very deeply Catholic man. He wanted to become a priest. He studied for this. The only thing he thinks about is how to portray the human aspect of Jesus Christ. Jesus, before he became the Christ. Jesus very humanly had fear and suffered when he climbed up to Calvary. Surely, this is a matter of approach. Did not Jesus Christ say, "Why have you abandoned me," and other similar things? He was a man and God. If not, how could he have felt pain? If not, he could think, "I am God, and if they crucify me, let them do it three hundred times." If you are a man, and you want to approach God, you feel pain with every nail that is put in your body, you feel pain when you go to the desert. And this is what Jesus Christ said.

PATROCLOS STAVROU: Kazantzakis was born in 1883. Eleni was born, it is written on her passport, in 1904. She says that she was born in 1903. So she was twenty years or nineteen years younger than him. They met in 1924. Kazantzakis was married already, but he was separated from his wife. He had not lived with his wife for many years.

It was very courageous on the part of Mrs. Kazantzakis to go to a man twenty years older. He told her from the very beginning, "If you come with me, you shall live in poverty, anxiety, and great toil. But you shall never have a boring day with me."

In 1945, after the liberation of Greece from the Germans, Nikos Kazantzakis was appointed a minister without portfolio. He was to be sent to the United States and Mexico, mainly to the United States, to collect assistance for the victims of the war. So Eleni Samios, his companion, had to accompany him. They could not go without being married, so they got married in 1945.

ELENI KAZANTZAKIS: I lived with Kazantzakis since 1928. Since the time we went together to Russia, where my body and soul became one with his body and soul, I understood only one thing. All his agony was about how man can endure, slowly, slowly, to cleanse himself, to make himself forget the mean things of the world, and *not* to forget that it is possible for the body to become spirit. To find God, the God that is within us. Nikos used to say, "All must become worthy of God in order to find God in ourselves."

He said that *The Last Temptation of Christ* was his best work, and I agree. The language is superb and the descriptions of Palestine are amazing. I remember that he used to send me to the library in Cannes because at that time we were living in Antibes. I brought him all the books connected with Jesus Christ. Some of the books said that Jesus Christ never existed because early historians like Plutarch did not say so. They say nothing about Jesus Christ, though they talk about Christians.

But Nikos never had any doubts about Christ, and many years before I knew him, he had written his first tragedy under the title *Christ*. When the book came out I remember that the Church, the Greek Orthodox Church, wanted to excommunicate him. But some people intervened and our Church eventually did not excommunicate him. Many write that Kazantzakis did not have a Christian funeral, but these are lies.

PATROCLOS STAVROU: He thought of writing this book in 1942, during the German occupation of Greece. Can you imagine? We have a letter of his dated May 16, 1942. He was living on the island of Aigina, and he wrote a letter to a friend of his, saying, "I have decided to write a book, *The Memoirs of Christ*, and I have started collecting documentation, all the material we need." So, he thought of writing the book under the title *The Memoirs of Christ*.

In January 1951, we have a letter in which he says that he has started writing his new novel, *The Last Temptation*. He continued writing throughout the year, because, he says in another letter, in June 1952, that he is deeply dedicated to the joy and the agony of *The Last Temptation*. In one letter he said, "Here in solitude, I'm working hard and well. I am writing a book on a Hebrew subject now, *The Last Temptation*. It takes place in Palestine, and you can understand how interesting it would be for me to see the Holy Land again. But that seems impossible."

He also writes, on November 16, 1951, "I am so deeply immersed in the joy and agony of *The Last Temptation* that I can't lift my head, and time passes. The moons get bright and fade away like lightning. My wife is away, I have nothing to prevent my withdrawing once again into my wide solitude, my own real climate. My wife keeps me still within human society, not permitting me to run wild. Once, when I had gone to Mount Sinai, the monks wanted to furnish me a desert hermitage, consisting of a little chamber, and a courtyard with two olive trees, an orange tree, and a tiny well of water. The Monastery of St. Catherine has a number of manuscripts which I would have read, and the most significant ones would have been published. And ever since that time, that place has loomed in midair in front of me. And if it were not for my wife, I should long since have gone back there. Nothing in my whole life has seemed so fascinating to me as the Arabian desert."

I have a letter from Kazantzakis, addressed to a friend of his in Sweden, dated May 1, 1954: "Yesterday, I received a telegram from a publisher in Germany. It said: '*The Last Temptation* on the Papal Index.' I have always been amazed at the narrow mindedness and narrow heartedness of human beings. Here is a book that I wrote in a state of deep religious exaltation, with fervent love for Christ. And now the representative of Christ, the Pope, has no understanding of it all. He cannot sense the Christian love with which it was written, and he condemns it. And yet, it is in keeping with the wretchedness and slavery of the contemporary world that I should be condemned."

There was a phrase from Tertullian that Nikos Kazantzakis telegraphed to the commission on the index of forbidden books, saying that he appealed to a higher court, the tribunal of God. "I appeal to your court, O Lord." In his response to the Greek Orthodox Church, he added, "You have cursed me, Holy Fathers. I *bless* you. I pray that your desires may be as clean as mine and that you may be as moral and as religious as I am. I am sending you this work of mine with great emotion. You please have the patience to read it, to go through it, and gradually it will dominate you. And I am sure that gradually the same emotions which I felt deep in myself while I was writing it will dominate you also. I attempted to revive the sacred legend on which the great Christian civilization of the West is based. It is not simply the life of Christ. The churches and all the clergy of Christendom, they have changed the form of Christ. Often my manuscripts, while I was writing, are smeared because I could not help my tears."

So he was crying, the tears fell onto the manuscripts, and the manuscripts were smeared with them.

Everywhere in the book, there are poetry, love for the animals, for the plants, to the people, trust in the soul of man, a conviction that life will dominate and win.

ELENI KAZANTZAKIS: Kazantzakis' agony went beyond the Christian approach. He always used to tell me, "I am not looking to find how I came to this world. I am looking to find *why* we came. What is our purpose." There was only one thing that preoccupied Kazantzakis in all his works, if you look at them. To turn the mortal part of man into immortal. To approach God. And further on, because he was always a fighter who believed in something, he was always upright up to the end. He was very much interested in man's soul. He wanted to remain upright and to the end, and to believe that man can become better than what he is.

The root of the book is that man needs love and great patience and great faith in order to endure the sufferings endured by Jesus Christ, in order to reach the highest point of sacrifice. And then, there, at this highest point of sacrifice, he becomes one with God. This is God. This is what is inside us. It is what is the best in us. When I sacrifice myself for mankind, I reach the highest point of myself and, therefore, I find God.

Well, what the book says is very concrete. It tells the youth that you must fight as much as you can to get into yourself, to *know* yourself and to reach to achieve the best in yourself—how to become better and useful to mankind, even if it be to sacrifice yourself. This is the message. There is no other message.

Kazantzakis was a very, very frugal man, content with very little things. He often said to me that it was better that we are poor, because if we were rich he would go around the whole world and he would not be able to write anything. When once I asked him, "Couldn't we travel second class?"— we were travelling all tourist class in those days—"Can we go to a good hotel?" he told me, "What would Gandhi do? If Gandhi were alive, he would travel fourth class, the last class!"

Many times I have seen my husband in tears when he was writing. From very, very young, when he was five years old, he wanted to be a great hero in the history—ecclesiastic history. He wanted to be a real scholar. To do what a student does. He asked me once, "Can I do what Christ did? Can I do what Schweitzer did? Can I be Schweitzer? No, I can't." You see, he knew how far he could go. He never chose a role not true. He adored Schweitzer, and Schweitzer liked my husband.

My husband adored Christ because he died because he believed in something. He found it wonderful to have this. To be fortunate enough to say, "I believe in this. I will suffer for this." And my husband believed this, too. He believed in Christ, but he could not be Christ!

PATROCLOS STAVROU: Some years ago, I entered a big bookshop in London. I looked around to see if there were any books by Kazantzakis. I saw none. I went to the fiction section—nothing; to poetry—nothing; even through the travel books—nothing. I felt terrible. So I addressed somebody there. "You have no Kazantzakis?" "Yes, we have." "But I have looked around fiction, poetry, et cetera, and I have not found any books." "Yes, you are right, but we have them just there, with the classics."

When I first read *The Last Temptation of Christ*, I was vehemently, strongly against Kazantzakis for this characterization of Christ, for the way he treated this holy story of Christ.

Years passed, and I began to think and think again, and pondered over everything. During the last twenty years, I have come to a firm belief in Kazantzakis, more and more, and I've been trying to just get deep into his own feelings and ideas. About ten years ago, I had to publish *The Last*

Temptation of Christ again. I had to read *The Last Temptation of Christ* at least five times, to get the proofs corrected as I wanted them to be, without mistakes in spelling or anything. Through reading and reading and reading *The Last Temptation*, I came to love Christ more than any other time in my life.

MARTIN SCORSESE: In 1961 a Greek friend, John Mabros, told me about *The Last Temptation*. I knew him at N.Y.U. and then later he was an assistant on *Raging Bull*. But it really started when Barbara Hershey gave me the book in 1972. When I first read the book, I liked it, but I was thinking of making a movie from a different novel, *King Jesus* by Robert Graves. But I liked *Last Temptation* because it dealt with the battle between the spirit and the flesh. I thought it was something I could understand.

Paul Schrader wrote the first version of *Last Temptation* in 1981. What he showed me by doing the rough draft was that the book could be conquered. He cut it to the essentials. I realized that there would have to be a rewrite, but the structure was there.

PAUL SCHRADER: On *Last Temptation*, I read the book and I listed everything, everything that happened, scene by scene—three to four hundred items. Then I created dramatic categories: Jesus' character evolution, disciples, comic relief, and the various themes of Magdalene and Mother. Then, after each scene, I put checks as to which ones were relevant and how relevant they were. Then I simply went through and took out all the scenes that had no checks. All of a sudden, this six hundred-page book was much shorter.

I thought of each theme. For example, I had to break down the revelation of God to Jesus. What does God want of him, and how? Jesus wonders, "What am I supposed to do?" The secondary themes would be the relationship to Magdalene, and the relationship with Judas.

The outline of *Last Temptation* was written in advance of the script, and with the exception of two scenes it is identical to the film that came out seven, eight years later. I projected the script to be 106 pages. When Marty had the outline, he had the movie. Everything was laid out. There wasn't any room for him to interfere with my writing process. He knew exactly what I was doing. At every stage, he *knows* how I'm doing, all he has to do is check his outline, and that way he doesn't interfere with me when I'm writing, and I don't interfere with him when he directs. And when I hand over a script, I'm on to something else. It really isn't big enough for our two egos. He has to step back when I write and I have to step back when he directs. It's better that way.

DAVID KIRKPATRICK: Paramount was initially attracted to the theatricality of Marty Scorsese doing the life of Christ. I think it was a unique idea because there hadn't been a strong theatrical picture about Christ in some time.

I truly loved the book. It showed a human side of Christ. I was very moved by the portrayal of Jesus wondering whether he was crazy or specially chosen. It was a remarkable achievement.

I read the book and the screenplay and my marching orders were, "Get this movie made, bring it in at a price, cast it well, and work closely with Marty, given the project needs a lot of care and attention and a lot of support." I decided to try and find as much history as I could about the project and get as involved as I could, without stepping on Marty's terrain. We started with noble intentions and those sustained us.

MARTIN SCORSESE: When it became a reality that *The Last Temptation of Christ* could be made, the only place that would make it was Paramount Pictures. It started, in 1983, on a budget of $11 million—average budgets, now, start at $15 million—and it rose to $14 million, and kept rising. The film was to be shot in Israel, and in January of 1983 we went to Israel, Morocco, and Paris. It was a big thing for me because I hadn't been out of New York City for two years.

I had an amazing time in the Holy Land. I liked it because the value of living was heightened; they were dealing with essentials, staying alive. I thought that was important. When I got to Jerusalem I had a powerful sense of the divinity of Christ, of all the centuries of faith and worship there. I felt it very strongly in the Church of the Holy Sepulcher at the Tomb of Jesus. I loved the idea of shooting *Last Temptation* in the Holy Land, because of the holiness of the place, and the seriousness with which all three religions regard it.

I came back to New York February 9, 1983, when *King of Comedy* opened. I remember I had to go back to L.A. for March 4, for a dinner for John Huston. The weekend right before that, I went to see Bobby in Paris.

There was speculation by the business that he would be Christ because we'd worked together in the last four movies, but De Niro was never really interested. I flew to Paris on the Concorde to see him. I was there and back in a weekend. He explained to me that he didn't want to do the project. Bobby knows that any script I have, I'm going to change. So it wasn't the script so much. He said he couldn't see himself in robes, and kept thinking of Paul Newman in one of his earlier movies, called *The Silver Chalice*. It was one of my favorites, but it was a terrible movie. He said, "It's just not one we should be together on." It would be hard to convince a guy to get up on a cross. You really have to want to do the part, to get up there and do it, and De Niro wasn't that interested in religion.

For De Niro to do a movie, he has to really be interested and he will start three years in advance. When we were doing *New York, New York*, he was already practicing at lunchtime for *Raging Bull*, though we didn't actually shoot *Raging Bull* until years later. But when he's really interested in something, I know it. We always check in with each other, we always talk. With the religious film, we never discussed it, we never had a meeting about it. It was kind of understood that I would give him the script and if he was interested, fine.

ROBERT DE NIRO: I was not interested in playing Christ. It's like playing Hamlet. I just didn't want to do it. Marty and I talked about it. We do things with each other because we like to work together, but also for our own separate reasons—I have mine as an actor, and he has his as a director. That's the best way.

Last Temptation was something I was never interested in doing. But I did tell him, "If you really have a problem, if you really want to do it, and you need me, I'll do it. If you're against the wall and you have no other way, I'll do it as a friend."

PAUL SCHRADER: I had thought of De Niro in the early stages of writing *Last Temptation* because of *Taxi Driver* and *Raging Bull*, but there is really no automatic connection between him and Marty. Nor is there with me. I'm not really part of Marty's circle. We see each other, and we get along, but it's a collaboration of sensibility, not of personalities. What we get from each other is a creative friction. I'm not interested in being his friend at the price of submerging my personality. I'm more interested in making films that invigorate than in being pals.

MARTIN SCORSESE: I realized at this point, after having seen movies about Jesus in the past, that there is not just one actor who can play Jesus, there are many—because Jesus has many different parts, many different sides. But I didn't tell the studio who I was thinking of. I tried to keep it all to myself, so I could just think about it. In the middle of September we decided Chris Walken was my choice.

The people at the studio were going through all kinds of painful deliberations. They had trouble with Chris Walken as Christ and wanted us to look further. We compiled some footage from a movie called *Reckless* with Aidan Quinn. I had liked him originally but thought he was too young. Then when I saw him in *Reckless* he looked a bit older. He had a lot of intensity. I liked the way he looked, he had guts, and he was willing to try the part. The studio loved him and approved him immediately. Irwin Winkler, in the meantime, had started to back away from the project.

IRWIN WINKLER: I was only involved in the production during the development of the script from the book. I withdrew because of my commitment to *The Right Stuff*. That movie just grew and grew. I couldn't see myself travelling between the Negev Desert, which was where we were going to shoot *Last Temptation*, and the Mojave in California, where we were doing *The Right Stuff*. That's an awful big commute. The budget on both pictures was getting bigger and bigger, and both needed close supervision. I couldn't be in two places at once and I didn't want to leave my kids for six months.

DAVID KIRKPATRICK: People in the company started to take a closer look. They started to question their original intent. I think everybody had nightmares. Not so much because it was an unusual picture, but because it could create a lot of confrontation.

BARBARA HERSHEY: When I read in the trades that Marty was doing *The Last Temptation of Christ*, I literally screamed out loud. My hand was shaking when I called my agent and said, "I have to try out for Mary Magdalene." Marty put me through three months of various tests. He told me the reason was because he didn't want to feel he gave the role to me because he felt obliged, since I'd given him Kazantzakis' book. I understood. I wouldn't have wanted the role for that reason either.

KEITH ADDIS: The first movie I worked on was *Taxi Driver*. When I heard that Marty wanted to do *Last Temptation*, I read the book. I told him, "Marty, I did the lowest things I've ever had to do in my whole life for you. I got you tea on the set for a year. I brought you Maalox when your stomach was upset. I've never asked you for a favor, but now I want a favor. I want you to have lunch with me and Sting." I took them to lunch at a restaurant in Los Angeles called Trumps. I didn't have to say a word. They sat down, and they were both so in love with the book, they talked for two hours about it. At that point we weren't talking about Sting playing Jesus Christ, because Aidan Quinn had been set; we were talking about him playing Pontius Pilate.

Marty tested Sting with Aidan Quinn. Sting flew in from London and they had the most marvelous time. They told us, "He's got the part." We agreed to do it for almost nothing, just about scale. Sting would have done it for nothing. Sting would have given him a thousand dollars to play the part, and paid his own expenses. And then everything fell apart for an infinite number of reasons, reasons and causes over which we had no control. It was a big disappointment for us.

STING: To start, I'd always wanted to work with Scorsese, and the Kazantzakis novel was one of my favorites. I also thought the script was staggeringly good, in comparison with what you normally are asked to read. I think Pilate is one of the most interesting villains consigned to hell. Pilate wasn't just the straightforward, two-dimensional villain, the guy who just washes his hands. He was a complex human being. I'd been very taken in by Bulgakov's portrayal of Pilate in *The Master and Margarita*.

As a child, I was always fascinated by Pontius Pilate because I thought he had such a neat name. When you're first taught to pray, as a child, there is a Catholic prayer that mentions Pontius Pilate. "Suffered under Pontius Pilate." And I always thought they were saying "pilot," and I kept wondering, "What's a pilot doing there?" I used to serve Mass at a Benedictine monastery near my house. I never went to the seminary or anything, but we were kind of conditioned that if you didn't have a vocation to join the priesthood, you weren't quite up to snuff.

Also, I'm from an area in the north of England called Walls End. I used to live near a huge shipyard. In the shipyard itself, there were ruins of a Roman camp. So all around, you had streets named after Roman things, a sense of the Romans. That might be another reason why I was so interested in Pilate. What a jerk Pontius Pilate was, I found out.

I don't know what the politics of making the film were, but I was hearing rumors about strong lobbying interests who were against the idea of showing Jesus having anything to do with a woman. People have this impression of Jesus as some kind of plaster statue—a middle-class, white, Anglo-Saxon Protestant. And he wasn't.

MARTIN SCORSESE: We made a first revision of Schrader's script in Palm Springs, Jay Cocks and myself. What I wanted was feedback from the studio, but what I started to get was criticism. There's a big difference. Feedback is, "I don't understand it." Yes, if you don't understand it, tell me, and I'll judge whether or not it is meant to be understood, and then I'll put it in the script or change it or whatever. But to criticize, to say, "This is no good," that stops the creative process.

The studio had problems with the script. They were beginning to feel the script was difficult to understand, and too arty. They were worried; they were moving, as they put it, "from a green light to a blinking yellow." I told them that making this film was like praying to me, it was that important. I can't remember exactly what I said, but when we walked out of that room, they were still going to shoot the film.

DAVID KIRKPATRICK: I was behind the movie and I wanted to see it made. We worked hard and long on it, and it was Marty's dream to see it through.

But since upper-management was not familiar with ongoing theological dialogues about Christ, the script seemed much more inflammatory than it really was. I think that was part of the problem. November is when things started to spark. A group of Protestant women called the "Evangelical Sisterhood" heard that we were making a movie of *The Last Temptation of Christ*. In an effort to block it, they put out a newsletter asking people to protest. Gulf + Western, which owned Paramount, was receiving five hundred letters a day on that. Upper-management at Paramount were being extremely cautious, and rightfully so, because as intelligent men they wanted to be able to frame our response in a rational way. Since they didn't know all the facts and didn't have training in that area, they wanted to know more about it. That's when we had the theological seminars. I thought the management at Paramount must realize the opportunity they had, and go beyond the negative voices already raised against the project.

．　．　．

The studio, through David Kirkpatrick, agreed to sponsor a theological discussion. Since I was already doing theological research on the project, I was asked to organize the seminar. Father John McKenzie, a noted scripture scholar, agreed to take part. Three or four other Christian theologians, both Catholic and Protestant, would be invited. Scorsese liked the idea. Anything to help get this movie made. And so, for probably the first time, a movie studio hosted a theological seminar.

For the more than twenty years we had known each other, an interest in religion had formed the unspoken but continuing bond between Martin Scorsese and myself. Both of us had spent much of our childhood and adolescence convinced we had a vocation to religious life. When I learned that Father John McKenzie was actually living in Claremont, California, only forty miles from L.A., I felt he and Scorsese must meet. We went to Claremont.

The focal point in the house where Father McKenzie was staying was a large glass case filled with artifacts from the Holy Land. There were coins, lamps, and pottery, all from the time of Jesus' life. We stood transfixed. An apostle or someone who knew Jesus or perhaps even Jesus himself might have poured oil into one of these lamps or carried one of these coins.

Father McKenzie and Scorsese found common ground immediately. Father McKenzie was in his seventies and had recently suffered bouts of illness, but he was still an independent thinker and on the cutting edge of theology. He was also a lifelong movie fan. He tried to describe the impact Gloria Swanson had made on the nation during his youth. No modern star, he said, could even come close.

Some people have trouble with Scorsese's elliptical style of conversation, but McKenzie entered right into it. He understood not only his questions, but also what lay behind them. At one point, Father McKenzie said, "The question is always the Resurrection." "The Resurrection?" Scorsese asked. Father McKenzie said, "Yes. A humanist thinker can accept everything about Jesus—his existence, his followers, his thought, his life, even his suffering and death. But it is with the Resurrection that we move from speculation into belief." Scorsese nodded. Here was the core of the debate in contemporary theology.

On November 5, 1983, Father John McKenzie swept through the Paramount gates in a studio car, just as Gloria Swanson had in *Sunset Boulevard*. He enjoyed the coincidence. Three other prominent and respected theologians, whose works were among the books Scorsese, Jay Cocks, David Kirkpatrick, and I were reading, also arrived for the seminar.

John Cobb of Claremont College represents a liberal Protestant perspective; Rosemary Radford Ruether, from Garrett Evangelical Theological Seminary in Evanston, is a prominent Catholic feminist and theologian; John Elliot of San Francisco State University is a Lutheran scholar and teacher. They assembled with Father McKenzie in the executive dining area of Paramount at a round table. Jeffrey Katzenberg, Paramount's president of production, presided. The transcript of the seminar was taped for studio heads Michael Eisner and Barry Diller, and for Scorsese.

Over brunch and the three-hour meeting that followed, the conversation ranged from Christ's dual nature to the significance of the bread and wine at the Last Supper to Jesus' relationship with his mother. Kazantzakis' book initiated the discussion, but what really emerged was a survey of current Christian theological thought. Rosemary Radford Ruether, whose book *To Change the World* had impressed Scorsese, spoke of the interplay between the political import of Jesus' message and its internal spiritual dimension. He calls his followers to set aside the very impulse to dominate. McKenzie hoped Jesus would not again appear as "a pious wimp," as he had been portrayed in past films. Elliot granted that the focus on sexuality was justified given contemporary society's preoccupation. John Cobb saw Kazantzakis as "hyper-orthodox," attributing to Jesus claims of divinity he did not make. All the theologians present were teachers, and questions about Jesus and his mission were a legitimate part of their work. But a movie theater was not a classroom, and as Father McKenzie remarked, "This is a dangerous job. Anything about Jesus is dangerous."

DAVID KIRKPATRICK: I think everyone was impressed by the caliber of people who came to the seminar of theologians at Paramount, and by the incisive and historical reactions they gave. There was a lot of humor and a lot of thoughtful consideration. The feeling was, "Great, this is wonderful! This gives us more courage than ever to go out and make this picture." The idea that something could lead to this intelligent discussion about Jesus was very exciting. But Barry Diller wasn't sure. The chairman of the board of Gulf + Western for the first time took an interest in what Paramount was making. This was the first time since the former head of Gulf + Western, Charlie Bludhorn, had died that someone said, "Why am I getting five hundred letters a day? What are we doing here?"

MARTIN SCORSESE: The theological seminars had been good, but also showed that there could be trouble. We had a meeting in which I talked about the issues raised by the theologians. There was no getting away from it; it is a volatile story. After two thousand years, people are still killing each other all over the world about this story.

The movie couldn't be *King of Kings*. *King of Kings* is a lie. A number of people complained about it because it lulls people into an easy way of thinking that they don't have to work at love in their lives. That's *not* what I wanted to say.

The opening scene, where Jesus is making crosses, should be reminiscent of James Dean in *Rebel Without a Cause*. In the beginning, in the opening shot where Dean's drunk and they pick him up and take him to the police station and he has such anger that he doesn't know how to direct it—that's the character in *Rebel Without a Cause*. And there should be something of that in the cross-making scene.

I was trying for subjectivity. In *Raging Bull*, it was what a fighter fears or feels inside his mind. What do these punches sound like after fifteen rounds? And, in *Last Temptation*, when Jesus is sitting for forty days in the desert, day and night, and that snake goes by, I don't care who you are, that snake is going to talk to you! That lion is going to talk to you. That's a real snake, no fancy special effects. All the miracles and all of those strange hypnotic suggestions are going to come from real things. You won't see a tree growing out of the ground. It will just appear there.

When you see Jesus in the valley, where the crazy people are, it has to have kind of a hyper-reality to it. In fact, the dream, the last temptation, should be very realistic—so realistic that people say, "Well, it can't be that this lunatic is really suggesting that this guy got off the cross and died an old man! I can't believe it," until the very last frame of the picture. That would be the beauty of it.

As far as Jesus' relationship with his mother is concerned, he must hurt her once, the way we all have hurt our mothers. It is very beautiful. It should be a very good moment, a very positive thing. He has to say he can only deal with a father who is in heaven, not with her. Nobody understands Jesus. Eleni Kazantzakis mentioned this to me when we met her. Nobody understands Jesus, not even his mother. The sense is, "I wish you could understand, Mother, but I don't even know who you are, basically, because I only know one thing. My father is in heaven." Of course, at the end he says, "Forgive me, because I was a bad son," in temporal terms. It is very beautiful.

I knew the heart scene was a concern. I think it's very important to know that our special effects guy, who flew in from Italy, had a model for the scene and showed me how Jesus reaches into his body. *No blood.* I suggested just painting the inside, like a little pink, and he said to me in Italian, "No blood—a miracle!" A miracle, of course. He understood completely. No blood. He pulls out the heart, and it's more the symbol of the Sacred Heart of Jesus with the flame and the sword through it. Drips of blood go into the pool and the water changes to red. It's the idea that he offers his heart to the apostles as a sign of love to create solidarity. They've been waiting for him to come out of the desert. They're grumbling and he comes and gives them his heart.

In addition to concerns about public response to the film, Barry Diller said that the shooting in Israel seemed like a runaway production already. He apologized for not having raised this six months ago instead of waiting. I said to Barry, "I understand that you really have to feel for this subject matter." He said, "That's right, I don't feel the same way you do. I don't feel enthusiastic enough to undergo all the problems I would have to undergo." "What if Marty took no salary and shot it in sixty days, would you be interested?," Harry Ufland asked. Barry said no. I figured this was it. The picture was dead. It was the unmaking of *The Last Temptation of Christ.*

So I said, "This film should never have been made through the Hollywood system. It should have been made like Pasolini's film *The Gospel According to Saint Matthew.* Shoot it for $3 million or $4 million in Italy somewhere." "That's exactly right," Barry Diller said. So I kind of perked up a little. I wasn't trying to convince them, I simply made a statement about the style in which the film should have been made. Michael Eisner said, "Well, listen, I'll help you get the film set up somewhere else. We'll pretend the film is not in turnaround." Turnaround happens when a studio decides not to proceed with a project and tries to find someone else to make it. I went for Thanksgiving dinner at Brian De Palma's house and the first thing he said was, "So, you're in turnaround already."

From Thanksgiving Day to December 21, I stayed home and made up shots and went to meetings about the picture. Both Eisner and Katzenberg wanted to do the picture. So we cut the shooting days down to fifty-five days—fifty-five shooting days all shot in Israel very quickly, and the budget down to $7.8 million, then to $6 million, including the $4 million we already spent. No salary for me. And I told Katzenberg I would do *Flashdance II* if he wanted. And no salary for Keitel or Aidan Quinn, who would play Judas and Jesus. On December 21, at a meeting, I asked Barry Diller, "Isn't there a figure we could reach that would balance the risk of the picture?" There was dead silence. I said, "Does this mean we can't make the picture here?" We all started laughing. It was no, no, finally no! He should have done this months ago, he said, and apologized, and he left. David Kirkpatrick hugged me, and Jeff Katzenberg said, "With my fifteen years in the business, I think that was a no." I said, "I think I got that impression."

Harry Ufland was running all over to different studios trying to get it set up, meeting with everyone, and we kept coming up against a brick wall. We learned that Salah Hassanein, the head of the United Artists film chain, at the time the second largest in the country, said that he would refuse to show the film. So a month later I met him in Great Neck, Long Island. He hadn't really read the script until a few days earlier. He asked me why I wanted to make this film. I told him that God can't be only in the hands of the churches. There are so many obstacles in between us and the spirit. In a sense, to make this film was to try to make God accessible to people in the audience who feel alienated from the churches. I said, "I have had three divorces, does this mean I can't speak to God because the church says I can't? No, no! I can talk for myself because I am me." He answered that he felt the same way as I did. His mother was a Christian and his father was a Muslim. By the time he was in college or high school, he felt the same way about God, but he chose to keep it to himself and not burden other people.

Then he told me about the movie called *Martin Luther*, which he had had bad trouble with. There was trouble also with *The Greatest Story Ever Told*, and then *Life of Brian*. The worst of all was *Mohammed, Messenger of God*, when they bombed the theater. He said, "You people can produce a film, you can act in it, you can direct it, and you can distribute it. But when the audience doesn't like something or when their religious beliefs are offended, they don't find where *you* are, they go where they saw it last. I don't want it in my theaters. Religious films are just too much trouble."

HARRY UFLAND: Michael Eisner was a great proponent of this picture. But it was tough for Barry Diller. It wasn't easy for him to face Marty and tell him that the movie was in trouble. The Thanksgiving meeting was a big surprise.

When I heard about Salah Hassanein's objections, I arranged a meeting. This was a few months later. We went out to Long Island, and he held court for about three hours. We found out early on that he hadn't even read the book or screenplay. He even said to us, "*You* make the movie. They don't come and cut up *your* seats, and refuse to buy *your* popcorn."

He would only say that he would see it when it was finished and make his decision. He's one of the key exhibitors in the country. And, contrary to public belief, the exhibitors all talk to one another. So for instance—and I don't know this to be true, but *if* one exhibitor told the others, "Don't run this," I'm not saying that they wouldn't run it, but it isn't a good thing to happen. I think it became like a hot coal, and people just didn't want to go near it.

PATROCLOS STAVROU: We have a museum of the life and works of Kazantzakis in his birthplace Vavare in Crete. Mrs. Titiki Saclabami, his relative, is in charge. All the correspondence about the movie was collected there. For a while we were afraid the film would exist only in documentation.

SEVEN

SURVIVAL

AFTER HOURS (1985)

"THE TRICK WAS TO SURVIVE AFTER *THE LAST TEMPTATION OF CHRIST*
WAS CANCELLED BY PARAMOUNT IN 1983."
—MARTIN SCORSESE

IT WAS LATE one September night in 1984, on Hudson Street in lower Manhattan. The last of the trucks that feed into the Holland Tunnel had bumped their way back into Jersey. The workers that clog this area of small manufacturers, wholesale merchants, and artists' lofts during the day had gone home. Night transformed the neighborhood into a frontier where ordinary city life confronted another world. This was the milieu of *After Hours,* a film Scorsese had agreed to direct in order to survive the cancellation of *The Last Temptation of Christ.*

On the first night of the shoot, Scorsese sat in his director's chair on the sidewalk, conferring with Griffin Dunne and Amy Robinson, co-producers of the movie. Dunne was also playing Paul Hackett, a non-descript computer programmer who meets a strange but beautiful girl, Marcy (Rosanna Arquette) in a midtown Manhattan coffee shop. She gives him her phone number. He calls. She invites him to her place in SoHo, the downtown neighborhood of artists' lofts, odd night clubs, and bizarre behavior.

On his way downtown, fate and an irate cab driver snatch Paul's last twenty dollars. The adventure soon becomes a nightmare. First, Marcy must drop her keys to Paul (no intercoms in SoHo). The shot is taken from the keys' point of view, and they become a threatening missile, hurtling down from above toward Paul's upturned face. They are a warning: He enters this world at his own risk. Paul climbs the narrow staircase into the loft Marcy shares with Kiki, a sculptress with a fondness for leather and whips. Marcy is the ultimate nightmarish blind date: As Paul waits for her to get ready, she kills herself. Paul escapes from her apartment, but nighttown has captured him and will not let him go. After a series of horrible encounters with strange women and hostile residents, he is turned into a living statue, wrapped in a linen shroud. Two thieves steal him, but then return him to the daylight uptown world. Scorsese and his collaborators struggled to find the right ending. "We need a resurrection," Scorsese said. So Paul was allowed to wake up in front of his own office.

After Hours is an anxiety dream. Paul Hackett can*not* hack it in the strange, foreign territory of lower Manhattan. Only when he gives up trying to impose reason on irrationality can he be saved. Paul, a representative of the ordered life, has entered the realm of art. All Paul wants is to get home—to be safe—but even this simple goal seems impossible. His plight is so exaggerated it becomes a joke.

When things get really bad in Scorsese movies, some character—Johnny Boy in *Mean Streets,* Joey La Motta in *Raging Bull,* or Peter Boyle's Wizard in *Taxi Driver*—laughs at the absurdity of it all. In *After Hours,* Scorsese, still frustrated in his attempts to make the movie most important to him, *The Last Temptation of Christ,* is the one laughing now. It's as if he says, "Can you believe what's happening to this poor guy? It's so awful it's funny."

The script and project did not originate with Scorsese, but his preoccupations mark the movie. In addition to exploring the theme of redemption in a new, more comical way, Scorsese again uses objects—the keys, the twenty-dollar bill—as symbols of emotional states. Scorsese liked the nighttime quiet and emptiness of pre-gentrified SoHo and TriBeCa. Like the Russian cemetery in *Mean Streets,* the taxicab sanctuary of Travis Bickle, the boxing ring roped off from the howling crowd in *Raging Bull,* SoHo is a place apart, especially "after hours."

MARTIN SCORSESE: The trick was to survive. That was the idea. The trick was to survive after *The Last Temptation of Christ* was cancelled by Paramount in 1983. That was four weeks before shooting was to have started. We had everything ready. It was devastating. My idea then was to pull back, and not to become hysterical and try to kill people. The idea was to not break things, and to try to be calm, and to think, "All right . . . be *really* calm." And I was very calm, very calm. Because in a funny way, I was almost relieved, because the picture was becoming too big. We may have been on the road to ruining the picture by making it one hundred days of shooting. It may have been a little too much.

So the trick then was to find *something*. First I said, "Give me anything. I'll do it. I've got to work. I've got to do something." And I was sent scripts, but I just couldn't do them. Part of making films is like playing. If you don't like the game, forget it. If you don't want to be there by six o'clock in the morning, forget it. To be up that early and to deal with the actors and all the physical problems, without the enjoyment of doing it—if it's not your first or second film, forget it!

MARTIN SCORSESE TALKS WITH GRIFFIN DUNNE (PAUL HACKETT)
DURING FILMING OF *AFTER HOURS*.

What eventually happened was that I got a script from my lawyer, who represented Amy Robinson and Griffin Dunne, called *Lies*, which ultimately became *After Hours*. The first sixty-five pages were fascinating and the dialogue was very funny, and I realized what I could do with it. Amy Robinson played Charlie's girlfriend in *Mean Streets*, and Griffin Dunne is a wonderful actor, and I thought they had produced interesting independent films with *Baby, It's You* and *Chilly Scenes of Winter*. I realized this would be made for about $4 million, in Manhattan, and I said, "Make it." I thought it would be interesting to see if I could go back and do something in a very fast way. *All style.* An exercise completely in style. And to show that they hadn't killed my spirit.

AMY ROBINSON: The great thing about doing *After Hours*, so many years after *Mean Streets*, was that all of that excitement and enthusiasm Marty had was recaptured. It was the same intense kind of fun.

Coming off *The King of Comedy*, he'd been tired, exhausted and disillusioned. *After Hours* was a little more on the edge, had a lower budget, and brought Marty back to a place where he had been. He was in the vibrant, creative mood he had been in when we did *Mean Streets*.

I had gotten the script for *After Hours* at the Sundance Film Festival. And it *was* so New York, and it was even darker in some ways than the movie. I called Griffin Dunne right away and said, "I have a very funny script, full of black humor, with a great part for you." So we optioned it.

In *After Hours*, Marty wanted to do a surreal movie realistically. That's how I had seen this script as well. The script was meticulously written— real and yet surreal.

MARTIN SCORSESE: *After Hours* was perfect. You could make it minimal. You're dealing with a guy in the street at night. It was all shot at night, eight weeks of night—that's great. I used to edit at night, too. *New York, New York* was edited mostly during the night, and so was all of *Raging Bull*. I prefer the night, because you don't get the phone calls.

I was living in TriBeCa at the time. The idea would be to take this one guy at night and deal with him. I mean, how difficult could it be? I was used to making films, from *New York, New York* to *Raging Bull* to *King of Comedy*, that were all one hundred days in shooting. And we were going to go into *Last Temptation of Christ* on a ninety-nine-day shooting schedule. I could do this one in forty days. That's the way I did it—in forty nights, very quickly, because I laid out every shot.

The idea would be to come up with a style. I thought it would be a parody of *film noir* and also a parody of a thriller. The angles themselves are parodies—the angles, the cuts, and the Fritz Lang–type shots, the Hitchcock parodies. Griffin goes into a room, and it cuts to a big close-up of a light switch on the wall, just a light switch, and the lights go on, but nothing else really happens. It's like a psychological twist each time, a joke. You think the lights going on is going to solve his problem, so he can get home that night. It's ridiculous! There was constant cutting to extreme close-ups for no reason, just to build up paranoia and anxiety—total anxiety. It's simple to do in camera movements. It was so simple, it was like an exercise. And Griffin, I wanted his timing to be like Jack Benny's— those pauses. There was also Michael Ballhaus's lighting, which was a takeoff on German Expressionism—the shadow of the walls in the staircase, a shadow against the wall. But nothing of *film noir* or psychological horror really occurs. It's all in his head.

MICHAEL BALLHAUS: When I first saw Martin Scorsese, he was in Berlin talking about film preservation and how to prevent colors from fading. I was sitting there and I said to myself, "One day I'm going to shoot a movie with this director." I didn't expect it would happen so soon.

The way Marty tells stories about people is the way I feel it should be done—the way he moves a camera and blocks a scene. Nothing is meaningless. Everything is thought out and specific. Marty has his brain filled with images—and with movies. You feel that when you see his work.

I had worked with Fassbinder for nine years. He was a fascinating director to work with, and had a vision similar to Marty's. He knew what he wanted and how he wanted it to be done. But Fassbinder always wanted to battle; whenever I had an idea he would make it more extreme. I learned that if in the context of the film it is right for the scene, no one will see it as weird or strange.

Marty takes chances too. For example, in *After Hours*, the camera sometimes looks at people in a different way or at an odd angle. In the beginning, in the coffee shop, the camera jumps over Rosanna Arquette to Griffin as if it were a hawk grabbing this guy. These moments look easy on-screen, but it's not so easy to figure out how to execute them. The camera had to really move, really jump down. I did it with a jib arm. The camera is mounted on a thirteen-foot arm, and moves up and down fast. We were restricted. We knew we had to do the film for less than $4 million. We had to be inventive, and for Marty it was like returning to his roots in moviemaking.

GRIFFIN DUNNE: Both Marty and I would come in after we'd been shooting for about a week, nearly blind, bleary-eyed, trying to get our energy up. And then after about two hours of shooting, his energy would just overcome all obstacles. A big flood of ideas would just keep coming in, and suddenly you'd start to talk like Marty, really fast, until you realized you weren't even finishing your own sentences. Neither is he, yet you understand each other perfectly, and it's entirely enjoyable.

It was only exhausting getting *started*. The real hard part was coming down. My problem would be, toward the end of the shoot, that I would get to sleep later and later. It used to be that I would get to sleep before "The Today Show" and other morning shows began. And then I found myself watching them, and the next thing I knew, I was into Regis Philbin territory, nine o'clock shows, and next thing I knew, it was eleven o'clock. I'd get so pumped up, I couldn't sleep right away.

The anxiety of the movie struck all of us as hilariously funny. We always thought it was a nightmare, and it was so scary that it was funny. The expression on Marty's face when we'd watch Paul Hackett go through something was like, "Oh, no! Oh, my God, oh!" I could hear him out of the corner of my ear during takes, saying "Oh God, that's awful." He had to turn away to not look at the take, because he'd be laughing. And you'd see the silhouette of his back, jumping up and down from trying to hold in his laughter. "Oh boy, oh God, what are we gonna do, oh God, this is awful, this is the worst!" And he would keep laughing.

Marty understands, and very few people do, the distinction between criticism and talking about your work. When you're working it's so easy to doubt. Everybody's so vulnerable. It's so easy to be a smartass and come up with the right twist of a phrase that just freezes everybody. A lot of times people think that's clever, to approach work that way. But it's really very destructive.

AMY ROBINSON: There was a shot that Marty designed, the famous key-drop shot. Kiki drops the keys out the window before Paul comes upstairs for the first time. Marty kept saying, "This is crucial to the movie." He wanted it from the point of view of the keys. She throws them out. Keys are coming down, and Paul is looking up at this weapon coming down at him, and, to Marty, it represented the ominousness of the movie.

So our crew designed this Rube Goldberg contraption, like a platform with a hole in it. The camera was attached to it. And then they had the platform tied up there on the fourth floor of the building with mountain-climbing rope. They dropped this entire platform down four stories of the building and it stopped just above Griffin's head.

It was the middle of the night. And we shot this scene a couple of times, and it was really terrifying to watch this thing come down right at Griffin's head. And it would stop and snap, and *snap*. Up and down. And the rope was fraying! Marty was a wreck, and then we did three takes and it was over. We went to the dailies, and the whole thing was out of focus. And Marty, *of course*, said, "Well, we've got to do it again!" And this was really the only fight we had. I just sort of flipped. I said, "We can't. I mean, it's lucky Griffin's not dead. We can't do it again."

But you never just say no to Marty. "You can't say no to me like that, Amy." And we eventually did do it again, except we did it with a crane, and it was very simple, which was the way we should have done it in the first place.

MARTIN SCORSESE: I thought one of the strongest scenes was with Griffin and Rosanna Arquette, when she was on the bed and telling him these stories, and when he goes to touch her, she gets up and says, "I'll be right back; are *you* in for something tonight!" Then he picks up a book on impotence. Everything possible that could go psychologically wrong on a date!

I tried to do it in an entertaining way. I enjoy telling a story and making people laugh, or telling a story and making people feel sad. I *enjoy* it. I don't think of the audience, but at the same time, I'm *always* thinking of the audience. There's no star today who guarantees an audience. It's amazing, not like ten years ago or fifteen years ago. It's the film itself that's got to be good. The film itself has got to be the star.

ROSANNA ARQUETTE: My sense of Marcy was that she was completely neurotic, so I lost a lot of weight. I even made up a whole background for

CARICATURIST CATHY HILL CAPTURES SCORSESE
WORKING THROUGH THE DEVASTATION OF HAVING
THE LAST TEMPTATION OF CHRIST CANCELLED.

her—a bad childhood. And it worked for the part, it really did. Marty kept telling me, "Gain weight. You're too skinny." But then he felt that it was right for the character. She was loony-tunes. She was just out to lunch, Marcy.

I am very comfortable improvising. My father was in Second City. Marty loves when you just go for it. It's second nature for me. I love to go *away* from a script. I'm sure writers hate that, but for me, I love it. Marty's very open to any kind of discussion, he almost never says no. He'd rather explore something than say no to it. And if it doesn't work, then it doesn't work.

THELMA SCHOONMAKER: Between *The King of Comedy* and *After Hours*, my life changed. I married Michael Powell in 1984. We actually got to know each other during the editing of *Raging Bull*. Marty and I would edit through the night. Michael would call at 3 A.M. We were the only night sessions. But in *After Hours* we began to edit during the day, rather than through the night, which was quite a change. We were working much harder, and much quicker.

With *After Hours* we started working in a very disciplined manner, not wasting money or time. Marty realized that the kind of films he makes don't necessarily have a big commercial value, but he wanted to keep making them. Therefore, he had to make them *cheaper*.

We were a very artistic generation. Art was everything to us. Marty loved Hollywood, but that doesn't mean he liked living there. The difference between all of us at N.Y.U. and Marty was that he knew, somehow, he had to go to Hollywood and make it *there. Then*, he could do what he wanted. We, on the other hand, were all thinking, "Oh, well, we have to stay in New York." But we were wrong. You have to prove yourself out there first. Marty really went through the fire for a couple of years. But once he realized that he would die if he stayed out there, he gave it up.

After Hours he made because nothing else interested him. Of all the things being offered to him, nothing interested him but that script. Being a comedy, of course, it had to be cut a certain way. We had to take out stuff we both loved in order to get it to work. And it was made for so little money! *After Hours* was very good for Marty. He wanted to prove that he could make a film very cheaply, quickly—and still create art.

AMY ROBINSON: Marty's always saying, in interviews, that trying to get *Last Temptation* made was his own personal *After Hours* for him—that kind of nightmare. And doing *After Hours* was getting it *out*. It was a creative way for Marty to exorcise his demons.

THE COLOR OF MONEY (1987)

"I JUST DIDN'T BELIEVE THIS GUY, EDDIE FELSON, WHO WAS SUCH A HUSTLER, SUCH A SELF-DESTRUCTIVE, THICK-HEADED GUY, WOULD EVER *STOP*. HE MAY HAVE MOVED OUT OF NEW YORK, BUT HE *WOULDN'T* STOP." —MARTIN SCORSESE

After Hours proved to Scorsese and Hollywood that he could work in the style of his youth and make low-budget films with high production values and wonderful performances. He had survived. But *Last Temptation* remained his major concern. Studios can be uncomfortable with film-makers who are obsessed with one project, but Scorsese had shown balance. He was willing to go on to do other movies while still working to get *Last Temptation* made.

Enter Michael Ovitz. As the President of Creative Artists Agency (CAA), Ovitz wields much power in Hollywood. His client list includes major stars and directors: Paul Newman, Dustin Hoffman, and Bill Murray are just a few. His phone calls are always returned. The workings of the agency, particularly its penchant for packaging—that is putting a star, director, and writer together and working with a studio to get movies made—has attracted more attention than any other recent industry development. Ovitz, who resists press attention, has nonetheless been the subject of a cover story in the *New York Times Magazine*, appeared in the *Los Angeles Times*, and has been called by *Time* magazine the most powerful man in Hollywood.

In 1985, Scorsese's longtime agent, Harry Ufland, moved from representing clients into producing. In the next stage of his career, Michael

SCORSESE AND CINEMATOGRAPHER MICHAEL BALLHAUS (SECOND FROM LEFT) SET UP A SHOT WITH PAUL NEWMAN FOR *THE COLOR OF MONEY*.

Ovitz would be Scorsese's agent. As so many times in Scorsese's life, a classic movie was the catalyst.

For years, attempts had been underway to produce a sequel to Robert Rossen's classic *The Hustler* (1961). Paul Newman wanted to reprise his role of Eddie Felson, but the right elements had never come together. After viewing *Raging Bull,* Newman wrote a letter to Scorsese complimenting him on the movie. Scorsese responded and the contact between the two led to the discussion of the possibility of Scorsese becoming involved in the sequel. As Newman's agent, Michael Ovitz worked to make the project happen.

Michael Eisner and Jeffrey Katzenberg, Scorsese's supporters at Paramount, now ran Walt Disney Studios, Eisner as chairman of the board and CEO of The Walt Disney Company and Katzenberg as chairman of the board of Walt Disney Studios. They could do what they wanted. The problem was, the rights to the sequel had been owned by many studios. It was a complicated deal to set up.

They said they would be interested in producing the sequel with Scorsese directing. Would Scorsese be interested in doing a film that had not originated with him—one that he had not spent years and years personally developing? He had taken existing material with *After Hours,* but that had a $4 million budget and a short shooting schedule. This movie would be a mammoth production and star Paul Newman. Of course, most of Scorsese's favorite films were made by directors like John Ford, Howard Hawks, or John Huston, who worked on assignment. Scorsese admired *The Hustler,* and could certainly relate to the milieu. And so he said yes. By the time the movie was released, Scorsese would be represented by CAA. For Scorsese, a deciding factor was that Michael Ovitz believed in the *Last Temptation of Christ.* And if anyone could help get it made it was Michael Ovitz. In March of 1986, he began shooting *The Color of Money.*

The Color of Money begins twenty-five years after Fast Eddie Felson's classic confrontation with Minnesota Fats (Jackie Gleason), the great pool player, and his sadistic manager, Bert Gordon (George C. Scott). Piper Laurie had played Sarah Packard, the crippled alcoholic, who committed suicide, and, in an ironic foreshadowing, Jake La Motta appeared as "the bartender" in the Robert Rossen classic.

The Color of Money had emerged in stages. Walter Tevis, the original writer of the novel on which *The Hustler* was based, had written a sequel.

In that bittersweet story, Eddie Felson falls in love with a college teacher. But Scorsese saw Eddie as a brother in spirit to Jake La Motta and to Jimmy Doyle and Johnny Boy—characters who are too thick-headed to accept defeat, who embrace the most painful parts of themselves and then somehow find a way to redemption.

Scorsese and novelist-screenwriter Richard Price, author of *The Wanderers* and *Blood Brothers*, made Felson an amoral liquor salesman who has lost his faith in his own talent. He meets Vincent (Tom Cruise), a young flake who plays brilliant pool. Eddie wants to cash in on Vince's ability, and so becomes his stake horse. He takes Vince on a road that leads through decaying pool halls in the midwest to the climactic tournament in Atlantic City.

Scorsese found in the story some of the themes that fascinate him. One is the paradox of the hustler, the street-smart guy, seemingly without a soul or inner-life, who discovers a hunger for spiritual fulfillment. Though Eddie teaches Vincent to betray his gift and make money his only value, the emptiness he has created awakens Eddie and forces him to work out his own redemption.

In *The Color of Money*, pool is an obsession that isolates the characters from normal society. Eddie, Vincent, and Carmen (Mary Elizabeth Mastrantonio) hit the road in search of the promise of big money. But, as in other Scorsese movies—*Alice Doesn't Live Here Anymore*, *The Last Waltz*, and, to some extent, *Raging Bull*—the flight from permanence into hotel rooms and bars becomes an end in itself. Though *The Color of Money* is an urban movie, the city is not New York, but a succession of the aging centers of middle-American towns, where decrepit pool halls recall the contained wickedness of the past. In contrast, today's legalized gambling is wholesome family fun, and modern pool sharks find their action in tourist-clogged Atlantic City. The final confrontation between Eddie and Vince takes place amid plastic chandeliers and muzak.

MARTIN SCORSESE: On *Color of Money*, I read the novel by Walter Tevis and I read the script. The script was fairly good, but I didn't want to get involved in dealing with a movie star like Paul Newman on the basis of a script that I had nothing to do with. I have to have a history with my scripts. I have to be involved with them. I eventually decided that I didn't believe what went on in the novel and I didn't believe what went on in the script either, so I had to come up with another idea. Eddie Felson, at the end of the first story, *The Hustler*, is told he can't play in pool halls anymore because he owes money to this guy Bert Gordon. In the book he doesn't play any more. He runs a small pool hall, and gets involved with an English professor. It's a love story more than anything else.

But I didn't believe it. I just didn't believe this guy, Eddie Felson, who was such a hustler, such a self-destructive, thickheaded guy, would ever stop. He may have moved out of New York, but he wouldn't *stop*. He'd say, "You want to see how bad I can be? I can be worse than you, Bert." And he becomes Bert Gordon. His business has become lucrative over twenty-five years. Then he sees this amazingly talented young kid. He gets bitten by the bug—if not to *play*, then to get more seriously involved with the game, because the arena of playing pool now has changed a great deal from twenty-five years ago. He takes this young kid under his wing, and teaches him everything on the road, but teaches him only the negative. And in the process, he has to come to terms with himself, as a man—does he remain dead, or does he come alive again? To come alive again, he's got to face himself. He doesn't have to win, but he's got to play. He's got to put his balls on the line—literally.

PAUL NEWMAN: *The Color of Money* is really about recapturing excellence, having been absent from it, and then witnessing it in somebody else. Eddie Felson reeducates himself and recaptures his excellence. Marty didn't think Eddie Felson in *The Color of Money* would wind up a victim. He'd be a successful businessman, not necessarily in a reputable business, but he'd be a success. And I think we started out with that, with the concept of the whiskey salesman. Starting with that premise, we developed a whole story line. After the second draft by Richard Price—it was his first produced screenplay—we knew that there was work to be done, but we felt that it had a great line. Marty liked the characters, he liked the style of the language, and we committed to it on that basis.

MARTIN SCORSESE: This was my first time working with a movie star. A movie star is a person I saw when I was ten or eleven on a big screen. With De Niro and the other guys it was a different thing. We were friends. We kind of grew together creatively. Not that we had planned it that way;

it's just what happened. But with Paul, I would go in and I'd see a thousand different movies in his face, images I had seen on that big screen when I was twelve years old. It makes an impression.

Newman is a wonderful guy. He would talk to me in certain ways, with a lot of sports allusions. Sports! I had no idea what he was talking about. I've had asthma all my life, I had nothing to do with sports; I had no idea what he was talking about. So I said, "How are we going to communicate with this guy?" Finally, at one point, we talked racing, racing, racing. I said, "Well, why do you race if you can't win? It's really a dangerous thing." He didn't have an answer for that. And that's when I realized that's what the film is probably about.

Richard talks like me—even faster. Imagine myself and Richard Price and Paul Newman in the same room. Paul didn't know what we were talking about in the first three sessions. He had no idea. We were talking so fast, Richard and I. He said, "You guys are crazy."

RICHARD PRICE: I was working on another script called *Night in the City*, and Marty was interviewing writers to see who would be willing to write *The Color of Money*. He had read *The Wanderers*, and he knew about me, and I certainly knew about him. I auditioned verbally, saying, "I'm the man for you!" At the time, he was working with Paul Newman on doing a rewrite, and they weren't happy with their progress. The project was dead in the water. They decided to take one last shot at it. Marty saw the work I was doing on *Night in the City*, and said, "Well, do you want to come out and meet Newman?" I went there for half an hour, and Newman said, "Do it."

I went off down South, where the pool hustlers were meeting at these so-called tournaments, which are really just excuses to get together and let heavy gambling happen after it's over. I wrote about eight pages. We made the mistake of writing for ourselves, when basically what we were writing for is Newman, who is not New York, who is not De Niro, who is not Pacino—he's Paul Newman. He's American. He's not New York, he's American.

Newman looked at it and said, "Fella, this is not me. I can't do this. This is too dark, grim and down." I myself didn't care if it was grim. But the reality is, you've got to write for Paul Newman, because he's got to *play* it, and if he won't play it, there's no movie! So either you write a script that

194

goes on the shelf, or you write a great script that caters to him. You're a tailor, you're not a fashion designer, and it's *his* body—you've got to cut the clothes for his body.

We spent about a year getting to know Newman. We'd come in and read ten or twenty pages with him, discussing it. If I had been left to my own devices the movie probably would not have been as appealing. It would have been much darker, grimmer, and probably more of a turn-off. And it probably would have played in Middle America for about a minute.

MARTIN SCORSESE: The film had already gone through a series of revisions. Several million was spent in other studios for the properties. So we had only a certain amount of money to play with. We wound up working about nine months on the script and, in that process, we really started to shape the film for Paul. We realized we were making a star vehicle movie.

Paul Newman, Richard Price, and I all worked around what I thought was best for Paul's persona in the movie, as Fast Eddie Felson, and if Paul had said, "Listen, I want the guy never to play pool," I'd have said, "Gee, that's interesting. Maybe that would work." In fact, in the beginning, Richard and I felt the guy *should* never play pool. But Paul said, "Listen, they're going to come and see Fast Eddie Felson. They're going to want to see him play pool at some point." And we said, "You're right. Absolutely."

There is a tendency to get really wrapped up in research and begin to lose sight of what a film is about. You get into too much detail. I think there was that tendency in *The Color of Money*. When you start to go to a lot of pool games, it gets to be ridiculous.

In *The Color of Money*, all the pool games were, of course, laid out way beforehand in drawings—all the shots of the poolballs, and how they were being hit into the pockets, and the cue sticks. Paul Newman is at the bar, and he says, "Yeah, the kid's got a dynamic break." The concept was to cut in movement and not let the camera come to a rest. That's the idea. All that sort of thing was done beforehand.

In some cases, I locked myself in a room to come up with the shots. But in other cases, I was listening to some music, or watching another movie, or just eating dinner with somebody, and an idea would come up. The important thing is *Post-its*. Post-its are the most important, because you can write on them, you can stick them around the house, and in the morning you can go around to collect them. I'm serious. I have them all over.

The rest of the scenes in *Color of Money* were designed pretty much the same way. There was one afternoon when a big hurricane was expected here, and I was doing nothing. So I picked up the script. The most terrifying thing to do, for me, are these sessions where I've got to come up with shots—absolutely terrifying, because it can come to nothing. For example, when Paul walks into the game room where he's got to play and there are all these kids, and rock 'n' roll is playing, and the camera is moving fast into his face—that was thought up the day I was just sitting there, waiting for that hurricane to hit.

RICHARD PRICE: In *Color of Money*, I liked the hustling, the thinking on your feet, the amorality, the street quality, the manipulation, the con. It felt very close to home. So did the feeling of envy I thought Newman had for the Tom Cruise character—you don't know whether to caress him or kill him. I know that mixed feeling.

We decided to think of these characters as guys from the Bronx with Midwestern accents. If things weren't working out we made something up. It's like Marty once wanted me to write about Modigliani and his circle of friends in Paris at the turn of the century. And I said, "I don't know anything about that." "Just make 'em guys," he said. "They're just *guys*. Make 'em guys, and they're on the make, and they want to be artists. I wanted to be a filmmaker, you wanted to be a writer. They're just guys." It's like reducing everything. You have to bring your little Bronx-in-a-cage, and open it up and let it come out and play, and look at what it does.

Newman's character is creating this golem of cynicism, this Frankenstein's monster—the character played by Tom Cruise. All of a sudden, it's on its own! He's gone, he's wreaking havoc, he's a sorcerer's apprentice. And finally Eddie says, "No, I'm wiser now." That's why he wants to play him at the end, just play-for-play. He's got to confront this thing he's created, which is a living testament to his own awfulness. He's got to bring Cruise back so he can live with himself. It's the same thing as Jake La Motta in *Raging Bull*—Scorsese's sense of redemption.

PAUL NEWMAN: Everything was comprehensively prepared. I thought, "My God, how long do you have? Ten weeks?" We had 392 setups. We were able to do it because the planning was so complete. And incidentally, these setups came out of rehearsals. Some he had obviously thought about beforehand, but for the most part, the rehearsals were very good for that. We had a cohesive two-week period with actors working, as we used to in live television, back in the stone age.

In the middle of the film I told Marty, "You know, I talked to Joanne last night, and I told her I'm really getting very nervous, because it's fun getting up in the morning. Everything seems to work, and when that happens, I really get nervous." And Marty said, "Fine! Use it in the movie." So on the phone, I tell Helen Shaver—my girlfriend in the film— that things are going terrific and my legs are great and I feel great, and she should come on down and give me some grief!

MICHAEL BALLHAUS: We had to approach the actors carefully. Paul Newman came to the set and he had some ideas about a scene. Our idea was different. Marty knew exactly what he wanted, and I knew what he wanted. So what we did, we just tenderly and slowly pushed him in the direction—from both sides, from my angle and from his angle—to do what we wanted. And he did everything; he was wonderful. He never said, "No, I don't want to do this." Paul started one day, and he said, "Marty, in this scene, I think I should be eating something." In about twenty minutes Marty explained the shots and what he wanted to do and why he really shouldn't eat. It happens in a lot of movies, actors bring in their ideas. Sometimes it helps, sometimes it doesn't.

I remember one shot in *Color of Money* when Paul Newman walks into a large room in Atlantic City. He walks in, and then you see the overhead shot, and then the camera swoops down, and then you see him from his back, and then it cuts again to the front. In Marty's shot list, he had in mind that the camera would start up real high, like forty feet high, then swoop down and turn around and find Paul in his position looking at the room. We set it all up. It was pretty complicated. We were all set up and we looked at the shot and felt it wasn't graphic enough; it wasn't going to work.

These are things that you can't exactly tell until you do it. In this case, it just didn't work. We had to change it. Marty was about to give up because it was a major thing to move these cranes again, and it was late in the evening. I stayed there until one o'clock in the morning, then the next day we did it.

JOE REIDY: I was nervous when I first worked with Marty in *The Color of Money*. After I graduated from N.Y.U. film school I entered an apprenticeship at the Directors Guild of America for assistant directors. Getting out of school, we all wanted to become directors. So I figured the assistant directors' training program would steer me in a certain direction. I was lucky to get in. And that's how I became second assistant director and worked my way up to where I am now, as first assistant.

Marty's like a hero to me, and I wanted to do a good job on *The Color of Money*. I was impressed with how easy he made my job. He was extremely prepared. He had a vision of the film and was very clear about how certain things would be done. All this made my relationship with him easier. He virtually had a shot list, and had copious notes by the director of photography, Michael Ballhaus. As a result, I could properly schedule this film, which made it easier for him and allowed the time he needed to work with the actors and do the specialized shots.

Several scenes involved trick pool shots or complicated games, where we had to plan out where the pool players would be. The pool room atmosphere and the dynamics of the game of pool didn't lend itself to experimentation. However, Marty invented some really interesting angles that showed off the game well. We had a pool technical advisor who helped the actors do the shots, but Marty had an idea of where he wanted the camera to go. It was not just a dramatic thing but a physical thing; it gave the camera a different kind of energy, following a ball, following a cue stick. The pool table became a stage.

MARTIN SCORSESE: I remember the most dramatic scene is one where Tom Cruise comes in and lays the money down and tells Paul Newman he dumped the game. There are no moves at all; it's all static and strained. I thought that would be more interesting and more powerful. That was done, literally, on the set.

Part of the thing that I tried to do was to set up some very difficult, complex shots. Take, for example, the pool scenes. The pool games were excruciating, because Tom and Paul did their own pool shots. There was only one shot that Cruise didn't do, which was the one towards the end of the tournament, where he hits a ball and it flies over the other. That's the only one he didn't do. He could have learned it, but it would have taken him another week.

PAUL NEWMAN: It was my idea to introduce the girlfriend, Helen Shaver. Originally the bar owner was a man, but I said, "Who's Eddie with? Who is his woman?" And we decided to make that character Eddie's love interest. During the movie, there wasn't any ritual dancing. No egos. Tom Cruise and I were just very, very open with each other. Inasmuch as any actors who travel so much can be good friends, Tom and I are good friends. When you have a working experience like that, nobody has an ego.

I'm a great admirer of Marty, a great admirer of the films he's done, especially the style, the scale, and the street majesty of *Raging Bull*. I think all three of us learned a lot working on *Color of Money*. This was as creative an experience as I've ever had.

Scorsese's got an incredible eye. You just don't get away with anything—he's on you *like a hawk*. You can't fall back on inaccessible mannerisms. He would hesitate, kind of creep over like a crab, and I would say, "Spit it out!" I couldn't quarrel. He'd be right on.

In the end, Eddie Felson reeducates himself and recaptures his excellence. Some people wanted a more "ending" ending. But we simply couldn't have stood another pool game! The ending is an admission that there were betrayals on both sides and they're pretty hard to weigh equally.

MICHAEL EISNER: Martin Scorsese has been, for many years, our premier director. We were glad to have him at Disney and we were determined that *The Color of Money* would have all the resources a studio could provide to make it an artistic and commercial hit.

Something that always impressed me when I was on his set was that Marty had such organization. He gets these incredible effects, and yet, it all flows very naturally. It seems so fluid and contained, yet he gets effects greater than more grandiose productions. *The Color of Money* was extremely successful for us.

MICHAEL OVITZ: I have followed Marty's work from the very beginning. As a young agent I shared an office at William Morris with Harry Ufland, who represented Scorsese and De Niro at the time. He was very supportive of them and I would go to screenings that he suggested. It was clear to me from the beginning that Marty was a great American Stylist. Anyone in the film business has to look to Marty. He has the most extraordinary set of eyes that anyone could ever hope to have. Extraordinary eyes, and his incredible knowledge of film blends with his view of life to create a very unique body of work.

EIGHT

PASSION

THE LAST TEMPTATION OF CHRIST (1988)

"JESUS HAD TO DIE TO GIVE US HOPE—TO GIVE US THE HOPE THAT GOD LOVES US." —MARTIN SCORSESE

THE COLOR OF MONEY was Scorsese's first true box office hit. The critical response was good. Richard Price's screenplay was nominated for an Oscar. After five previous nominations, Paul Newman won his first Academy Award, for Best Actor, for his performance in the film. The time was right for Michael Ovitz to move forward with *The Last Temptation of Christ*. He called Tom Pollock.

As a respected entertainment lawyer, Tom Pollock had spent years hammering out deals with the studios for his clients—writers, actors, and directors. In 1986 he joined the other side, the studio, and became the head of Universal Pictures, moving into the executive suite of M.C.A.'s tall, black tower in Universal City in Hollywood. But his sympathies remained with the talent.

TOM POLLOCK: I first read *The Last Temptation of Christ* in a freshman philosophy class at Pomona College before I transferred to Stanford. I was fascinated because it was a book about an *idea:* What would have happened if Jesus had not chosen to die? My own religious background is part Jewish and part Theosophist, and I have always been interested in religion. So when Michael Ovitz called and asked if I was willing to talk to Martin Scorsese about *The Last Temptation of Christ,* I said yes. I am a great admirer of Marty, anyone in my position would be. He is a great filmmaker.

The meeting went very well. Though I knew there had been problems at Paramount, I felt the movie could be a spiritual awakening for people. I felt that to be true even from a commercial standpoint. We live in an age of secular humanism, where people look down on religion and don't really feel that believing can make them happy. And I actually thought, when we were making this movie, that on some level it would strike a chord for thoughtful people. Faith is not normally something you think yourself into, I realize. You have faith or you don't. But this movie encourages thinking your way into belief through the exploration of an idea. The idea is powerful, and it works on your emotions. It is the idea of the man Jesus at odds with the divine Jesus, and *choosing* to die for the sins of man. It's his choosing that makes the sacrifice meaningful. Otherwise it is preordained.

I then talked to Garth Drabinsky at Cineplex Odeon, and he was extremely enthusiastic. I doubt we would have made the picture if we had not been a partner with Cineplex, because they are the second largest theater chain in North America. The fact that they co-invested in the movie with us assured us of exhibition. In fact, the week the picture opened, it only opened in Cineplex theaters, but by the time it expanded in the second and third weeks, and there had been no violence, other chains joined in. All of the major chains, except two, ultimately showed the movie; those two were General Cinema, which later apologized to me, admitting they had made the wrong decision, and Carmike Cinemas, predominately in the South, which has never apologized. United Artists Theatres eventually showed it because Salah Hassanein, who had stopped its production at Paramount, was no longer there.

So at one time, before all the controversy started, I thought that the film would work for those individuals who, on a basic level, believed but had fallen away. They would be the audience. Marty then said he could make the movie for $7 million. Now, for making a biblical epic, $7 million is absolutely chicken feed! But it was the only way we could have made it. It meant great discipline in shooting and on all levels of production. But Marty was determined.

MARTIN SCORSESE: We had only fifty-eight days to shoot the picture, which was based on a 120-page script. The film was incredibly physical. Normally I shoot in bars and pool rooms and streets, and that's it—a couple of churches, tops. I don't even go in a courtroom; it's too big. So I wasn't prepared for the physical demands it placed on us.

It turned out to be pretty good for me. It was really wonderful because you are working very quickly, and expending a huge amount of energy just to get through the day. But it was an agonizing shoot, too—such a difficult way to make a film.

My view had been to pull back, to make it a smaller picture. The only thing about it being a smaller picture is when you get there, it's big anyway. You're stuck because it's big. It's Jesus walking into the frame, not just anybody. The concept of Jesus in this picture is to make him look like somebody you might know. If every time Jesus appeared he was bathed in radiant light, as in other films, then why didn't everyone automatically follow him? First I had to get an actor to play Jesus. I had wanted Aidan Quinn again, but he felt he couldn't do it.

AIDAN QUINN: I never did get to play the part of Jesus. When Marty called, I was in the Seychelles islands finishing *Robinson Crusoe*. It was a very, very difficult shoot. I was completely exhausted and told Marty I was afraid I couldn't give the part the energy it needed. I was terrified I might just physically fail him if I went right into the movie. It was really unfortunate, but the timing made it impossible for me.

MARTIN SCORSESE: So I was looking for other people to play Jesus. I had seen Willem Dafoe in *To Live and Die in L.A.* He was good in that, but he had played a villain. When I met him I liked him, I liked the look of his face, and he really wanted to do the film. He had no fears or physical problems with it—it's a very physically demanding role, as demanding as Jake in *Raging Bull*. I looked at him in *Platoon* and I was convinced.

He looked like Jesus as we know him in religious images. They all had blue eyes. That seems very nonhistorical. But when you look at the faces of the Moroccan extras, some are white, some are black, some have brown eyes, some blue eyes. They are all different. In Judea and Israel during the time of Jesus, there also was assimilation. There was lots of mixing, even though Jewish law tried to prevent it to keep their culture distinctive. So we thought Jesus could have had blue eyes. Willem looks like the Jesus we've known over the years. This was kind of nice in a funny way. It made it comfortable, especially after he comes out of the desert and takes his heart out. From that point on we intentionally made him look more like the Jesus we know from the traditional art.

WILLEM DAFOE: Years ago, when I heard Scorsese was planning to film *Last Temptation*, it didn't even cross my mind to play the role of Jesus. Later, Marty essentially outlined the character, and I read the script. I was

MARTIN SCORSESE AND WILLEM DAFOE (JESUS) IN MOROCCO
FOR *THE LAST TEMPTATION OF CHRIST*.

really struck by the way he talked about the end—the sadness and the victory. There were lots of things that I didn't understand. But Marty's passion was really infectious.

The role of Jesus is very difficult to put in place. In acting you have to put yourself in a neutral place. It is very important to start out in a place where you can struggle with the project itself. As an actor facing the part straight on, I could only deal with it in human terms. I think the movie brings out the heart and the spirit of Jesus. It was a difficult movie in *every* aspect. We were shooting very fast, with long hours, and physically it was draining. But I was working on a great role with great people.

BARBARA HERSHEY: At the time it was cancelled, and whenever I hear anything controversial about *Last Temptation*, my first feeling is to be protective of Marty. I was so hurt for him when it was cancelled. He told me, "I'm not going to give up until I make the film," and he wanted to know if I was with him. I said, "I was put on earth to play this part." He said, "That's how I feel about directing it." My inner fear was that I might someday be too old to play Mary Magdalene.

Among the books I was studying during this phase, waiting for the film, was the Book of Thomas in the Gnostic Gospels. Society in Jesus' time was very patriarchal. But before that, in ancient times, society was very matriarchal in that part of the world. So the patriarchal establishment became very anti-female in order to suppress the older religions where women had power. The fact that Christ welcomed women among his followers made an important statement. The women are at the crucifixion when everyone else has run away. Kazantzakis talks about the looks between the women. They knew. Marty had me walking with Jesus and the disciples in many scenes. The only scenes I couldn't appear in were the ones at the temple where women weren't allowed. He even embraced the idea of Christ's having women at the Last Supper.

I met with Marty in New York and brought my list of questions about what Mary Magdalene should look like, and he had his list, and we sat down and talked. On both of our lists were tattoos. Marty had, by then, been to Morocco and seen the tattoos on women. He'd seen henna on their feet, and we decided to make them red. It's more beautiful, it would show up more, and it seemed like something a whore would do. Because the research was so contradictory it liberated us to do what we wanted.

The right arm had a design Marty found on a cover of an old *National Geographic*, it was an Afghani design. And the left hand and the feet I planned with a Moroccan woman. I *loved* the idea of the tattoos. Jewish women were not supposed to use tattoos but Magdalene is trying to make herself despicable. She's trying to be the lowest of the low. If she can't be what she feels she's destined to be, which is Jesus' bride, she'll be mud. Kazantzakis said the sweat of a thousand nations was on her. She was the most famous prostitute. People would come from all over the world to give her gifts. At the same time, she was spat upon by her own people. The tattoos, I felt, would give a feeling of a woman marking herself. And yet, they were beautiful.

MARTIN SCORSESE: I got to Morocco and I thought, "Oh, beautiful. If we could shoot ten thousand extras, it would be great." But we couldn't afford extras. But then I realized, of course, it's all in the landscape. I realized that in these villages, there's nothing. They have no electricity. We went from village to village. We shot the first five-and-a-half or six weeks in one village, maybe twenty minutes out of Marrakesh.

And there's nobody there. When you see somebody in the movie going for water or whatever, they really *are* going for water. What is interesting is that the people don't hang around. They may congregate in the village square, if there is a village square, or maybe by the well, if there is a well in the town. We built a well in one of the villages for the film. But the look of the landscape was very poor and very, very sparse. So for the Sermon on the Mount, instead of having one thousand people, we had twenty-five, and that seemed right somehow.

We started shooting on October 21. We would leave the hotel in the dark so we would get the dawn. For half an hour, the first part of dawn wasn't that good. We wanted to do what they call a "magic hour" kind of shot. And then we figured we'd shoot until six o'clock, like in New York. But at four o'clock we'd start losing light. We'd get the guys in makeup and robes. Their robes have to look a certain way; they can't look too clean— these are people who live in the dirt, they've got to be filthy. But they'd be all set and the sun would start to go down!

MICHAEL BALLHAUS: *Last Temptation* was a struggle from day one. We had sixty days to shoot. We had a number of rainy days, and numerous problems with the weather. We'd start a scene like the Sermon on the Mount, which was supposed to take five or ten minutes, and it would take two or three days. On most movies you would shoot about two hours, until the light wasn't good any more, and then wait for the right light to come back, but that was impossible. We just had to go on. Sometimes I was desperate. We'd shoot the first shot when the sun was up and the last when the sun was almost down. Yet it was supposed to be the same light in the same scene. Everything had to match, but sometimes it didn't. It was a constant struggle to balance the light. On top of this, the crew wasn't experienced, compared to guys I've worked with before. But I did have my son Florian as my assistant cameraman. He and his wife Pam, who worked on the film, were a great help.

Sometimes we were moving so fast that we had no time to communicate. We were under such pressure that when Marty thought he had the take, there was no chance to say, "Okay, let's do another one just to be safe, or for the fun of it." We had to go on to the next one.

The colors of the location were all warm yellow, brown, and beige, which was wonderful for the look. The light was fascinating because it was so crisp and clear, like you could imagine it was two thousand years ago. There was no pollution, just poor peasants and farmers living there. They live there now the same way they lived two thousand years ago. It was about half an hour's drive from Marrakesh, but the people who lived there looked at us like we were people from the moon. They were fascinated by things like plastic caps or plastic bottles; they were carrying them around like treasures. They worked hard as extras and helping the construction people. Marty had designed his storyboards and shot list back when we thought we'd be filming in Israel. Now we were using them in Morocco. Looking back, I think it was better that we didn't do the movie in Israel. I think it's more fitting the way we did it, as a "poor" movie, with little money and under rugged conditions. It was true to the subject and better for the. movie.

MARTIN SCORSESE: There were things to be decided on the spot. How does an apostle walk up and ask for something? I don't know. I had to work all that out. I had the shots worked out but it was extremely difficult. Then we had no rushes. We couldn't get the film back. When we finally got to see the rushes, they put the first reel on and it's the secondary shots of the moon going up and the sun. We have a tape of me saying to Michael Ballhaus, "That's good. That looks fine." He says, "No, it's upside down. No, it's fabulous. Wait, it's not right. No, no, that looks like the moon. That looks like the sun." By the time they got it straight, it was eight o'clock at night and I had to be asleep by 9:30 so I could be up and out by 4:00 A.M.

Eventually, what happened is that Ballhaus looked at the footage, and looked at a selected series. He had a video machine and I saw about four of the major dialogue scenes. I had a video assist while I was shooting. I knew what I was getting from the camera. I knew I got the performances. As best as I could, I got the performances. So I didn't look at the rushes.

Bernardo Bertolucci couldn't believe it. He said that even when he was shooting *The Last Emperor* in Mongolia he saw rushes. Bertolucci told me, "If I don't see my rushes, I die of anxiety." But he shoots differently. He said, "Every morning until twelve o'clock I was sick from anxiety because I hadn't made up my mind what to shoot yet. By around twelve noon, I'd get this shot." I said, "Well, that's the way *you* work." That is the way he works. For me, one scene is fourteen setups.

I remember one scene in the first half of the picture. Jesus is in a monastery cell and he wakes up and he hears two snakes, who come out of a hole in the ground—two cobras. The cobra handlers in Marrakesh were great. Of course, I was in another room because I don't like snakes, I'm terrified of them. So I used a little monitor. "Oh, that's good, men," I'd say. "That's good. Keep shooting."

The snakes came out of this hole and Willem is looking at them. He has some voice-over saying, "What are they trying to tell me?" Everything from God has two meanings—one physical, the other abstract. "What do they mean? What are they trying to tell me?" And then the snake speaks to him in Mary Magdalene's voice. It says, "Jesus, I forgive you." My original drawing was: medium shot, dolly in fast to his hands—real, real quick. A dolly, not a zoom, because the dolly you can feel. The audience can feel itself propelled into action. We used a lot of that in *After Hours*— dollies instead of zooms. But I had trouble getting it.

The monastery in the book is really ancient, the kind that was in *Exorcist II*, John Boorman's picture, where they go to the monastery in Abyssinia. It was like the one Kazantzakis was in, where no women were allowed, or even female animals—no hens, just roosters. So when Jesus sees snakes coming out and one is female, it's very interesting. I felt the monasteries that existed in Jesus' time were basically mud huts. So ours were huts made of wood, pieces of wood covered with mud, with an animal skin for an opening. But a mud hut is not very wide. Jesus is sitting here with a mat and his little light. But you couldn't track.

I built the interior of the huts in the ruins of an ancient palace. We were able to track a little bit. We had rented a little crane but we couldn't get it there. It had to come on a barge from Spain to Tangier. Then it had to be driven. But it was always getting stuck. We'd get reports that it was stuck somewhere else: "It's coming—the crane is coming!" But we never got it. So we had this jib on the camera that we were barely able to move. Michael looked at me and said, "Just move it so fast with a jib on it, and we have a zoom." So it's a zoom. I still feel that it would have been better if we had the tracks dollied and just went *boom*, right in. But it works anyway, it works. And the idea was to get the thing on film and to get on to the next scene. That was the idea. Not to rebuild the set for a shot like that.

We worked in a state of emergency. The budget of this film itself was an emergency. I learned how to work the minimal way for *The Last Temptation of Christ*—that you don't have to have three thousand people in each scene. I had to do some scenes of Mary, the sister of Lazarus, all at once. The actress, Randy Danson, had to leave because she had a terrible toothache. The only dentist there operated out of a storefront with a sign that had a picture of a big tooth.

We had to finish by Christmas. In fact, as we got closer, some members of the crew just started leaving. I'd look up and there would be a group of Italians waving to me: "Ciao, bye-bye. We love you. Bye-bye."

J O E   R E I D Y : In *The Last Temptation*, Marty had no time to direct. It was Michael Ballhaus and I setting up the shots Marty had talked about. Actors would come on the set, and Marty would need time to talk to them. At first he wanted twenty minutes but we had to cut it down. He got five quality minutes, which meant no carpenters hammering, no crew activity, and that was about all. He acknowledged the fact that everyone had to work quickly, including himself, in order to accomplish the film within the time and money allotted, and also in the amount of daylight we had. Very often we were fighting sundown.

It was exhausting, but everyone worked together. They had to make it happen. Beyond the long hours, and getting up early and getting to bed late, working in Morocco was also a challenge. Rather than walking on the sidewalks of New York, we were charging up and down hills, and into dry riverbeds, and sometimes in the mud. It was physically exhausting as well, having to carry equipment. It was hard physical work. Everything the crew had to go through the actors had to deal with as well—the walking, the locations. But the actors were in sandals, and didn't wear that much clothing. And when it was hot and sunny, they were exposed to the sun. And as the shoot went on, they were subjected to cold weather, especially at night.

The first half of the film was shot in a village near Marrakesh. And that worked as Nazareth and for the early part of Jesus' mission. And then Meknès, which is in the northern part of the country, was our Jerusalem. It was much colder there, but it was green. The marketplace is probably very much like a marketplace of a thousand years ago. They may sell transistor radios, but it still has that caravan atmosphere.

Apart from the filmmaking, we had a couple of acts of God that were just horrible to deal with. One was a flood during a heavy rainfall when we were shooting in the village of Umnast, outside of Marrakesh. The roads were cut off, and we couldn't get back to Marrakesh. There was no communication, and we didn't know what to do to find out how we could reenter the city. But we had to get back so that we could go to work the next day. It was frightening. I remember fording this rushing river of water in a Land Rover with Marty and Barbara De Fina and Willem Dafoe and some hardy souls from the Moroccan crew who helped get us across. It was memorable. But every day there was the beauty of Morocco to see and the chance to do something so different and interesting.

One day we got a report that the weather was getting bad in the north. Already in the south we could see snow on the Atlas Mountains outside of Marrakesh. The location we had picked in Meknès for the crucifixion was becoming muddier and more difficult to deal with. Michael Ballhaus and I went out on our one day off. We'd been driving all day and had just about given up when we found our location. We were amazed at how wonderful it was. The light was running out, and I remember the photographs of the location we had found were not exposed properly, but we knew that we had found the right place.

MICHAEL BALLHAUS: It was almost like war. We had to have a plan for every shot. We were counting minutes. Marty was so wonderful, but he felt everything so much because this project had been living in his head for years and years. And now we had to rush through it. He'd have to say okay even if each shot wasn't 100 percent. He had to decide, okay, this was as close as he could get and he'd have to accept it. We would go ahead and do the next shot. But this takes a tremendous amount of energy and concentration.

BARBARA HERSHEY: We never had the luxuries that you get even on a B movie. Although the makeup men were extraordinary, they had so many people to do every day—false beards, false noses, false hair, false this and that—and they were so overworked, I knew they couldn't handle the tattoos, except the flame on the forehead and the other tattoos on the face. Other than that, I took charge of the tattoos. They washed off constantly, every time I took a bath. So I hunted for something indelible. I even went to England on my time off to visit makeup departments, special effects departments, I tried everything— all kinds of inks, all kinds of paints, hair dye, black nail polish, anything I could thing of.

Finally, after a month of this—and this is a real lesson in non-resistance—I resigned myself to the fact that I was going to have to constantly reapply the tattoos, and I did. It took about two hours every day. Every time I took a bath I had to redo them. At night, I'd do my feet before I fell asleep. And because they would wear right off in between almost every take, I'd have to redo them. Marty made fun of me when he saw me sitting there on the set, doodling on my hands. But it was actually a perfect thing to do. It was sort of like knitting; it became meditation. I missed the tattoos after the filming. I mourned them because I grew so used to them and found them really beautiful.

Working with Marty, when you really take off is when he says, "Okay, we've got it but now let's try something." We never had the time to do that. We had to be ready, take one. If I had to break down in a scene, I had to be preparing in makeup. I remember that for the stoning scene I had to obviously be in a wild state. I started preparing during makeup and the makeup man said, "Oh look, she's crying." He didn't understand what I was trying to do.

BARBARA HERSHEY (MARY MAGDALENE) AT THE FEET OF WILLEM DAFOE
(JESUS) IN THE STONING SCENE FROM *THE LAST TEMPTATION OF CHRIST*.

HARVEY KEITEL: Central to my desire to play Judas was my loathing, my abhorrence of prejudice. The notion that some man, woman, or child's quality will be judged by the contours of their bones disgusts me and fills me with anger. That's why I had myself made up in the image of a stereotypical Jew—the hooked nose, the curly hair. Judas would have been a man of qualities who someone would point to and say, "Look at that hooked nose, look at that protruding chin, look at that bone structure. There must go a low Jew."

That was one element of the characterization. The other was a man who was outraged at the injustices of his time—the economic inequality, the oppression of religious freedom, the rape of his people, and a man's spirit rebelling against that, willing to give his life for it.

In the village of Umnast, where we shot most of the movie, I used to have children around me before I'd come in to shoot a scene. These could have been little Jewish children, who somebody wanted to burn or starve or kick. The image of children was important to me in creating this part.

Marty and I spent hours and hours and days and days discussing religion, discussing theology. These weren't just discussions about what the dialogue would be, or the historical Judas; these were discussions about things we believed—things we didn't know, but felt. Our blood went into it. We felt we had to make a total commitment, because that's what people had given before us, thousands of years ago, up until the present time—their blood for these beliefs.

VERNA BLOOM: Marty told me that Mary was a mother, a Jewish mother. I'm a mother and I'm Jewish. As I worked on the part, I thought of my own son, Sam, and how much I loved him and would want to protect him. In fact, during the crucifixion scene, the identification I'd made became almost too painful to think about.

For me working on *Last Temptation*, playing Mary and working with these people, was an amazing experience. Because we had no time to prepare for each shot, we had to be ready, have our performances and everything in place. But the costumes helped. The fabrics, the way they fit and flowed around the body, you really felt when you put your costume on that your character might have worn this. The costume designer, Jean-Pierre Delifer, came from the Middle East, and he had a real feel for what was right. In fact, he absolutely refused to let me wear a bra under my costume. It wouldn't be authentic.

The morning of my first scene, I got very sick, the Moroccan version of *turista*. I knew there wasn't time for me to be sick, but I couldn't even sit up in the car on the drive to the set. I didn't tell Marty. There was a Moroccan woman who was wonderful. She came into the trailer all veiled and mysterious looking. She brewed me herbal tea, and then took out these wonderful oils and proceeded to massage me. After a while, I really felt better. I went onto the set and Marty said, "You look really weak. Great! It will work in the scene." Marty was sorry I was sick, but he felt that the drawn look I had was just right for the performance.

In that scene, the extras were told to throw stones at Willem. I heard one man ask another, "Who are we throwing stones at?" "Jesus," the other replied. With that, the first man screamed and charged the crowd, yelling for them to stop abusing one of God's prophets. About that time, I had to push my way through the mob to get to Jesus. An old man saw me and came to help. He told others, "Let her through." This, of course, was not in the script, but he became my protector, and even between setups he stayed with me.

PEGGY GORMLEY: In the early scenes, Marty wanted me to play naturally. Those are the scenes that take place in real time. But during the temptation sequence, when Jesus comes down from the cross and lives with my sister Mary and me, Marty told us to make the scenes like tableaux. We were to play our parts in a contained, quiet way—religious pictures brought to life. I had originally wanted to put a lot of emotion into it, especially when Jesus seems to prefer my sister to me. I had all these things from within all planned, but Marty said no. He wanted our scenes to look like paintings.

■　■　■

Scorsese purposely chose actors comfortable with the naturalistic New York style of his earlier movies to portray the apostles. After all, the men Jesus called were working class—fishermen, laborers, shepherds. Initially, these actors were slightly bemused to find themselves playing saints who had been revered for two thousand years. In an early study session at my apartment, their reluctance dissolved as an impassioned religious discussion began. In fact, it became so heated that two delivery men, who had arrived with furniture to assemble, did the job and were gone in record time. Ten minutes later their boss called. The men had told them they had stumbled into the meeting of a religious cult.

The apostles continued these discussions on the set. They became a band of brothers depending on each other through the difficulties and the joys of the long days of shooting.

PAUL HERMAN: We apostles became a real unit. We spent our free time in the hotel playing music. Most of the guys were musicians. I remember one night we were in someone's room working on "Under the Boardwalk." Harry Dean Stanton was singing with us, and David Bowie did the background. We did it over and over, just enjoying the harmony and the effects we were getting. There was a knock on the door. Marty was standing there in his bathrobe. "It's getting better guys. It really is. Every time you do it, it gets better, but I have to be up at five o'clock to direct a movie and I'd appreciate it if you would call it a night."

WILLEM DAFOE AS JESUS, SURROUNDED BY THE TWELVE
APOSTLES, IN *THE LAST TEMPTATION OF CHRIST.*

On Halloween there was a night shoot in an olive grove. It was very cold. Marty was shooting a scene with Harvey and Willem in the foreground and we apostles were supposed to be sleeping in the grove. All that you can see of us in the scene are lumps—we were well out of the camera's range. Bales of hay could have played our scene! I was shivering on the ground with my Walkman in my ear, trying desperately to tune in the World Series. Halloween in New York is one of my favorite holidays and I was wondering, "What am I doing here?"

VIC ARGO: Playing Peter in *Last Temptation*, I did a lot of reading and thinking about Peter and the apostles—what they thought about Jesus. We would sit around and discuss this during the filming. Michael Been was one of the apostles, and his wife was a seminary student. When Marty was busy or there was no one that we could ask, we would go to Michael. He became our expert on the set.

The most amazing thing about the experience is that we're still together. We play music together. In fact, Michael Been has a musical group, The Call. Harry Dean Stanton played with them during one tour.

I'm a Puerto Rican from New York and my mother was Catholic, but I was never religious. I received my first communion, though. I found myself really thinking about the whole thing in a different way. Probably one of the most impressive things was the love between all of us.

MICHAEL BEEN: I was in the cast of the first *Last Temptation*, and so had thought a lot about my part and the story itself. On the set in Morocco the actors would come to me and ask, "Was this in the Bible? Did this really happen in the Bible?" If I said it didn't, they would ask, "What did happen?" or "How does the Bible tell it?" They liked Kazantzakis' book more than the Bible—the book was a much more practical approach, without the mystical leap of faith that the Bible requires. I got the feeling that this was the first time in their lives that they had questioned these things. Some of these discussions would go on until dawn.

Before, most of religion for them was just rigid orthodoxy and rituals of going to church with all the rules and regulations. It turned them off so much as children that they never got the "meat" of the theology itself. So this was like the first time they got the details of the story, and it was fascinating to them. As artists they heard it like a story with parts they could act out.

I read the book *The Last Temptation of Christ* in my twenties, and I suddenly realized I had a bit of a "messiah complex." I thought I must be mad. When I read the Bible I never confused my experience with that of Jesus. I could never read it deeply enough. My interpretation of the Bible was that Christ was *above* the things that I'm subjected to. You had the feeling it would be disrespectful to think that you should be on his level. I felt incredibly earthbound. Kazantzakis' Christ was earthbound, too. *Last Temptation* became the story of God coming to earth as a man, rather than coming down and being this radiant, glowing being from the clouds. He had to struggle like we do. That's how it started for me—the awakening of the spiritual life.

I'm from Oklahoma and I've been playing rock and roll since I was six. I always wanted to make music the way Scorsese made movies—exploring the dark side of human beings, the struggle for the infinite. The Call, my group, started in 1980. Garth Hudson from The Band played with us for three years—another Scorsese connection.

At my first audition, when I was waiting to meet Marty, I thought, "What am I going to say to this guy?" About five seconds later, Marty comes running out. He immediately starts talking about how much he loves The Call. He had been following us for a few years, had the albums, knew the lyrics, loved the music!

We had a wonderful conversation about *Last Temptation* and theology and our backgrounds—how I was this tortured southern Christian and he was this tortured guilt-ridden Catholic. It was as if all of a sudden you met somebody with the same life experiences, and the same kind of artistic intent. I read the part of John, the apostle. I had never really acted before. What Marty wanted, though, was not the dialogue, but to see what we were like as people. Still, I left there thinking, "I am *sure* I didn't get the part." I was so glad when I did.

I was really trying to get into this character. I did all kinds of reading, but Marty threw me off. The first scene I was in was the stoning of Mary Magdalene, and Marty told everybody, "Okay, we're going to stone Mary Magdalene, so I want everyone to pick up these rubber rocks and start pelting her with them." Everybody went to the bucket and got a rock except me. He said, "Michael, do you have one?" And I said, "No. I really can't imagine John, this gentle John, stoning someone." He said, "Bullshit, pick up a rock!" Marty had a talk with me. He explained that he wanted me to be the gentlest and most sensitive of these disciples, but he wanted me to think about the times they were living in. These were tough guys! You can't compare a sensitive person of *that* time to a sensitive person of *our* time. From that point on, my character was set for me.

There's a scene which was totally improvised that Marty kept in the movie. The apostles are camped out for the night and Jesus and Judas have a great talk. We're all by the campfire and getting ready for bed, and Peter—Vic Argo—comes over and wants to lie down next to me because he's cold. And I said, "Well, go lie over by Phillip, we're all cold." And Peter says, "Shut up." That whole bantering back and forth between us was completely improvised, and it's in the movie.

ALAN ROSENBERG: I had done a play based on *The Last Temptation of Christ* when I was in graduate school at Yale in 1972. I played Jesus. This was an adaptation written by Christopher Durang, who was a playwright there at the time. But we ended up taking most of the dialogue verbatim from the book. The set was a boxing ring. And all the temptations were different bouts. It was really a fabulous idea. It was very powerful. I remember people from the seminary came to see it and they loved it. We had many discussions about it. But, you know, it was kind of a liberal college environment. I had no idea the thing was so controversial. Our college production should have been controversial. In one scene, I was in red bikini underwear.

During my first interview, I talked to Marty about how important the story was for me. If people in the world asked themselves what Jesus had to suffer in order to attain what he attained, and if they took to heart his message of love and justice, a movie like this could make a difference. The movie *did* make a big difference. It made more people talk about Christ and his message than anything in recent memory.

When we were filming the scene in the temple, and Jesus' palms are bleeding, all of a sudden, the sky got black. When the scene started, there wasn't a cloud in the sky. And when he opened his hands, there was thunder and a lightning bolt and then huge hailstones came falling down. It was unbelievable. Unbelievable!

There were four Moroccan disciples who didn't speak in the film. Leo Burmester and I, in particular, became very close friends with one of them, Ahmad. He was so hungry to learn. He started out knowing very

WILLEM DAFOE (CENTER) PLAYS JESUS CURING THE BLIND MAN AS
JON LURIE (JAMES) AND HARVEY KEITEL (JUDAS) LOOK ON.

little English, and every day he would come to us and ask words and he was just desperate for knowledge. One day we were sitting next to each other at the Last Supper. I asked him if he was married. He didn't understand what I was trying to say, so I pointed to my ring finger and said, "Are you married?" He thought I was admiring his rings, so he gave me this ring his grandfather had given him. I said, "No, no," but he would not take it back. That is how they are. If you go into their house and point to a picture and admire it, they will give it to you. They are the most generous people I ever met in my life. Morocco was such a spiritual place. You'd get up at 4:30 A.M. to go to the set, and you'd hear prayers over the desert. Maybe five times a day, those people get down on their knees and they pray.

But if we were affected by them, working on the movie changed their lives too. For example, there was this guy who liked to be called Spud. Spud's job is to sell ties out of a suitcase in the marketplace. All of a sudden, he's making a Martin Scorsese film about Jesus Christ and he's bringing Jesus into the temple on a donkey! It became a joke that we were all apostle-jockeying. In a lot of scenes, the apostles were standing in the background, and some were better than others at getting their faces in front of the camera. Pauley Herman was one of the best at it. So the joke was, stand next to Pauley if you want to get on camera. But then it became, go stand next to Spud. Because Spud had developed his own technique for getting on camera!

People back home would ask me about my involvement and I would say that it was one of the most intense spiritual experiences of my life. Many of the people involved with the film felt the same. I have always been an agnostic. I played Thomas, the doubter, and I felt he was a doubter because he was afraid.

LEO BURMESTER: The first time I read for a part in *Last Temptation* I didn't get it. When I heard that the picture was cancelled, I thought that maybe I would have another chance. I was asleep in Central Park in the Sheep's Meadow—I was playing Thénardier in *Les Misérables*, and during the break between the matinee and the evening performance, I would go to Central Park and relax. I called home and my wife said that I was supposed to audition. I went down and read and I got the part. I was Nathaniel.

To work with Martin Scorsese is a privilege, and to work with the incredible people associated with the film was fantastic. The apostles will always be "the apostles." Even now, I say to my wife, "I'm going to get together with a bunch of the apostles." We've all stayed in touch. *Last Temptation* had a tremendous effect on all of us. It gave me a new perspective on Christianity.

We stayed together in the hotel in Marrakesh. We'd start the night out just jamming, having a few beers, and pretty soon we'd be talking about Jesus. We'd sit around the pool and look over at Willem. I'd say to him, "I know you're Willem, but I look at you and I see Jesus." People would ask Willem, "How can you play Christ?" And he'd say, "I'm not really playing Christ. I'm just trying to play myself in that situation."

There were some very strange, mystical moments during the filming. I'm sure other people have told you about one of the last scenes we filmed, when Willem extended his hands and there was a *huge* peel of thunder. It was really something. Everything in that scene—the wind, the darkening of the sky, the thunder—it was *real*! We knew that there was something special going on. There was a sense of deep meaning, of spirituality. We knew that we were doing more than just making a movie.

One evening Michael Been looked at all of us and said, "What are we here for? What has brought us here?" And I said, "I guess we're here for love." That started Michael writing a song called "For Love." We started writing it that night in the hotel and you'd hear Michael; the words would start to come, and he'd mumble a little, then sing "for love," and mumble some more. The words started to come to him. The questions and the answer. Why are we here? For love. It's a great song. It's about the experience of making the movie.

The first time I saw *Last Temptation*, I couldn't really react because I kept watching myself. But the second time I saw it I was profoundly moved. I was disturbed, too. I'm German Catholic, and I don't necessarily agree with all of Kazantzakis' ideas. In one review it talked about his "humid world" and the conflict of flesh and spirit. People sometimes confuse temptation with sin. It's only a *temptation* to sin. But there are other parts of *Last Temptation*, like the vulnerability and humanity of Christ, that I really loved.

MICHAEL BEEN: We were doing the scene where Jesus is in Nazareth and the priests are coming out of the synagogue and he's saying, "I've come to you to tell you first, my brother, that I'm the one you've been waiting for." Well, it was a hot, hot day in the middle of the desert. Willem was really into it and he was just wonderful. Marty yelled, "Cut," but everyone was really quiet, still into the scene. All of a sudden, a white dove came over the top of a building and flew right at Willem. Willem actually had to duck, and then the dove vanished. There was not a bird in the sky.

Most of us still keep in touch with each other. What we were doing as a group was more important than what we were doing as individuals, and you got that feeling. The camaraderie, the closeness, was just amazing. I'd never had it before, and from what everyone else said, they had never had it before either. Nobody who was involved with this movie was ever the same afterwards.

I felt that different forces had led me to this movie, and that it must be something very important. And if something is very important in this world, there's usually an attempt to destroy it. When something gets that close to the truth, that close to the bone, there's always an element in our world that tries to kill it. I think *Last Temptation* is probably closer than any of us knows.

TOMAS ARANA: Harry Dean Stanton and I got together and started working on our scene. As Paul, he comes to kill me. Jesus has raised me from the dead and that makes people believe in him, and Paul is against Jesus. Instead of Paul jumping on me with a knife, we changed it. He says, "Give me your hand," and he takes my hand and kills me. I seem to know what's going on. It's sort of like, "Let's just get it over with, no hard feelings." We were afraid Marty wasn't going to like it. Maybe we'd gone a little bit far. But as soon as he saw it, he said, "Oh, that's great, guys." He gives you a great freedom, and a lot of confidence, and that's important for an actor. Even if you are doing something small, it's very important.

GARY BASARABA: Marty told us that at the beginning the apostles are just this group of n'er do wells following a prophet they're not too sure of. Each one does have a spark inside that will come out later, but now they're just these regular guys who have left everything and are wondering, "When do we eat?"

There's an early scene in an apple orchard where Jesus and Judas are talking in the foreground and we're sleeping in the background. It was the first time we were in full costume and we'd been given this very authentic underwear—basically, yards of cloth we were supposed to tie into loincloths. Well we couldn't do it. We ended up like swaddled babies. Eventually most of us threw them under a trailer and went back to our own. I mean, under those robes, who could tell? But in the beginning we were "actors" taking it all very seriously. So I was there on the ground trying to get used to my costume and scratchy underwear yet amazed at what we were doing. Marty was trying to direct us from far away, and finally in exasperation he yelled out, "Will the third heap on the left please move!" That was me, and I became "The Heap" for the rest of the shoot.

We were really always switching among three or four different roles—first our characters, then we were playing actors in an exotic location and then, of course, befuddled tourists. I'm from British Columbia and have studied French, so that helped, but Morocco was a mystery to us. We became this tremendous unit, marching out of that hotel in the half-light, past the exotic market place. Then we'd get on the bus and drive to the location, and it could have been Nebraska—empty miles stretching out. We'd sing on the bus: "We Shall Overcome," and old Wobbly songs. Then, in this vast, trackless waste, a guy would just be standing there, leaning on a stick. There wasn't a car, or a house, or anything. Just this lone figure.

Of course, at times we got bored and mangy and were the venal, squabbling group Marty wanted. Jesus would be doing a miracle, and we'd be mumbling, "Is this the curing of the blind man? Haven't we seen this already? What's next?" Initially it was very hard to enact scenes from the Bible that are so famous. I mean, whatever your religion, everyone's seen these scenes depicted in art. Like the stoning of Mary Magdalene—you have a vision of that, and of Jesus saying, "He who is without sin cast the first stone." But Marty wanted us natural—real. He said to us, "You're pissed off. You're really pissed off!" It was extremely challenging, but we knew how important it was to Marty, and so we tried to discover the truth of every moment. But from an apostle's point of view, we didn't know if we were making great art or just fools of ourselves. I don't think even Marty knew what he was getting.

The experience prompted a lot of soul searching in all of us. The most dramatic moment came for me when we did the scene where Jesus throws the moneylenders out of the temple. We were filming in this ancient stable complex in Meknès. Willem was supposed to open his hands and reveal the stigmata at the end of the scene. Well, there was this Italian special effects guy—very blasé, a cigarette hanging out of his mouth—just off camera with the syringe of fake blood attached to the tubes that went up Willem's arm. So we do the scene. Comes the cue, the guy pushes the syringe, but it doesn't work. Just a little blood dribbles out. So we have to do it again. They clean up, reset everything. On the next take, Willem held up his hands, opened them, and blood just poured out. At that precise moment there was a tremendous crack of thunder and huge hailstones fell. We ran into the stable and stood there in the soft light under the mud arches. We could smell the straw. Marty was there, and Willem. We all just looked at each other. A few jokes were attempted, but what we were really thinking was, "What does this mean?"

JOHN (MICHAEL BEEN) AND THE WOMEN KEEP VIGIL AT THE FOOT OF THE CROSS (LEFT TO RIGHT): PEGGY GORMLEY (MARTHA, SISTER OF LAZARUS), VERNA BLOOM (MARY, MOTHER OF JESUS), RANDY DANSON (MARY, SISTER OF LAZARUS), AND BARBARA HERSHEY (MARY MAGDALENE).

MARTIN SCORSESE: At the Last Supper in *The Last Temptation,* women are present. Jesus was so great, I just couldn't see him telling the women at the Last Supper, "Wait in the kitchen." I remember saying, "How could he say 'wait in the kitchen' to these ladies?" Especially since he was a man who broke the rules. He broke the Hebrew rules, he broke all the other rules, and he would have had women there. He would have them take part in the first Mass. I don't think he made a distinction between men and women. Why should he? They're only half-known to God? They can't know God fully? And God doesn't know them fully? What is this? Not that I know very much about women—but they're humans, right?

I said to myself, "These women have been with him the whole movie, they've stuck with him and they're the only ones at the Crucifixion." The only ones at the Resurrection are also women, although in one Gospel John was there too. But Jesus appears to the women first. He's telling us something. And so I said they had to partake of the Last Supper. They had to.

BARBARA HERSHEY: In the script of *Last Temptation*, my introduction into the film is the scene when Christ comes and visits me in Magdala. I said to Marty, "I really think there's a problem. In the book you have a whole history about what they have meant to each other. I don't know if this scene will have much meaning if you don't have a hint of what their relationship has been." Almost before I got the words out of my mouth, he said, "What if, at the first crucifixion, she walks up and spits at him?" It was so brilliant, it was perfect. You know they have something going on, that she's a woman, he's a man—to be angry enough to spit at someone, there must be something going on.

In the script, Magdalene reacts with horror in her death scene. I said to Marty, "This is God, wouldn't she be happy to see him?" And he said, "Yes!" And I said, "Do you want me to try the horror?" And he said, "No!" Within a second he changed the whole concept of that scene. He loved the idea of her being ecstatic. It's Christ who mourns her death, not her.

My most important scene, as a prostitute in Magdala, was also the most difficult, because I was going to show Magdalene with a series of men. Even though Marty's films have a lot of sexuality, there hadn't been any nudity in them—and he asked me if I wanted a double, so at first I said sure. Every atom of me wanted a double. But I didn't feel a double would be Magdalene, I didn't feel she would move like I would move. I knew if I did the scene, I'd really feel like a whore.

Marty did get a double and I knew immediately she was wrong. I just said, "Take her out." The men who were extras were nonprofessionals, and I don't know what they thought the scene was going to be like, but the reality of it was nightmarish. The first man was crushed and embarrassed and didn't know what to do. We were under the gun. The clock was ticking, and we had this major scene to do. We had no time and this man was very, very nervous. He was so nervous that I had to reassure him and that helped me with my nervousness.

I had to be in the throes of making love in front of these people with Willem watching, and the skeleton crew—we had closed the set. It was very difficult. And Magdalene was supposed to be fantastic, to warrant the fact that men would come from throughout the world to see her. Finally we were done with the first man and he left. Then the second man came, and he was *horrible*. He started mauling me, and Michael Ballhaus and Marty screamed, "Stop! Stop! Stop!" I turned to Marty and I saw horror and panic in his eyes. I saw horror, but also panic, because he had no time, and so I turned to him—and it was just such a great moment between us —I turned to him, and I said, "Do you want me to express this on film?" And he said, "Absolutely." He rolled the camera and I expressed what it felt like to have this man molesting me and I was in profound pain.

That's how the scene got that tone of pain. I thought, "What is more difficult for Christ to watch, her pleasure or her pain?" Watching her in pain has got to kill him because he feels responsible for her being there.

In the second part of the scene, Magdalene looks up and sees Jesus there. Marty shot that in subliminally slow motion. He does that occasionally, you know. You don't notice it, it isn't obvious, but in that moment when Magdalene turns and looks at Jesus, there's that subliminal stretching of time, the kind you have in an emergency.

There's the scene in Magdala, when he's visiting me in my house. Marty had a contraption built for that. The camera would come in past Willem onto me. He had a reverse shot you don't even really notice. I'm lying prone, but the eye moves with the camera. He had to have this whole thing built, he had planned it. We had no dailies and he really had to shoot the movie blind.

There was one shot, just a simple shot, where an Indian man is watching me make love. Christ is sitting out of focus in the background. The camera goes up to the man's face and you see him in the foreground on the left side of the screen with Christ out of focus in the background. Then, the camera slowly starts to move in and you think it's going to move onto Christ, but it swoops slightly and moves into the close-up of the eye of the Indian man, and then it locks focus and Christ is in focus as well, in the background. When I saw it I said to Marty, "How did you think of that?" and he said, "I thought of that four years ago. I woke up in the middle of the night with that one." I realized that he had been preparing for this film his whole life. He told me that he had a storyboard for a movie about Christ when he was a little kid. Who knows what talent is? Who knows what that is? I don't think talent is as rare as the need to express it or the strength to handle the rejection. I don't think Marty can help it; there's nothing else he can do with his life.

MARTIN SCORSESE: In Kazantzakis' book the snake represents sex. It represents needs, the bodily needs. Maybe I should have changed the voice, not used Mary Magdalene's voice for the snake, but it seemed that the three main people in the film are Magdalene, Judas, and Jesus. So you have to keep that together. For me, being a Catholic from before Vatican II, sex has always been portrayed as the most evil sin. Now we know the balance there, we know it's off, but I can't help it. That's what's in my mind. And it stayed with me that sexuality is evil.

The snake represents sexuality in all its forms—even in thought. When the two snakes are uncoiling, the image is very sexy. It has a very erotic feel to it. It's sex in all its forms, not just male/female. The greatest gift from God still seems to pull us toward evil. I think it's totally wrong. I think we're crippled because of it.

Kazantzakis' book was not really factual. It's not Gospel—it's fiction. It's an idea, a book made to set off discussion—not necessarily controversy, but to get people to take Jesus seriously. If you take him seriously, then you take his ideas seriously—the ideas of love, loving God, and loving your neighbor as yourself. I think those are the most important and hardest things to do.

That was my point of view, and my personal relationship to the material. To make a movie I have to feel something about the subject matter. And this is what I feel in this case. I wanted to take Jesus seriously. In Woody Allen's *Hannah and Her Sisters*, when he decides to become a Christian, he's perplexed when he sees a 3-D Jesus winking at him. How do you take that seriously? Or that Jesus you put on the dashboard, or the Jesus on velvet? That's a low blow in the movie, but we deserve it. We let these images take over. Of course people don't worship the images, they worship the God that the images represent.

Kazantzakis opened up my sense of Jesus, pushed me beyond these kinds of images and helped me decide to take more risks. The film takes risks in dialogue, in accents of actors and costumes and locations— everything. I figure the more risks, the better. It puts you in a state of emergency all the time.

Much of the film centers on Christ's passion. I've always been attracted to that—I liked passion plays, dramatizations of these events.

JOE REIDY: The Crucifixion was very important for Marty. He wanted the cross to have an authentic ledgelike seat carved out of wood. I believe it's called the *sedile* in Latin. It was meant to prolong the pain for the person crucified. We had to stop shooting at one point to make sure that the seat we had on the cross was true to the realism of the scene. Marty insisted on it. In this case it was on screen for just a moment, but he had to have it because he felt it was important.

MICHAEL BALLHAUS: In the Crucifixion scene there is one shot when the image of Jesus starts to tilt while he is on the cross. This incredible moment breaks all the so called "rules" of composition, but people accept it because when it's right for the emotions they don't feel that something is wrong with it.

We did almost thirty setups a day for the Crucifixion scene. Can you imagine Willem hanging on the cross in the bright sunlight hour after hour? He didn't complain; he didn't say a word. When it came time to shoot, he was there. These are things that take tremendous physical strength. Willem was living for this movie. He was up in the morning, at four o'clock, for three or four hours of makeup, and sometimes we were shooting for more than ten or twelve hours. Sometimes he didn't sleep more than six hours and then had to play his part. I had great admiration for him.

PEGGY GORMLEY: We all had such respect for Willem. He was such a wonderful person, so ethical. To understand the difficulty of what he had to do physically during those scenes was to have a glimpse of what Jesus

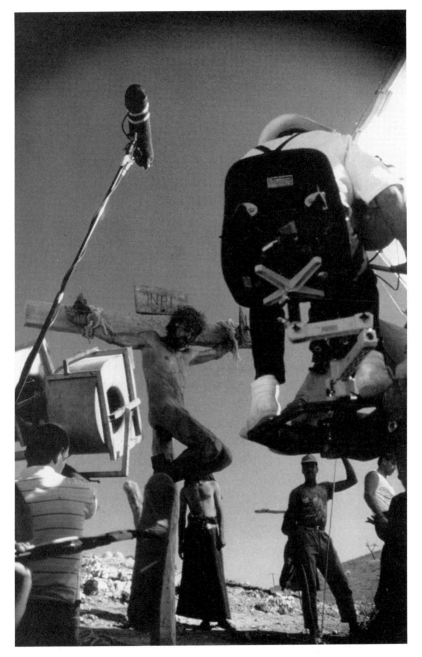

FILMING THE CRUCIFIXION SCENE FOR *THE LAST TEMPTATION OF CHRIST*.

must have gone through. The Crucifixion was a very affecting, very terrible scene—and wonderful, too.

WILLEM DAFOE: Even though the Crucifixion wasn't the last thing shot it was an emotional completion. Still, when we finished I really felt very strongly that I was finished, too. Luckily, when we stopped shooting it was really finished. On other movies they usually come to you later on and say, "We have to shoot two more days." This one felt so complete. But the role never left me.

HARVEY KEITEL: In the film's last scene, when I return as the elderly Judas, I asked Marty if when the camera was on me, he would play Jesus. Jesus is stretched out on this pallet on the floor dying in the scene. Marty was very nervous about it. He called me up the night before and said, "Can I talk to you for a minute?" He came down to my room, and he said, "What is it you actually want me to do tomorrow?" I said, "Just lie on the pallet and be Jesus for me." He said, "But what are you going to do?" I said, "I'm going to stand there!" He said, "Oh, you're just going to stand there?" I said, "I'm not going to move." He said, "Okay, okay, okay, fine." He was nervous, and the next day, he lay on the deathbed for me, and when I'm talking to Jesus in the movie, it's me talking to Marty, who's lying on that pallet.

MARTIN SCORSESE: During the editing we faced difficulties. There was a series of scenes where Jesus cures deranged people and then cures a blind man. When he cures this man, the idea was to track around his head. You start with the blind man, then track back over Jesus' shoulder while he's looking at the man. Then you tilt down to Jesus' hands. He puts herbs and sticks in his hands and then he puts them on the blind man's eyes. Then you track around and Jesus takes his hands off the man's eyes, and the man's been cured.

The point of this scene is not necessarily the curing, but rather the expression on Jesus' face. Because in this story, every miracle, everything that gets him closer to his destination, also brings him closer to his death, closer to the Crucifixion, and that is something he doesn't want.

We go from that to the wedding at Cana, but what's the cut from Jesus curing the blind man? What is the last thing you see in the curing of the blind man and what is the first thing you see in the wedding at Cana?

I wanted to begin with the slaughter of the lamb for the wedding dinner. Now, this is Morocco. The lamb is there. So you see the butcher kill the lamb, he hangs it up, and it's the wedding at Cana. I wanted to cut from a close-up of Jesus' face—his reaction to the blind man's cure—to the lamb. This is what is going to happen to Jesus. He is the lamb who will be slaughtered. The image is so shocking that you don't think of that. Later on, you piece it together. But you don't think of it at the time.

For the wedding itself, we did a lot of research. We finally combined some Jewish and Bedouin customs. We also saw some Moroccan weddings. We ended up with a compilation of Moroccan, Bedouin, and Jewish, all of these together. In the scene there are four cuts. The first shot is the lamb being slaughtered. The shot tilts down from the butcher cutting the lamb to a dish. People walk by and throw coins in the dish to help pay the butcher. That was a custom. Then the second cut would be when they brought the bridegroom in on a litter.

But when the camera tilts down, with the butcher cutting the lamb open, it takes him a little too long. It's a little too long. He cuts. I said, "Gee, that's a little bit much." Now, the picture is pretty brutal already, and to see this lamb . . . I tried cutting first from Jesus' face to the hooves hung up, and then tilt down as the butcher starts with the knife. But it looked awful. The lamb hanging there looks like it's in a butcher shop. It looks too normal.

So I tried it another way. The butcher starts, then you cut to the husband being brought in on the litter in wedding clothes. He has an iron mask over his face and there's drumming. Then you cut back to the lamb, then cut back to the husband. Then you cut to the wife, then back to the bridegroom, and then you cut to the dancing. But then it's not a montage anymore.

If we go back to the wedding ceremony, there is a letdown, because the drums stop. So instead, we went right to Jesus coming in with Mary Magdalene, Judas, and a couple of his other apostles. They are stopped by one of the guests at the wedding who says to Mary Magdalene, "You don't belong here." Jesus tells him that the kingdom of God is like a wedding. God is the bridegroom and man's spirit is the bride. The man looks upset and says, "It's against the law." "The law is against my heart," Jesus says, and walks away, and you cut to the bride. So these were the decisions and the things we were doing during the editing.

THELMA SCHOONMAKER: I started crying in the dailies. I was so overwhelmed that for three days I couldn't talk to Marty! That hadn't happened to me since I saw the scene in *Raging Bull* where De Niro embraces his brother.

There's something so sweet about the feeling of this film, and the way people feel about it who worked on it—not only the crew who were on the production in Morocco, but the editing and sound mix people. People still stop me in the elevator and say, "We'll never work on a film like that again." It's an incredibly strong feeling. You've heard how the crew felt about each other: tremendous love between all the disciples and their incredible love for Willem. It continues; they really are a kind of family.

A girl was explaining why she didn't like the film: She didn't like the accents, didn't like this and didn't like that. And then she said, "I cried all the way through it." I've heard a lot of people say that. That's power.

Marty's very good at keeping his films from veering into cliché. He'll stick with a shot that isn't camera-perfect, because it's got the right emotion. He's not afraid of awkward moments or of making people feel uncomfortable. It's *supposed* to make you uncomfortable. For example, Peter Gabriel said, "I didn't want him not to be on the cross. I wanted him to die." That is what you are supposed to feel. It should be like a nightmare you're trying to wake yourself up out of. But that's what is happening to Jesus. God's trying to wake him up; you should feel that. Marty forced you to look at Jesus as a human being. When Jesus does die, you react the way a human being reacts to another human being dying. And it's a tragedy. You feel devastated.

PETER GABRIEL: For me, music is directly connected to both emotion and spirituality. In most societies, people use it to get in touch with their deeper needs and feelings. Music can be a vehicle for social change, and I thought, as I was doing the score for this film, that if Jesus were also trying to bring about social change, music would play a role in that. I think there are moments of ecstasy in the music. Perhaps that's a bit of a bold word, but we're talking in a religious framework. When it's really right and happening, there's *magic*. It's similar, I think, to some sort of religious experience, and that happened when we were doing the score.

Some of the musicians I worked with on *Last Temptation* were African, some were Middle Eastern, and some were Pakistani. There was a wide range of influences and sources. I spent a lot of time with the National Sound Archives in London. Lucy Duran there acted as a sort of researcher. She turned us on to various bits of music, and I would select pieces and play them for Marty—two or three of which got used in the film. For example, in the monastery scene with the monks, the singers are actually pearl divers from Bahrain. There's some Egyptian music in the market which was one of Lucy Duran's finds, which we augmented with some other rhythms and flute stuff. The opening is a traditional Armenian melody.

I knew Marty wanted me to create a physical reality with the music, as he was doing with the visuals. The carrying of the cross sequence was very strong for me. I think the scene is a stunning piece of filmmaking, that ninety-degree turn. I would have the tape ready and the mikes all set up and show that sequence of film, and then press the record button. We tried to keep the flow and the feel in our playing. In that scene we used a Pakistani Qawwali singer called Nusrat Fateh Ali Kahn. Baaba Maal, a Senegalese singer, did the traditional Moslem call to prayer which is used in the Last Supper scene.

My parents are now regular churchgoers, but they weren't really when I was a kid. At school, chapel was a pretty important part, and I know that the hymns inspired me, and still do. I think quite often that religious music is the closest that a white man gets to soul music. So *that*, if you like, made an impression. People on both my mother's side and father's side were into classical music, and some of that was religiously inclined. In the first school I went to, at age ten or something, I was in a school choir. But I purposely tried to avoid it in my second school, when I was a teenager, because it meant you had very little spare time to do anything else. And though I felt drawn to spiritual things, I wasn't, probably still am not, a practicing Christian, although I think I have faith.

At various points, when I felt my soul in danger, I've prayed. Once I thought I was going to lose my daughter—at times like that, in danger, stress, proximity to death, you have a tendency to fall back on your faith. I

THE WOMEN OF JERUSALEM WALK WITH JESUS ON THE VIA DOLOROSA IN
THE LAST TEMPTATION OF CHRIST.

think my own beliefs are a hodgepodge of Christianity, Buddhism, and Taoism, which is somewhat typical of someone who was a teenager in the sixties. There is some of that in my music—an openness to various influences.

There's actually a piece with Lazarus' sisters that we did with synthesizers. We did one piece with a boys' choir. We tried using it for the scene when the angel/devil takes Jesus off the cross. It was the only traditional religious music in the entire film. I liked it—I loved it, in fact—and I was disappointed that Marty didn't want to use it. It would have been the only time we used traditional church music. The devil's music, if you like, would have been religious. There would have been that paradox.

You know, the flap over *Last Temptation* is absurd. If people's faith is so weak that it can be destroyed by a film, then it's not much to begin with. I think people may find themselves reviewing their own lives and their own points of view on religion as a result of the film. I'm very proud to be a part of it.

MARTIN SCORSESE: When the demonstrations began on the West Coast, we were editing in New York. The studio was getting most of the heat. The first demonstration was around July 14 or 15. We had invited some of the religious groups who were trying to stop Universal from releasing the film to a screening on July 12. They didn't show up. At 10 A.M., when the screening began, the only people who were there were me and my crew and Jack Valenti, Paul Newman, and a man from *Time* magazine. At two o'clock some other religious people saw the film. Some were hostile—but overall they liked it. We had dinner with them that night.

When the demonstrations started later in California, they were aimed mainly at the studio executives, and focused on the fact that they were Jewish. Demonstrators held caricature drawings of Lew Wasserman, head of MCA, with a crooked nose. This was at his home in Beverly Hills. Lew Wasserman, to my knowledge, had not even seen the film. The demonstrations were pretty ugly. They were picketing outside the studio. They also started tying up the phone lines at Universal, and doing all sorts of gremlinlike activities that we didn't know about. There were threats at the studio that a man was going to immolate himself in the parking lot at three o'clock on Thursday, the day before the film opened.

PAUL NEWMAN: *The Last Temptation of Christ* made me think for a fleeting moment of actually getting involved in a formal way with religion. My father is Jewish and my mother is Catholic and I was raised Christian Scientist, so I'm not sure exactly where I would affiliate. But it made me think more about God than I had in years. It's a powerfully devout film. I don't understand how it could be considered sacrilegious. I can't believe that Christianity is so fragile that it can't stand inspection.

PAUL SCHRADER: A lot of the protest about *The Last Temptation of Christ* was really from an anti-intellectual wing of social and political Christianity. It doesn't have that much to do with Christianity itself. They preempted the debate for a number of reasons. It didn't even matter whether they had seen the film, that was irrelevant to what was in it for them. They preempted the debate by saying *Hollywood* is seeking to defame our Lord, *we* are seeking to defend our Lord, please send us money, help us in this fight. Well, when couched in those terms, mainstream Christianity has to ally itself with fundamentalism—it's not going to ally itself with Hollywood.

TOM POLLOCK: The protest emerged almost as soon as the Tim Penland issue arose. He was hired by Universal as a consultant, to advise us. Penland's company is called Christian Marketing, and he had been employed earlier by Warner Brothers on *Chariots of Fire* and on *The Mission*. His relationship with the fundamentalist Protestant community was quite strong. We thought that we would show the film to the fundamentalist community so that even if they did not approve of what was being said, they would not attack the obvious sincerity of the people who were saying it. We never got that far, because what was attacked was not the film. They circulated an old Paul Schrader script that had things in it that were never in the film; it was really Paul's first draft of the script. Marty told me *he* did not even have it. No one knows how they got it, but they got it. They used quotes from that script and claimed they were from the film. So when I walked out to speak with some of the twenty-five thousand people who came to protest at Universal, and I said, "Why are you here?" They said, "Because you are portraying Jesus as a homosexual." That reference could only have come from the early Schrader draft.

By and large, good people were misled, and all of this takes on extra meaning these days because of Salman Rushdie. Penland left us to join the protest. I believe he was a man who got stuck in the middle. But he had read the *actual* script, and must have known the other one was a phony. After all is said and done, I don't bear anybody any ill will. In the spirit of the film I forgive him.

JAY COCKS: I had worked with Marty on the script very intensely. It was hard not to get a credit. In some of the early posters I shared credit with Paul Schrader, but he challenged that, and the Writers Guild, who arbitrates these things, decided that Paul would get sole credit. I found out that in projects adapted from a book the first draft of the screenplay takes precedence, but no one can take away my pride in the work I had done and my work with Marty. They can take your name off, but they can't take your work away.

Schrader's good. He does have this very single-minded, focused approach toward writing—very contained. He can really get that momentum going, keep it sustained, as he did for *Last Temptation*. That was a major accomplishment for such a dense novel, and he came out with a workable structure. But I thought we added a lot of color and nuance. We did the monastery sequence. Everybody wanted us to take it out, but I'm glad we left it in.

Everyone connected with *Last Temptation* seems to have been hit by some kind of lightning bolt. But Marty took the brunt of it. Everybody complained about the length and the dialogue, apostles talking like longshoremen, but there's one thing that no one complained about. No one didn't *get* it. Everybody understood.

We knew that as soon as we succeeded in making Jesus real, many of the people who have a vested interest in what you might call the Jesus on black velvet were going to get very upset, because a real Jesus would be threatening. What the book did was to make him human, because of his doubt, and it was his doubt and the fact that he wanted to be human that was upsetting. I had this idea in my mind that it was like John Lennon: You're lying in the street dying in a millisecond, and all you want is what everybody takes for granted—you want life. That's all the Jesus in this film wanted.

BARBARA HERSHEY: The irony is that the last temptation, the greatest temptation of all, is the most ordinary of miracles—which is our lives, our everyday lives, the fact that we can eat and drink and make love and have babies and get sick and become old and die. The fact that we can just live is the greatest gift of all, though we don't think of it that way.

TOM POLLOCK: Before this film, you could scarcely find an executive under thirty in the movie business who had spent an hour over the last ten years talking about the nature of Christ. They talk about the grosses, or about Arnold Schwarzenegger's performance, but they'll never talk about the nature of Jesus. With *The Last Temptation of Christ*, it became an issue upon which you had to have an opinion. Not only the freedom of speech issue, but the humanity of Jesus. People who hadn't gone to Sunday school in twenty years were having to think about that. It became a topic of conversation in offices, in the halls, over lunch. I even started reading theology.

I've read studies that suggest that the strain of fundamentalist Protestantism involved in protesting the film goes back to St. Paul and St. Augustine. The fundamentalists are very uncomfortable with the idea that Jesus is fully man, because if he *is* fully man, and all men are evil, then Jesus is evil. They would prefer Jesus to be fully *God*, and only God. Although everyone says that they accept the Council of Nicaea, which said that Jesus was both fully man and fully God, they really do not. If Jesus was only God in the form of man, then Jesus is not only without sin, but without temptation, or any human foibles. But the idea of this film is that a Jesus who is human and is tempted to remain so has so much more to sacrifice. He sacrifices himself for man, and it becomes a much more meaningful sacrifice.

In the European countries, we had very little trouble. Ireland showed the movie with little protest. We only had trouble with it in two countries in Europe; one was France and the other was Greece.

France was, I believe, a special case. Bishop LeFebvre, who had just been excommunicated by the Catholic Church, got together with the right-wing candidate for president, and they used this, as it was used in the United States, for fund-raising. They did it as a political issue to embarrass the Catholic Church into taking a position against the film. The protest was also highly anti-Semitic in France, and there was a lot of violence. Although there were protests in other countries, only in France were there the same overtones of anti-Semitism that there were in the United States.

In Greece, the Greek Orthodox Church was forced to relive what they did twenty years ago in condemning Kazantzakis. Of course, ultimately, the film opened to huge business, but after two weeks it was condemned and pulled by the Greek Orthodox Church, overriding the liberal Papandreou government, in which Melina Mercouri was minister of the arts. The film was pulled, and it has not been shown again. Kazantzakis died once again in ignominy.

ELENI KAZANTZAKIS: When the book appeared, many said that it was a masterpiece, the best novel that had ever been written about Christ. So often those who said the book was blasphemous had not read it. It was the same with the film.

I liked Willem Dafoe—*beaucoup*. He was simple, very natural. After I read the script I wrote to Martin Scorsese. I wrote, "I am Orthodox, but I am not maniacally religious, not at all. Still, people will be shocked if they don't clearly grasp that Christ is married only in a dreadful dream. He *dreams* that he has had the last temptation. The last temptation is a dream. His path crosses ours. But it was not possible." But Scorsese did the nightmare a little too natural. When Christ is shown with his children, it should be like a very happy dream. People should understand that there is the Christ on the cross, and all this is imagined. And I thought it was too long. But Nikos did the same thing. I told him while I was typing the manuscript I thought the temptation scene was too long. When you have a nightmare, you see it for one minute, one second, and you think that you have been the whole night with it. But it is not true. It takes seconds.

But that is Nikos, and I had told him. So it was not Mr. Scorsese's fault.

．．．

In New York, demonstrations against the film took place in front of the Ziegfeld Theatre, but the threatened violence never occurred. On the afternoon the film opened, August 12, the people in the ticket line with me one afternoon did not suffer the taunts of protesters in silence. Rather, they simply invited the demonstrators to attend the film. Director Michael Ritchie, taking advantage of a break in his shooting schedule on *Fletch*

PROTESTERS OUTSIDE THE ZIEGFELD THEATRE IN NEW YORK THE DAY
THE LAST TEMPTATION OF CHRIST OPENED IN AUGUST 1988.

Lives, happened to be near the head of the line. He offered to pay the admission of one particularly vociferous man. "Come in, see it. If you want to protest, fine. I respect your right to do so. But at the same time, look at the movie before you condemn it." The man declined.

I tried to discuss the film with a member of a group from Westchester County, which carried large red banners embossed with golden lions. He refused to respond, but directed me to a spokesman for the group, who explained that they were called the American Society for the Defense of Tradition, Family and Property. They had been founded in Brazil to "denounce leftist progressive infiltration in Catholic circles," and had previously demonstrated against Kissinger and Planned Parenthood, as well as socialism in all its forms. About twenty members had come to the Ziegfeld Theatre by bus. They departed when the TV cameras left. But those same news crews captured something else for the evening broadcast. For the first time, regular filmgoers responded to the movie. Audience members interviewed as they left the theater said things like, "I was deeply moved," and, "this is a beautiful film." A priest said he would recommend it to his congregation. The director of a center for homeless men said he had finally seen a Jesus his dispossessed people could love.

Earlier, in Los Angeles, the Reverend H.L. Hymers, pastor of a fundamentalist Christian church, had led a demonstration in which an actor portraying Lew Wasserman pretended to drive nails through Jesus' hands into a wooden cross. Hymers staged such scenes at Wasserman's house and at a synagogue. Even more moderate groups, who tried to distance themselves from such extreme behavior, exhibited a kind of fanatic opposition to artistic expression that presaged things to come. They tell their own story in the book *The Last Temptation of Hollywood*, by Larry Poland and Robert Holmes.

After a month of calling the movie "the *most* controversial ever," the media began, in typical fashion, to take the opposite tack. Now it was, "What was the fuss all about?" Some critics dismissed the movie as a typical biblical epic. It became almost impossible to judge the film on its own merits. Lost in the controversy were the more humorous aspects of *Last Temptation*.

MARTIN SCORSESE: Judas is really very funny, in a way. He's like me. He gets confused when Jesus is upset. Jesus says, "I have to die," and Judas says, annoyed, "Every day you got a new plan. Last week it was cures, now it's dying." There is a lot of humor in the film that some people aren't getting. The paying audience gets it, the paying audience in America, they laugh. Because it's a biblical film no one's supposed to laugh? These people were human beings. Jesus must have said, "Pass the bread," or, "I'm tired," at least once.

In a certain sense, the life that we try to lead to follow Jesus has the same kind of struggles and doubts and anxieties as Jesus' life, but it has exhilaration, too. In the film Jesus says, "I'm the farmer, the farmer's me?" He's very happy. And his enthusiasm elicits laughs from those around him. Not laughs of ridicule, but laughs of enjoyment. Here's this fellow, and he's suddenly enjoying himself, suddenly getting the right answers. "I used to think God was angry, too," Jesus says, "and then he blew over me like a cool breeze and said 'stand up,' and here I am." This also gets laughs from people. He's not communicating with his audience yet. It's still a dialogue between him and God. He's saying, "I got it. I got what you're talking about, and I'm so happy about it." He starts communicating after that, when the people say, "These are children's stories." He says, "What do you want? You want justice, right? You want respect?" Then he starts communicating. He says to the widow, "You're mourning," and he embraces her. But up until that time, he really isn't communicating; it's all within himself. He's thinking it's all within the beat. He's getting the language and the rhythm of it. It's kind of funny in a sweet way, a nice way. It's watching a guy get himself together and it's great. When he gets it, he feels terrific about it. He says, "Here I am."

In his discussion with Judas, Jesus says that getting rid of the Romans is not enough. There has to be a change in the spirit of the people. Changing the spirit means changing what's important to all people—greed to generosity, hate to love. If life were not based on greed, or the subjugation of other people, or power for the thrill of power, then it wouldn't matter who was in charge. I think that is Christ's message.

I'm a devout Catholic even if I'm not a "good" Catholic. I'm not even a practicing Catholic, but I believe and I pray. During the mixing of the film we would choose a reading for the day from the Bible, because we were getting hit with so many things from the fundamentalists that we were searching the Bible to find things to support our position. Tom Fleischman, who was our mixer, is Christian, and he'd find about two or three things a day, and he'd read to us.

I feel closer to Jesus now. I feel closer, but again, people have said that this is *me* seeing myself in Jesus. But I don't think there's anything wrong with that if you can see yourself in God, because it's your attempt to come to some sort of terms with God. It has to start somewhere. It has to start on some level. It starts on the lowest level, which is ourselves, and tries to get to the highest level, which is God. There has got to be some way to get there.

MICHAEL POWELL: I'm a very simple Christian, brought up in Canterbury in cathedral school. Mine's a simple religion, based upon the Bible and the hymn books. The picture, because of the attacks on it, will take some time to find itself. But it's one of those movies that can change lives. You know, with Marty I have often thought it's as if someone says, "I'm bringing a friend to dinner," and he brings Christ.

BARBARA DE FINA: When I was a little girl, a Christian was someone who believed in Christ and wanted to be like him. Everyone was a

Christian, there were no "born-again" Christians. It's hard to believe someone can say, "*You're* a Christian; *you're* not a Christian because you don't believe exactly as I do."

MRS. SCORSESE: What hurts me is people do not understand this picture. They still don't understand, they'll never understand. And you know what Marty said at the end, what he told me? "I don't care. I made it. I got it off my chest. I'm happy. I've wanted to do it all these years. I made it. I'm satisfied."

MR. SCORSESE: I understand my son. I know why he made that picture. And he made it from his heart.

FATHER PRINCIPE: Marty's movies do have an Easter dimension. I remember in *Taxi Driver*, the young prostitute is saved, and she goes home. People forget that. In the Last Supper scene in *Last Temptation*, Marty gave us a sense of the Real Presence as physical, real. When the wine literally became blood, that was as strong an understanding of the Eucharist as you can imagine. In the Passion and Crucifixion, Marty showed Jesus dying not because he was a zealot or a political agitator, but because of the horror of sin. He sees the perversity of human vice that causes death and destruction, especially the death of the just man. But in the film there is the Resurrection. For me, Marty is communicating the Christian message. His is a kind of vocation and a priesthood in and of itself.

MARTIN SCORSESE: I do believe in the Resurrection. I can't exactly say what it means, beyond a kind of transcendence. But I prefer to believe in it, and I believe Jesus is divine. But Jesus' last temptation is very human. The human side of all of us doesn't want to suffer. It wants peace. It wants tranquility. It wants to be assured of happiness. The drama of life should be in family drama, not something like war. And Jesus is given this temptation. He's had enough drama in his life. He's had enough sacrifice and hardship. Now he can rest. He can have a pleasant death, which is a great thing. And why not? We call earth a "vale of tears." If you could be assured that you wouldn't suffer anymore, that you'd have a wife and children, time to enjoy yourself and them, and on top of that, to have a good death . . . well, it's a great temptation.

He resists that temptation because he comes to terms with his own nature, the divine nature. He had to die to give us hope—to give us the hope that God loves us. He had to become one of us by dying for our sins. It's the idea of relinquishing, of cleansing, the idea that God understands exactly what his creatures go through. And God has sympathy for us and pity for us. That's what dying for our sins means, I think—but then I'm not a theologian. I ran into Father Principe a few years ago at the Museum of Modern Art. I was looking at Georges Rouault's *Christ Mocked by Soldiers.* Soon after *Last Temptation* opened, he sent me a postcard of the painting with a quote from Pascal: "The heart has reasons which reason cannot comprehend."

NINE

GANGSTER/PRIEST

NEW YORK STORIES: LIFE LESSONS (1989)

"THERE'S A LOT OF MOVEMENT IN YOUR HEAD WHEN YOU'RE PAINTING OR WRITING OR DIRECTING. I WANTED IT IN THE CAMERA." —MARTIN SCORSESE

IN HIS NEXT film, *Life Lessons*, Martin Scorsese turned inward. For the first time since the earliest N.Y.U. films, his main character was an artist. *Life Lessons* would be part of *New York Stories*, a trilogy of short films by New York's premier directors; the other two were Woody Allen and Francis Coppola.

Scorsese's movie is drawn from *The Gambler*, by Dostoevski, a novel influenced by the writer's obsession with a young bohemian, Polina Soslova. In *Life Lessons*, Dostoevski becomes Lionel Dobie, a successful downtown painter, played by Nick Nolte. As the movie opens, Dobie cannot paint. He tries, but he can do nothing. His canvases remain blank. And in three weeks, he must mount a major show.

The first segment of the movie was shot in a TriBeCa loft. Dobie's agent (Patrick O'Neal) ascends in an old, battered freight elevator. The camera, from an extreme high angle, watches Dobie waiting for him. Nolte's face presses against the wall of the elevator cage, as if he were an animal in the zoo. The suave, fashionably dressed agent enters the messy, ramshackle studio. He pauses before a large canvas daubed with a few graffitilike strokes. He is the adult businessman here to discipline this unruly child. For the agent, there is only one rule: deliver. There are new geniuses in the wings. Dobie must work, and work quickly.

But Dobie's inspiration of the moment, his assistant Paulette ("just Paulette") has left him. Rosanna Arquette plays the latest in a long line of young and beautiful muse/companions. Dobie persuades her to return, but Paulette sets a condition: no sex. She will stay with him, in her section of the loft they share, but concentrate on her own painting. He accepts her conditions. With Paulette both present and absent, Dobie's frustration feeds his obsession with her. Now he works with frantic intensity; the paint from his brush splashes on his clothes, his arms, and his five thousand-dollar Rolex watch. He's oblivious. Pure talent pushes away self-destruction and surges forward once again.

Dobie's redemption comes from his art. It is the one thing he will not betray. His moment of truth comes when Paulette asks him to judge her paintings. "Say I can be a great painter, and I will stay with you as your lover," is the unspoken message. Dobie wants her desperately, but he cannot say her work is good. She has only a pedestrian talent. Paulette would welcome even a clumsy lie, but he cannot bring himself to speak falsely. Art is the only morality in his life. If he loses that, he loses himself. But she has served his purpose. The paintings are finished; Paulette leaves. The show opens. At the gallery, the young woman serving drinks accepts Dobie's offer of "life lessons"—to serve as his new assistant—and the cycle starts all over again.

With Lionel Dobie in *Life Lessons*, as with Jake La Motta in *Raging Bull*, Scorsese neither interprets nor justifies his character. He simply makes him present. Just as we were in the ring with Jake, we are in that loft slashing paint across the canvas as "A Whiter Shade of Pale" blares from the portable tape player. Layers and layers of paint build up as Scorsese piles image upon image—a hand, the brush, Paulette's ankle, the slap of a basketball on wood as Lionel shoots layups in his studio at 4 A.M. Dobie battles to make visual the emotions churning inside him, but his struggle requires only space and materials. Scorsese needed a crew and a cast that included almost a hundred extras.

Joe Reidy again acted as first assistant director. Nestor Almendros was the director of cinematography; his work with François Truffaut had inspired Scorsese.

In his desire to recreate the downtown club scene, Scorsese used clouds of billowing smoke. It added to the atmosphere of arty decadence, but it also interfered with his breathing. Between takes he had to inhale oxygen from a clear plastic mask.

JAY COCKS: *New York Stories: Life Lessons* says a lot about Marty and Marty's priorities, and about his ability to deal with, focus, and transcend his obsessions. It's quite moving. He has to forgive the obsessed artist; if he didn't, he'd be hanging himself in effigy. The movie is Marty's act of self-justification. It's very honest. Artists use people up in a way. He's got a nice little irony working here. Dobie uses this woman up, but for what seems to him a good reason. But he can't lie to her. His moral life is in his art. I think *Life Lessons* is a metaphor for the process of creativity.

Marty's strength comes from his bedrock belief in the sustaining power of his gift, his talent. In the period after *New York, New York*, he had a Mexican standoff with mortality, and mortality blinked. Not many people can get away with that.

MARTIN SCORSESE: It was Woody Allen's idea to do a film sort of like the old Italian and French compilation films of the late fifties and early sixties. Woody and Francis Coppola got the two comedies, and I got the serious one. During mine, people will probably be running around the theater, not paying attention, like I did as a kid when the fight films came on. My film, called *Life Lessons*, examines a painter's obsession with his mistress. We examine something that's either dead or dying. It also made me examine something in myself.

When I was casting, an actor said to me, "The guy starts off bad and ends up bad." He's looking at it negatively; I'm looking at it positively. Let's try to understand it, and maybe in the understanding there's a sort of exorcism of what you do in your own life. I've had some close friends of mine say, "You know, this is depressing stuff again. You're just doing more depressing stuff." I say, "All right. But that's the reality I see." So it's not necessarily uplifting, or whatever you call those movies where they say, "It uplifts the human spirit." I always get nervous when I see those things.

RICHARD PRICE: Marty said that he was interested in doing something based on the diaries of Polina Soslova. He had a book, *The Gambler*, and in the back, as a supplement, they had excerpts from her diary. This woman, who was twenty-one or twenty-two, had been a lover of Dostoevski's, and she dumped him for an Argentine medical student, who in turn dumped her. She took out all her rejection and humiliation on Dostoevski, but Dostoevski would do anything to be with her. At this point, Dostoevski was a famous writer, and she was a callow, shallow, would-be bohemian—a talentless individual. Marty was intrigued with how he would debase himself for her. When Dostoevski finally left her, he wrote *The Gambler*, in which she played a very central role. Then he married the woman to whom he dictated *The Gambler*.

I think Dostoevski knew what he was doing; he needed this passion to write. I can relate to the feeling that propels you to write: You want to be loved, you want to dazzle and amaze people, and make people love you. But you have to have an object in mind. You can't say, "People will really love me." You say, "This woman doesn't love me. I want *her* to love me."

That's how I started writing *The Wanderers*. I was with some girl and she dumped me. At her house on Thanksgiving weekend she left me to see her old boyfriend. I started writing *The Wanderers* just to show her what she was missing. I tried to create a parallel story about a writer who is an acknowledged master of his art form, but needs a prop to write. He needs a Polina Soslova.

Marty said, "It has to be a New York story." Writing is not visually exciting—you have a guy tapping away, a Fred MacMurray with a pipe who says, "I'll be with you in a minute, dear. I'm finishing up my novel." If it's New York, I said, let's make him a painter. Painting is very visually demanding and challenging. And New York owns the art world, like New York owns the theater world. Outside of New York, whether it's Paris or Topeka, there's nothing. Okay, I thought, I'll have a guy, and I'll give him his Polina Soslova. He's got a show coming up, and he just can't work, and she wants to leave him. She lives with him, and she won't sleep with him, and he yearns for her, even though he's got nothing in common with her; he's fifty, she's twenty-two.

NICK NOLTE (LIONEL DOBIE) AND ROSANNA ARQUETTE (PAULETTE)
IN *NEW YORK STORIES*.

What does he see in her? What did Dostoevski see in Polina Soslova? He saw in her that he's not being allowed into her bed. You need an erection to paint and this one never goes down because it never gets used. So Nick can paint all night. Then the minute he finishes the paintings, she leaves. And at the opening he finds his next muse for his next show. That's how he operates. He lives in his own personal hell, never changing, never having anything deep with anybody. He's a slave to his art, but even more to his own glory, his own need to be glorified. He sacrifices everything to that. The girl even says to him, "If I was as good a painter as you, maybe I'd be a bastard, too—I don't know."

ROSANNA ARQUETTE: I have a line in *Life Lessons*: "I feel like a human sacrifice." To me, that one line is the thread to my whole character. She's young, and trying to be an artist, and living with a very famous painter. She's there to feed his art, and to stimulate him in every way. But he can't accept her as an artist, and it starts to make her crazy. She is a strong woman, strong enough to see that the relationship is going to kill her. So she gets out. She *has* to leave. She leaves him, and you don't know if she's going to be okay, or if this has destroyed her. But she's smart. She's twenty-two, but she's not stupid. Marty said, "You've got to be twenty-two." In this, I have the emotional range of a twenty-two-year-old.

I write a history for every character I do: where she came from, her favorite color, her astrological sign. This one lived in Philadelphia. Her parents are middle-class. She was an artist, won all the awards in college. But then she came to New York, to real life, real artists, the real world. It was a lot different. She found she wasn't as *great* as everybody had been telling her.

NICK NOLTE: The story is a little bit Dostoevski, a little bit Richard Price, with some Marty Scorsese thrown in. When I read it I immediately recognized that balance between excessiveness and creativity—how to get in and out of those creative states and still keep a relationship going. I had to examine the emotional side of Dobie's relationship with Paulette.

At one of our first meetings, Marty was explaining the story to me. I just sat there and listened. After about an hour or so, he says, "Well, I could sit here and tell you the whole script, but go to some of these painters' lofts. Once you see a loft, how they live, you'll understand exactly the story we're going to be telling." And I did. Their whole life is in that loft—their painting, their living, their whole existence. You can imagine how they might get lost up in there. They struggle from image to image.

We also talked about where Dobie fit in historically, especially in relation to the New York scene. We put him right between the Beat Generation and the hippies. He knew of the Beat Generation, but was a little older than the hippies. He was stuck between those two elements, which is a good place to be. When he talks about the war, he's referring to the Korean War, not Vietnam.

I think originally Marty and Richard Price had conceived this piece to be about a writer. Then, as they thought about it, it became obvious that the process of *writing* is so internal that there's nothing visual to see in the film. I think it was a great idea to make the character a painter. This piece deals with his ego and his fame. Very few painters are recognized; many are known only after death. Marty's own fame is in his lifetime, his fame is contemporary. You don't find that too much with painters.

In the original script, we would not see the actual finished painting, we would just see brush strokes. As we read the script, we saw an opportunity to add another character—the painting itself. I said to Marty, "You read it and you see the relationships and the chaos and the process, but you never see the beast." The beast is the creative thing. The final beast would be the image. So Marty decided to show the painting, to see a real painter's work. But would an artist allow us to invade his world this way? Some of the artists said yes, but then their dealers read the script and said, "It's terrible. Artists are not that way." Finally, Marty found Chuck Connelly. I worked with Chuck and we painted. We'd go down to our studio loft, and Chuck and I would stay there and paint.

It was hard for Chuck, at first, to understand the film process. The crew would be setting up and we would be painting and he'd say, "Well, shoot this, for Christ's sake, we're doin' it right now! You're strokin' great. Look at that thing you're painting!"

NESTOR ALMENDROS: When I read the script for *Life Lessons* it looked like a normal story of infidelity and incomprehension between a couple. It could have been done straight, like a little play. But of course that is not how we did it. Nowadays, any TV show is correctly done. Everything is known, digested, and predigested. Everything looks the same, because it is very naturalistic. They just reproduce human vision. Martin goes beyond that, and stylizes things. We reconstruct space so that it looks the best it can. It doesn't have to look like real space.

Other directors put the camera in places which are logical to the human mind. But with Martin, it seems that the camera is like God. It can be in the weirdest places. It can be everywhere. I think people get disoriented by all of these camera angles. Anything goes. Anything is possible in lighting, too. But since the angles are so expressionistic and offbeat, in a way it makes things easier. You can do lighting that is less realistic than I usually do, with high contrast, for interest. His films are very expressionistic. They remind me of German expressionism in silent movies, with its very strong movements, and of the Russians, and Orson Welles. Martin's camera is at weird angles, with extreme close-ups followed by faraway shots. Everything is very far out, very strange. And yet it *matches*. Things may seem not to match when you are shooting them, but everything cuts once the soundtrack follows. Most directors are not that daring. Martin knows there is nothing to be afraid of. As long as you keep following a story, it doesn't matter *where* the camera is.

NICK NOLTE: The camera is doing a lot of wild things, which is great for an actor, because sometimes that camera can bring across an emotion as much as the actor himself! First we rehearse and discuss it. Marty will tell you to start your investigating, and then he'll wander off. I think he makes you *search*. Every shot is challenging for the operators, the actors, and the technicians. He's a visionary, and it's fun to work with the vision he has.

MARTIN SCORSESE: I wanted to use theatrical lighting. For example, to have a light on her foot, let's say, with darkness all around the foot. Or he would be alone in his loft and there would be a spotlight on him, a theatrical spotlight. When he goes to answer the elevator, all the lights would come up around him and you see the loft, and the windows. But how do you make it all dark when the point of the loft is all light? So I used an iris shot to do what a spotlight would do.

A woman who really liked *Life Lessons* said that as a feminist she felt that the girl's point of view should have been there. I think that is a good idea. Maybe it should have been a big feature, with one version from a man's point of view, and one from a woman's, but I couldn't do that. I could only approach it as honestly as possible. I asked Richard Price to do it from his point of view, to try to deal with her as compassionately as possible. The painter, Dobie, loves her. He loves her but maybe his love is wrong for her. She needs something different. On a scale of one to ten, maybe he's only capable of four-and-a-half. She, being a good, normal person, needs about a seven, eight, or nine. But she is his passion. She becomes like an obsessive object, a fetish that he needs to do his work.

I love the idea of paint on a five thousand-dollar Rolex watch. And I love the song "A Whiter Shade of Pale." I liked the movement, the excitement of the scene with the music. I really wanted movement. It can be boring to shoot a static event. There's a lot of movement in your head when you're painting or writing or directing, and I wanted it in the camera.

NESTOR ALMENDROS: The look a movie should have is determined by the location, the period—many, many things that tell you how the look of the film should be. Marty decided to give his piece of *New York Stories* an expressionistic look, which is not really the look of a comedy, more of a tragedy. That determined that this could become a comedy and a tragedy at the same time.

With a project like this, it was important that we not try to copy or to imitate. The three stories should look as different as possible. They have three different styles, three different stories. We have not seen the other stories; we don't even know the subject. I only know in what neighborhood they take place; I haven't the faintest idea what they are about. I know the one by Coppola is about rich people, and I know the one by Woody Allen is about middle-class intellectuals, the Upper West Side. And ours is about artists and SoHo bohemians. That's all I know.

A year ago, I worked with Martin on a black and white fashion film produced by Giorgio Armani. It was a little preview of what *New York Stories: Life Lessons* was going to be like: There were many camera movements, many cuts, and a lot of editing. *Life Lessons* also resembles *The King of Comedy* a little bit. There's a famous man and one person who is not famous. It's about the relationship between the person who has arrived and the one who hasn't. Of course, this situation has a personal interest for me, because in my profession I am someone who has arrived, who has gotten recognition. Young people approach you, and they know your name and think that you are great. And the fear you have is of being used, the fear that those who surround you, like in *The King of Comedy*, are trying to get something from you. You never really know if people are sincere or if they just want something from you. That kind of subject interests me.

RICHARD PRICE: When Rosanna Arquette leaves Nick Nolte, he is looking into the abyss of the only thing that changes about him— his age. He will always be a famous artist. He will always be alone. Once people get wise to him, they leave. He stays in the same place. People just keep going through. He chews them up and spits them out, and they go on to have a life. He is stuck, and he always needs new blood, innocent faces. He is confronted with the terror and awfulness of mortality. That's the price he has to pay to be a famous painter. Marty must feel this in some way—it's the price he pays to do what he does. I also sacrifice to do what I do, because the most important thing to me is to be adored and loved for being an artist. But you've got to pay.

In *Raging Bull*, Marty made no effort to excuse or explain Jake. The question "What makes a man like that tick?" is never answered. He is a cipher. He is the *bad man*. We all root for the prodigal son. You want to go down with them. At the very end there's that moment—the turn. Maybe it doesn't go up any higher after that, but that's enough. It's like when Jake says, after that terrible beating, "I didn't go down, Ray." *That's* the character Marty will do over and over and over again—the bad man. We follow him down, see him graze the bottom, then see the beginning of a trajectory up to some kind of salvation.

The Nolte character throws his desire to be loved by people into creating his work. He says, "At any cost to myself and to others, I will be known." And the cost is terrible. He finally gets a glimpse of the abyss and of the cost of his actions, but covers it right up to go on. We get a sense of the ghastly deal with the devil he has made. The thing about Marty that separates him from other filmmakers of his generation is that there's a burning heart in the middle of his stories. It's like when Jesus takes out his heart in *Last Temptation*. I always feel like there's a moral center to his work.

BARBARA DE FINA: It is a hard story to tell and a hard character to play, because he's fifty, and he's been through a number of wives and girlfriends. He could come off being very uncaring and sort of a slob, who uses problems with his relationship to work on his paintings. But Nick does a good job. You don't hate him. You care for him a lot. You understand. Nick's a very lovable guy.

NICK NOLTE: Marty always takes care of his actors, lets you know where you're at. He keeps you informed. I like the fact that he keeps the work disciplined. It's very controlled work, very precise, and yet he lets you examine and experiment and explore.

ROSANNA ARQUETTE: When we shot the nude scenes, Marty closed the set just for me because I don't like people watching. But on screen, you never see anything—just stomach, lips, eyes, and hands. This was one of the most erotic love scenes I've ever done in my life. But it was erotic without showing anything.

Marty and I don't really discuss acting. When he hires someone, he knows they are going to give him what he wants. I've said this before and it's really true: It's like he plants the seed. For me, he plants it and waters it, and then it grows. On his sets, I have the best times I've ever had in a movie. I look forward to working. That's not to say that I don't like to work in other movies, but here there's an ease with Marty because he knows what he's doing. He's always open for any kind of change or suggestion. When he goes on the set, he has the shots. He knows how it's going to cut. He really knows his craft.

This is my second time working with Marty. I've worked with a lot of directors, but there is an energy between Marty and me that's like an unspoken word. We don't even have to say anything; I know exactly what he wants without him even telling me. He'll say, "Hey, Ro," and I'll say, "Right!"

NESTOR ALMENDROS: Actors here are much more disciplined than in Europe. They're more patient; they work harder. Like Richard Gere—if he has to fall in the ice water in Canada, ten or eleven takes, he'll do it again and again and not protest. They'll work until four in the morning, one take after another, and not complain. Americans have a workaholic quality. Also, actors in America are very physical. They can climb mountains; they can fight. There's a scene in *Life Lessons* in which Nick Nolte plays basketball inside. He was fantastic! He was actually not missing one shot. In Europe, actors are more intellectual. They don't know how to do things like the Americans, like De Niro and his boxing. American actors are not afraid of going through things, like Willem Dafoe on the cross suffering for hours, or getting fat, like De Niro in *Raging Bull*. Do not ask that of European actors!

NICK NOLTE: I've always felt film is a director's medium. I don't like it when the actors are put in the place of the material; they end up in something with a narrowly restricted viewpoint. I liked the idea of three directors for *New York Stories*, each with his own concept. I like the idea of short hunks of film, instead of long, drawn-out films. We had a lot of fun in this. I think our story feels very good, very solid. The writing is excellent. It's well thought out, and it works.

Marty's been real comfortable to work with. He helps you get prepared for the role, and if you get it right, then he lets you go with it. He gives you hints. He guides you in the direction you should go. And if you get a little off course, he kind of corrects you. He lays out a physical way to approach the character, then he lays some literature on you, and directs you, so you go for the character.

BARBARA DE FINA: I always like the shooting and the pre-production. Marty likes the editing—that's easier to control. I think what came out of our relationship in terms of work is that he has learned to have more control, to be more disciplined. The studio doesn't even call him; now they trust him artistically. They know he's not going to go wild financially, so they leave him alone. I think he's learned that through discipline he has more control.

I think Marty's pretty reasonable and that we are both on the same wavelength. As long as he realizes that, although I'm the producer, I'm not the studio, and I'm not calling the studio saying, "He's going crazy, he's ordering three thousand extras." I also think that together it's easier to get work done and to have some sort of personal life. I think working all night and sleeping all day was Marty's way of not dealing with being a human being as well as a film person. I think everyone, as they get older, soon realizes that.

Marty loves movies and could watch them twenty-four hours a day, but to me a movie is work, and I have trouble just accepting it as a form of entertainment. For Marty, though, movies are not just a reminder of work, because he studies them and always finds something new. They're his life.

JEFFREY KATZENBERG: It is very inspiring to work with Martin Scorsese. He's so intelligent, so immersed in his work. He can make any subject fascinating. I'm dazzled by his ability to compose images, tell stories, and break new ground. He really is one of a kind.

Marty is exciting to work with. He makes it fun. I saw his passion with *Last Temptation*. That's why I wanted him to make *Life Lessons*—because of that passion.

MICHAEL EISNER: *Life Lessons* was essential Scorsese. It shows the ways he can use music, acting, and the emotion of the piece in his own efficient style. Nick Nolte has never been better. I think Scorsese is one of our greatest directors.

NESTOR ALMENDROS: Martin reminds me strangely of François Truffaut, for many reasons. Like Truffaut, he is a film buff and has in his films many references to old movies. Also, like Truffaut, he is always smiling, always laughing, and he doesn't create terror on the set. He is very friendly to the crew. Also, his small size, and his body, remind me of Truffaut. Sometimes it feels like a resurrection. At times it's uncanny.

I've been very lucky. I've always worked with very kind people. I have not worked with tyrants. Nasty directors can make great movies, too. Fritz Reiner, apparently, was a tyrant, an unbearable person; so was Hitchcock. But if someone is unbearable, I will not work with them. I don't need that aggravation. There are people who are both talented and nice.

Truffaut was much more cheerful on the set than in life. In life, he was sort of depressed—not depressed, really, but quiet and unexpressive. He was always sick. Every time he made a film, he was cured; he didn't have any more colds or stomach aches.

The thing I prize most in a director is style. I like to work with directors who have a signature. Martin is one of the few directors in America who *has* a signature. You could come into the middle of one of his films, not knowing who made it, and you would know it was his work. Woody Allen also has his own signature. Nowadays, most films look like they're made by computers, by machines. They're all the same, all equally well done. Scorsese is a man with a signature. Truffaut used to tell me that he expected that one day I would work in America with some director who *had* style. If he were alive, he would be very pleased about that.

GOODFELLAS (1990)

"GOODFELLAS IS GOING BACK TO THE SAME PERIOD AS MEAN STREETS, THE EARLY SIXTIES, TO THE WORLD I GREW UP IN."
—MARTIN SCORSESE

The Hawaii-Kai, a down-at-the-heels "theme" nightclub on Broadway and Forty-ninth Street, offered welcome respite from the humidity that hung in suffocating waves over the New York streets. It was another hot summer, like those of *Taxi Driver* and *The King of Comedy.* Scorsese was again shooting on the streets of New York.

In *GoodFellas,* Scorsese returned to the subject that had always fascinated him: the "wiseguys" who live beyond the law. Theirs is a world of soldiers and hit men, of making spaghetti in your jail cell and getting to know your children in the prison visiting room. Here, being a stand-up guy, a "goodfella," means never talking to the police, never informing. But in this story of the Mafia, Henry Hill (Ray Liotta) does not stand up. He does not do the right thing. He turns in Paul Cicero (Paul Sorvino), the mentor who has sheltered him throughout his life of crime.

This is not your typical gangster movie, the kind that glamorizes organized crime. There are no dramatic gunfights, no precisely planned bank robberies. In today's scene, the wiseguys unload the cases of liquor (Cutty Sark), fur coats, sides of beef, even piles of tablecloths and linens, being delivered to a rundown restaurant, the Bamboo Lounge. The wiseguys have forced the owner of the Bamboo Lounge to make them his partners. All the merchandise bought on the restaurant's credit will be taken in through the front door, then sold out of the back. On the set, even the crew has the terminology down. After each shot, they shout, "Strike the swag!"

Tommy (Joe Pesci), the volatile, hard-to-control partner of the more sane Henry Hill, has a crucial part in the scene. The partners have wrung the owner dry; now they plan to torch the restaurant for the insurance. As the scene begins, Joe Pesci and Ray Liotta find their positions. They stick rolled wads of toilet paper into flammable liquid. These will be the wicks of incineration. Ray Liotta carefully reaches up to place his incendiary device in among the bamboo fronds overhead. Pesci acts disgusted: "You look like you're decorating a Christmas tree." The cast and the crew break up. Scorsese says, "Not bad Joe, not bad. Leave it in." It would become part of the scene.

Joe Pesci elaborates a little more. "What kind of a guy would torch a restaurant as if he was putting an ornament on a Christmas tree?" Ray Liotta asks the shorter Pesci, "Can't you reach it, Joe?" Pretty soon, it's difficult to separate the give-and-take between Pesci and Liotta from the scene developing between Tommy and Henry Hill. But whatever the motivation, it works.

After a hiatus of seven years, Scorsese and Robert De Niro were working together again on *GoodFellas*. De Niro played Jimmy "the Gent" Conway, the amiable Irishman who masterminded the six-million-dollar Lufthansa Airlines heist, and then murdered all his accomplices.

In Scorsese's other movies the main character experiences a moment of redemption. But in *GoodFellas*, Henry Hill is not saved. Consigned to obscurity by the Federal Witness Protection Program, he ends the movie in a suburban housing development in the Pacific Northwest. It is cold. It is rainy. It is boring. It is hell.

MARTIN SCORSESE: *GoodFellas* is going back to the same period as *Mean Streets*, the early sixties, to the world I grew up in and knew from an angle slightly different from that in *Mean Streets*.

The script is based on Nick Pileggi's book, *Wise Guy*. It's Nick's book, but the visual styling had to be completely redone in our writing sessions. So we decided to share credit. It's the first script I've put my name on since *Mean Streets*. And because I worked on the script for *GoodFellas*, I controlled the picture right on paper—it was like a movie already. It's really more like the control I had over *Raging Bull* or *Last Temptation* or *Taxi Driver*. But the emotional depth varies on these things. *Raging Bull*, I think, is a much more emotional film, and so is *The Last Temptation*. *GoodFellas* is more of an exploration, with a lot of black humor.

I'm interested in the book's structure. You see all the levels. The subtitle is *Life in a Mafia Family*, and the documentary approach interested me. It doesn't focus on the overdramatic. Most gangster movies focus on the big gunfights. The book *Wise Guy* gives you a sense of the day-to-day life, the tedium—how they work, how they take over certain nightclubs, and for what reasons. It shows how it's done. And it shows the emotion of these people working and getting caught up in a vortex of passion.

NICHOLAS PILEGGI: *Wise Guy* started out as a piece for *New York* magazine. I chose Henry Hill as my subject, not necessarily because he was the most interesting, but because he was the one willing to talk. The book was on the bestseller list. One day I answered the phone and this guy said, "My name is Marty Scorsese and I'm a movie director." "I know who you are," I said. "I'm trying to finish a film," he told me—but he didn't tell me what movie it was. He said, "I read your book, *Wise Guy*, and I've been looking for it for years. I'd love to do it." And I said, "To tell you the truth, I've been waiting for this phone call all my life. If you want to do it, you can do it." He told me he was tied up. I said, "Don't worry about it. I own the book, and I can do anything I want with it. Finish the movie you're working on, then we'll sit down. But if you want to do it, it's yours."

The next morning I called my agents and said I had committed the book to Scorsese. They were going crazy because they were trying to get more money from this one and more money from that one, but it turns out that Irwin Winkler, who was in Paris, had called up about it. Happily, Winkler found out that I wanted Marty to direct—and that Marty said he wanted me to do the screenplay, and that he would do it with me. Winkler is a great friend of Marty's, and he said, "Hallelujah!"

IRWIN WINKLER: When I was in Paris, working on 'Round Midnight, I was thumbing through New York magazine, and I came upon Nick Pileggi's excerpts from his book Wise Guy. I read it and I liked it a lot. Then I talked to Michael Ovitz, who was handling the sale of the book, and he told me that Marty Scorsese was also interested. By then I had negotiated to buy it, and had made an offer. Marty was in Chicago at the time, doing Color of Money. I called him and said, "Let's do it together," and we made a deal. He said that this time he wanted to write the script himself, with Nick Pileggi, and I made all those arrangements.

I think Wise Guy is a mature version of the modern American success story. This picture looks in nonromantic terms at what success has to offer us. It's a success of gangsters!

NICHOLAS PILEGGI: I broke the book down into the scenes I thought would work. I wrote them and I gave Marty a copy. He made tremendous, voluminous notes all over the copy. We taped our conversation, and we went over it scene by scene, and I incorporated his comments. Then we went through revisions. We met again and again. We did about eleven or twelve versions, until we got it down to what looked like the screenplay we thought we wanted. Every one of those twelve drafts was fun. I felt at ease with Marty from the beginning.

I was born in Brooklyn and grew up in an Italian-American neighborhood like Marty's. We have almost exactly the same family background. My parents owned a garment factory, coats and suits. Marty's and my conversations often wound up being about growing up as Italian-American kids in New York, not necessarily as tough guys—I was never a tough guy, nor was Marty. Marty had the additional problem of the asthma.

Marty's movie *Italianamerican* captures a lot of this. All those bloody saints and all that absolutely sanguinary Southern Italian Catholicism that Marty is a part of. Everybody's house has pictures of Jesus opening his chest with a bloody heart pounding.

In my family, the Church really did not play a major role in our lives. My father once went to Midnight Mass at St. Patrick's Cathedral on Fiftieth Street. He found the turnstile in the doorway, and he said, "They put a turnstile in the doorway of a church. I'll never go in that church." And he never went back. Italians are very vendetta-conscious people. One thing wrong and they never talk to you again, that's the kind of people they are. On top of that, the Roman Catholic Church in the United States—in New York, certainly, at the time—was Irish, and they didn't even want the Italians to be there. Italians were praying to saints the Irish had never heard of, basically pagan holdovers. There was a saint for toothaches, and all their religion seemed too pagan to the Irish. In Old St. Patrick's Cathedral on Mulberry Street, the Italians went to Mass in the basement.

My fascination with the mob has a lot to do with wanting to know more about who I am and where I came from. We do not have an Italian literature in the sense that Southern Italians are written about. The Irish have a real literature. You could spend the rest of your life reading Irish literature and never read the same book twice, but that's not true of the Italians. It's mostly an oral tradition. If you're Italian -American, and looking for a clue to your background and to the world your parents came from, the whole history of organized crime is an interesting source.

Everyone's fascinated by characteristics of their ethnic group, because it's the key to your identity. You see little things about yourself—the Italian opera, the Italian mob, the Italian artisans, the Italian immigrant experi- ence, the structure of the family. In all of this you will find clues to yourself and your family.

I think we all feel ambivalent about the wiseguys. Everybody who has grown up in the Italian community feels that they have been victimized in one way or another by wiseguys. My father had a little coat factory, and he had to put people on the payroll who really didn't do anything in the office, just to make sure we had no labor disputes. Downstairs from my father, some guys hung out at their club. My father thought he knew them.

They were all from the same part of Italy, and my father felt really close to them. One weekend they stole everything out of his place. They went up there—they had seen a lot of bolts of cloth being delivered—and they cleaned him out. There was nothing he could do. Report them to the cops? But the cops were already taking money from these guys; they were not going to do anything.

But when my father was a kid and he first came over from Italy, he lived on Fourth Avenue and Union Street, in South Brooklyn. There were five guys, all cousins, living in the same house. They didn't have any money for the rent. My father was a trombone player at the time, in the Capitol Theatre, playing in between movies, and the other guys had jobs here and there. They would all go home and cook spaghetti with oil. That would be their breakfast, lunch, and dinner. Whatever money they could scrape together they used for rent. One of the major wiseguys at the time, who knew my father and these cousins, said, "Listen, don't worry about it. You keep working. You'll be okay. When the guy comes to collect the rent, you make sure you get a receipt from him." "Yeah, we always get a receipt," they told him. He said, "Make *sure* you get a receipt." So the landlord came, and my father gave him the money, and as the landlord left, the wiseguys stuck him up. They gave the money back to my father to pay the next month's rent. They did this every month. So, it was the same seventy or eighty dollars that kept getting paid to the landlord.

How do you deal with that? These were the same kinds of people who robbed his store! A lot of the people in the Italian community have cuckoo stories like this about some different kind of larceny. The wiseguys might do little things like pay your rent, but the bottom line is, they are bad, and they are going to victimize you. They have to rob you. It's endemic. Maybe my father shouldn't have accepted the money. If my father were a Presbyterian, maybe he wouldn't have. He would have said, "Thank you, but I'm sorry. I cannot accept this money. I paid my rent and I will struggle and pay my rent next month." So maybe my father is a little to blame. Italians are both victimized and amused by it; I think it is an in-house drama that has gone on for a thousand years.

MARTIN SCORSESE: People think gangsters kill people. Yes, of course they do. But the main purpose of the gangster, especially in *GoodFellas*, is to make money. That's why, in *GoodFellas*, Tommy is killed. After a while, he was making more noise than money. He started killing people for no reason. So they had to get rid of him. He was messing up the whole plan!

MRS. SCORSESE: My husband Charlie was playing Vinnie, one of the gangsters. He'd come home and I'd say, "So Charlie, what did you do today?" And he'd say, "Well, today they killed so-and-so." And the next day he'd come home and I'd say, "Well, what did you do today?" And he'd say, "Well, they dumped the bodies today." Day after day after day. I said, "Marty, what's going on? What's this movie about? Only killing?" He said, "Ma, it's the book. It's the way it is." I played the mother of Tommy, and *he's* always killing, too.

JOE PESCI: First we had to change the name. The real Tommy was six-foot-something. I'm not tall. Marty and I were laughing about that the other day. Every time somebody tells us something about these guys, they get bigger and bigger. Pretty soon he's going to be Kareem Abdul-Jabbar. But acting has nothing to do with that kind of reality. People ask if I want to know about Tommy DeSimone. I know a lot about him, I read and I talked to people, but I don't take that stuff into the film with me. Now, Bob De Niro will find out everything about his character, and take those traits and little things with him, and let it start to feel like that for him. What I do is think of somebody that I know very well who is the same type, and play him. I do *my* Tommy DeSimone. I do Joe Pesci as if I were this killer, this crazy, funny, wisecracking person.

Marty has his own thoughts about the killings, the guilt and the religion. I have my own religious ideas. But I believe the wiseguys justify what they do the way any soldier who goes to Vietnam, or Korea, or Germany does. They fight people they don't know. How do they justify that? How do you justify killing someone you don't even know? Because a government person says it's okay? They give you a gun and teach you how to shoot it. And if someone in Brooklyn or the Bronx that helps you feed your family and clothe them, but who, say, runs a bookmaking business or whatever, if they tell you there's a piece of garbage on the other end of town who is looking to take something that doesn't really belong to him . . . They kill their own, within their crime families. They don't go out on the streets and kill ordinary people. My character Tommy goes overboard. I think he's a psychopathic killer. He just kills anybody.

But evidently they don't just kill to kill. They kill for reasons. As far as they're concerned, there are only certain things that a person deserves to die for—stealing from another or having an affair with somebody's wife, things they hold very dear. You are then messing with their families, and they'll kill you for that. So their thinking is—and I'm not condoning this—that that's who deserves a good kick, not some stranger in Germany or a kid in a village in 'Nam.

PAUL SORVINO: My character in *GoodFellas* is Paul Cicero, the neighborhood boss. I guess you'd say he's a don, and he wields an awful lot of power. And yet he has a very vulnerable side, so much so that he treats Henry like a son. He really loves him—in fact, that love is his downfall. He ends up in jail because of things that Henry did.

There is a curious, fascinating dichotomy in these characters, who are capable of such extreme evil and such extreme tenderness. To their families they're one thing, and to their enemies or their business adversaries, they're another. I find it extraordinary that in the human psyche such a thing is possible. I suppose that's what makes it possible for soldiers to wipe out villages and then go home and put their children on their knees. I don't think anyone can explain that. I think there's a certain part of us that, if unleashed, will run amok. As humans, we are capable of extraordinary polarities. All my life, I've been concerned with the reason one stays within a so-called moral life, and the reason one steps out of that life.

No one ethnic group has a monopoly. The officer at My Lai was not Italian American. Italian Americans have no patent on criminality. There are just as many people involved in crime that come from other walks of life, other races, other nationalities. I grew up in Bath Beach, which is not a "Little Italy." I really didn't come up against organized crime. I knew it was there, but you had to be part of that life to experience it, and I wasn't. I never saw it in the streets. We would see people that we would occasionally know were tough people, were in organized crime, and we just avoided them.

I think there are wiseguys who make moral decisions. I don't think all the people are the same in that walk of life, if you can call it a walk of life. It's more like a kind of descent into hell.

CHRIS SERRONE: As a kid growing up, Henry had a role model. Now I had a role model, Mickey Mantle, but Henry looked up to the hoods. He

CHRIS SERRONE (YOUNG HENRY HILL), PAUL SORVINO (PAUL CICERO),
AND ROBERT DE NIRO (JIMMY CONWAY) IN *GOODFELLAS*.

saw them as the bosses. They owned his neighborhood, Brownsville. Henry loved the mob. He ate, drank and slept it. I don't think Henry saw it as right or wrong. He just saw it as what he liked to do.

I think the reason Martin hired me was because they needed a kid who was very energetic, and fast. In the movie, like in real life, he needed someone that can get the orders straight. Because at the Mafia card games they needed someone who could keep the people happy, who was quick and on the ball.

Tuddy Cicero is my role model in the movie, he teaches me the ropes. He's played by Frank DiLeo, Michael Jackson's ex-manager. He's a very heavy-set man. He smokes cigars like a foot long. I had to drink espresso. I don't even like coffee—but Frank helped me. So I sipped it and it was over in one take. We did a couple of other scenes where I was running down the hill, bringing policy bets to the bookies.

Later on I got to drive the car. A hood's car, which is a 1955 Caddy. It's blue—a beautiful car. And the hood gives me the keys and I drive it and park it in the parking lot. That's like graduating. I'm moving up in the mob. I also had a scene with Robert De Niro. He bails me out of jail when I get pinched for phony credit cards at age thirteen.

One night we were shooting until 11:30. I had to stand perfectly still, because they wanted to catch my eyes, see? My house is directly across the street from the cab stand. And I'm fascinated. So I'm looking out, watching them do their thing. The camera's right here on my eyes, and I had to be perfectly still. I was there for about an hour. Marty came over and was very supportive. He gave me some soda and said "it's good work." I love acting. But if it doesn't work out, I want to be either a pediatrician or a center fielder for the New York Mets.

FRANK DILEO: We first met when Marty directed Michael Jackson's video, *Bad.* I was Michael Jackson's manager at the time. *Bad* was like a street song, and I had always felt we should make some sort of street video. And who knows more about the streets than Martin Scorsese? When Quincy Jones mentioned Marty to me, I almost fell out of the chair.

The first couple of times Michael and Marty met it was kind of weird. Because Michael didn't quite understand Marty. I showed him *Raging Bull,* and I showed him *Mean Streets,* and I showed him *The King of Comedy.* He liked them and wanted Marty, but Michael, like Marty, is a control freak. They're both control-oriented people. And I remember I showed up one day and it seemed to me there was a little tension, a little bit of a problem. And so I had to explain to Marty how Michael was, and I had to explain to Michael how Marty was, and then they both understood they were similar, and then it worked out. There was never anything after that. Just, I guess, crossing the line—like two guys sort of seeing who's going to take the first step.

Michael loved doing the video. I'm sure we drove Marty crazy, because we had a lot of unorthodox requests. Michael takes his time, especially when it comes to doing the dance. He believes there has to be so many angles, whether it's needed or not. He got this from his conversations with Fred Astaire and Gene Kelly. One day I was walking into the subway station where we were shooting, and Marty and Mike Chapman, the cinematographer, were discussing me.

I said, "What are you guys looking at? My zipper down or something? What's the problem?" Marty said, "Ah, nothing, nothing. I might do this movie, and I might have a part for you. You look just like the character." I said, "Ah, great." I was thinking to myself, "Yeah, right. I'll never hear from this guy after this video." I said, "Call me up and if I'm not busy I'll do it." I had never had any intentions of being an actor. About three years later he called me. And here I am, working on *GoodFellas*, where I play Tuddy. It's a great part for me, especially because I've never acted before.

Tuddy is Paul's brother in the book. He sort of discovers Henry Hill as a child, and raises him in the cab stand and through the ranks of the mob. Tuddy is an underboss within the mob. He does whatever it takes. He's a fun-loving guy, with kids around him a lot. But yet he's very serious. Towards the end I execute Tommy. Joe Pesci plays Tommy, my best friend. I hated to do it, but it's strictly business. I believe the mob really looks at killing as strictly business. It's no different from being fired at IBM or some other place. The only problem is, they can't fire you from the mob because you'll talk. The only pink slip you can get is a death certificate. I don't think they mean to harm anyone else. I think they just keep it amongst themselves, and that's the way it is.

Thank God that Marty won't hear this until after I'm done with the film, because I certainly don't want to sound corny, but if he'd asked me to do this film for nothing, which I practically am, I would have done it anyway.

Working on this film I've learned so much about directing and acting— I couldn't buy this at UCLA. I've seen every movie Marty's ever directed. I'm one of the very few people in Pittsburgh, because it didn't run very long, that ever saw *Mean Streets* in a theater! I saw it the first week it came out.

I came from a middle-class neighborhood. But I loafed around in a rough Italian section of town. I was there every waking hour. I would go home only to sleep. That's why I liked *Mean Streets* so much. I related especially to Harvey's character. I was raised Catholic, too. I went to all Catholic schools. I was going to be a Christian Brother. I'm still a Catholic; I still go to church every Sunday.

In another ten years, people in this country will understand what Marty Scorsese is really about. They're just starting to catch on, going back and seeing the first movies he did over again. This one, *GoodFellas*, will be a classic.

NICHOLAS PILEGGI: While the wiseguys love *The Godfather*, seeing it as ennobling them, their favorite Mafia movie is Marty's *Mean Streets*. Henry Hill and the others loved it so much they kidnapped Paul Vario, upon whom the character Paul Cicero is based, and made him go see it. Vario didn't even own a television set, let alone go to the movies. They snatched him off the street and dragged him to see *Mean Streets*. He was their boss. This is a home movie to them—maybe not the religious part so much, but the pettiness. All this about having millions and millions is all just dramatic baloney. People envision them as having endless piles of money, but they don't. Some of the bosses do. But there are organized crime bosses who make twenty, thirty, forty thousand dollars a year, and don't have the money to pay a hundred dollars to a bookmaker when they lose a bet. Cops have tapes of them staying in the back room, not wanting to leave because the bookmaker they owe the money to is out front, and they don't want to pass the guy without paying him. They wait until the bookmaker leaves; then they can leave. You're talking really human.

That's what I wanted to put in *Wise Guy*—the way it really *works*. I find that far more interesting than the fantasy surrounding these guys. I used to know a lot of them, and the one thing they all have is an unbelievably high metabolic rate. They are, almost every one of them, highly manic, highly energized, tremendous energy sources. In school they were the kids who you couldn't control; they were *spielkas*—that is Yiddish for "ants in his pants." *That's* who these kids are.

One of the great quotes of all time came from my friend, Danny Jack Parisi, who died about a year-and-a-half ago at ninety-four. He was one of the hit men for Murder Incorporated. You don't even want to think about how many people he murdered, and he took communion every day! Once a year he would make a special pilgrimage. He would walk barefoot from Brooklyn, across the bridge, and all the way up to 116th Street and Pleasant Avenue to Our Lady of Mt. Carmel Church. Two bodyguards followed him. My friend asked him, "But, Jack, how do you do this? How do you make sense of going to church every day and then going out and killing people?" He said, "I go to church every day and I pray to God to give me the strength to rob again." Now, that's who you are dealing with.

RAY LIOTTA: I was born in Newark and grew up in Union Township, New Jersey. We had our little tough guys, but they weren't at the level of the guys in *GoodFellas*. I got into acting at the University of Miami, where I graduated in 1977. Then I came to New York, landed a commercial, and within six months was on a soap opera. I did that for three-and-a-half years.

I wanted to get into film, and was very influenced by De Niro and Scorsese. Things started happening. And now, here I am with both of them. They're great. I like their commitment and passion. What's interesting is, as you're working with them, it's so loose and relaxed. Maybe I'm catching them at a great time of their lives, in terms of their age, maturity, and the successes they've already had. But they work with a wonderful, self-confident kind of ease.

I really wanted to do this movie. I was going to go to the 1988 Venice Film Festival and so was Marty. We talked about *Last Temptation*. It was in the middle of all the protesting, and through all of that, he was able to talk to me, as an actor, without being all frazzled about what was going on. I knew that he had seen *Something Wild* right after Jonathan Demme finished it. I was amazed that someone of his caliber was even seeing a movie I was in, and that he liked it!

He wanted me to send him a tape of me and said that he would see me when I got back from Venice. That night I went home and wrote a very honest letter, telling him it was nice meeting him, here's the cassette and view it at your leisure. About a month-and-a-half went by. We were both in Venice, and I saw him walking through the lobby of the hotel, and there were about seven bodyguards around him. The controversy over *Last Temptation* in Europe was almost triple what it was here. When I saw him, I wanted to tell him, "Good luck and don't let these people get you down." One of the bodyguards grabbed my arm, but Marty saw me and said, "Ray, how you doing? I got the tape, I haven't been able to view it yet." Now, here is a man, with what seems like the whole world coming down on him, and he remembers! It was as if we had talked two days before.

PAUL SORVINO: Marty has such extraordinary sensitivity and a sense of truth. I consider him as gifted a director as we've ever had, and the natural successor to Elia Kazan.

I'm impressed with the climate he establishes for the actors. It is obvious that the actors are kings on his set. The crew are not maltreated, but they know that they're there to serve his vision and the actors' work. It also is clear that he really *likes* actors and has respect for their creativity—he inspires, encourages, and develops it. He says, "Okay, let's just try this." He doesn't give you a lot of verbiage, or an avalanche of meaningless facts and information. He says only one thing at a time, and that one thing, for a good actor, is plenty.

In one scene he said to me, "If he's not convincing you, question him." There are two verbs in that sentence. Almost all directors speak in nouns, results. They say, "You're happy here," or "You're glad about this," or, "You're really angry at him." Marty doesn't speak in those terms; he speaks in verbs. As Sanford Meisner points out, "Acting is doing." Konstantin Stanislavski believed that "acting was the simple accomplishment of tasks." Well, when you speak of accomplishing tasks, you are talking about verbs. "Straighten him out; beg for this; question him; convince him." These are all things I can do. When I'm told to "be happy," what do I do, smile? If I'm told, "Ingratiate yourself with him; entertain him," I can do that.

I think there's an operatic style in Marty's work. Opera is a metaphor for very vivid life. His ideas are powerful ideas, vivid ideas, and yet he has great subtlety. He doesn't splash with heavy colors the way some modern artists do. He uses the most powerful colors in the palette, but then uses the lightest, most sensitive brush strokes to execute them.

His Italian background contributes to it. Italian people have a license to be emotional. It's fine to explode and let all kinds of things out, and yet Marty's movies seem to call for leading men who don't express much, but express it deeply—like an Al Pacino or a Bobby De Niro.

JOE PESCI: My character will kill you for the weirdest things, and I can draw on my temper because it's terrible. My father had a terrible one, and my brother and I have it, too. I have to calm myself down. I've learned as I've gotten older to control it or to walk away from people, to stay clear of somebody that I don't like, that will upset me in a way that would make me want to strangle them or beat them to a pulp. So, as Tommy, I use those urges to kill. It becomes nothing after a while. I did one of the murders like it was absolutely nothing.

ELAINE KAGAN: I have a scene where I send Henry off to school. For this scene, Marty said, "What do you do when your kid goes to school? What would you say? What would you feel?" I said, "I'd say, 'Watch how you cross! Drink that milk!'" It's what is real that always works. That's what makes his films so special.

I think some people are afraid of that. Because I worked with John Cassavetes for so many years, I'm comfortable with improvisation of any kind, with a spontaneous—"Oh, how about this!"—at the last minute. It's important to have the freedom to do that. When I worked with John, he would dictate a first draft screenplay. Then we'd read it back, playing all the parts. Whoever was around would come in, and we'd all read the parts, and we'd play with it. Then I'd take it down, and we'd change it.

John was crazy about Marty. He laughed all through *The Big Shave*. He liked the early films. He could tell that Marty could see, even twenty years ago. He sees everything, very much like John. John was always observing. Anybody who stopped us on the street to talk, we would talk to. He was always interested in what people had to say, and how they said it. Marty's like that. He has time for everyone, and listens. That shows in his work. It makes it real. He shows how real people behave.

One of my favorite scenes is when Henry gets married. It was at the bride's parents' house. All of the bride's side of the family were on one side and the groom's side of the family on the other. They're not too happy that she married an Italian boy, and we're not too happy that he married a Jewish girl. That's very funny, because I'm Jewish and I'm playing a Sicilian mother. Lorraine Bracco is Italian, and she's playing a Jewish girl. So I said to Marty, "Mediterranean is Mediterranean!"

MRS. SCORSESE: I made sixty meatballs for Charlie to take for his scene. In my scene, Tommy brings his friends home and his mother cooks for them. I play his mother, so I said to Marty, "What am I going to make for them?" And he said, "Make pasta and beans, just like you used to make for me—or scrambled eggs." If he'd come home late from a date or from being over at N.Y.U., I'd get up and make him something to eat, and then I'd go back to sleep. And, you know, it was in the middle of the night, so I'd make him something like scrambled eggs or pasta and beans. He said, "If it was good enough for me, it's good enough for them."

PAUL SORVINO: Marty has that Italian visual sense. It's rich, not pale. It comes from the earth, from Tuscany and Sicily. There are things in the geography and topography of Italy that make one sensitive to beauty. If you sit in the Bay of Naples and look at the water, with the reflection of the white city on the water and Vesuvius on the left—if you don't cry, there's no soul in you. This kind of beauty creates a certain kind of person.

His Catholicism also influences his visual sense. We were all brought up in churches that have marvelous windows and statues, and big ideas were presented weekly. The question of good and evil is a serious question for Catholics, and it is related to the question of beauty, because the history of the Church is a history of art. There's an awful lot for him to draw on there.

Marty is terribly honest about what he's doing. He doesn't lie when he makes a movie. He tells it *exactly* as he sees it. I've done some painting, and very often I'm tempted to do a standard thing to get by. I constantly have to tell myself, "Draw what you see. Don't draw what you think you see." Marty draws only what he sees.

MICHAEL BALLHAUS: It's a tough movie. First of all, it has to be right and Marty knows so much about the subject that he wants everything to be

RAY LIOTTA (HENRY HILL), JOE PESCI, CATHERINE SCORSESE (TOMMY'S MOTHER), AND ROBERT DE NIRO IN *GOODFELLAS*.

absolutely correct. So we spend a little extra time to get it right. The clothes, the crimes they commit and how they commit them—all must be done the right way. We are not experts on that, so we need help from people who know better than we do. All that is time-consuming. We are making a movie about a world that we are not that familiar with. In the first week, we had five dead bodies and that's something I'm not used to.

The results are great. Everything looks really authentic and right. How they do things, they way they move, has to have very special style. And that's amazing in this film; it all looks real. This is totally different from what I've done so far on other movies. We are using a lot more wide angles, up to extreme wide angles, and extreme high angles. We're using a lot of long lenses, so there's nothing in between, no 32s—it's like 24 or 28 or 18, and then it's 50 and 85. The light is not soft and not bounced. It's more harsh, direct light, with a lot of darkness in it. It's rich colors—rich reds, rich blacks. It's not smooth and soft; it's dark, shadowy, direct lighting.

IRWIN WINKLER: Marty's been very good lately on budgets. We planned this one well. He's very, very prepared, knows exactly what he wants, and that saves a great deal of time.

He knows what he wants, but he still has the freedom of improvising and trying new things. He knows how to seize the moment when an actor does something a little different or a little special. Knowing what he wants makes it easier for him to do these improvisations, because he has, at least, a standard by which to keep it under control. He's like a jazz musician. He doesn't know all the notes he's going to hit, but he knows the melody he's going to stick to.

MARTIN SCORSESE: The idea is to play around and fragment structure, and to make a film that's *almost* in the style of a documentary. It has the style and freedom of a documentary, where anything can happen, with a lot of narration and voice-over. I can take you three years ahead, and then pull you back. The film has a lot of characters, and the plot may be extremely confusing. But it doesn't matter. It's the exploration of a lifestyle. It's about what it means to be in a life of that kind, minute-by-minute, day-by-day.

In a funny way, growing up as a kid, you'd learn a kind of tolerance. They'd say, "Well, that's Don so-and-so, and you've got to be nice to him.

He took care of my uncle when he was . . . you know, he has our family under his wing." Then there's another guy down the block, he's got another family under his wing. And when there are problems with the two families, the two guys talk it out. And this way, people don't get killed. And that's where the love comes in, you see.

But then, another way of looking at it, as my father always pointed out, was that they are basically bloodsuckers. There was a whole group of guys who were doing little more than taking money. In other words, protection. A lot of people say they're bastards, really. But not all of them are. In a sense, you're paying protection to keep other gangs away. It's very complicated. It's like paying tribute to the duke, who takes care of the village. It's security. Yet, these men kill people and usually the killing isn't personal, it's business. I don't know if I can put these things together and understand them.

These guys actually don't make money that easily. I've tried to point out in my movies that they work more hours a day than if they had a nine-to-five job. You know, Joe Bono, who was one of the actors in *Raging Bull*, came in the other day, and we laughed about this—these guys kill themselves working! And a lot of guys who work legitimately may make more money in certain cases. We talked about a friend of Joe Bono's in his neighborhood, who owned a little coffee shop. The guy would be there twelve hours a day. Twelve hours a day, cleaning up, for a few dollars here and there. You know he never had a life to himself and he'd go home late at night. And one time Joe asked him, "Why do you do this?" And he said, "Joe, anything beats carrying a lunch bag. I can be my own boss, you know? I'm not making money for somebody else."

I was at a press conference before I started, and I talked about *Good-Fellas*. I said it was kind of a nostalgia piece for me, the days of the late fifties early sixties being the period when I was growing up. I had a nostalgia for the old-time, Italian-American gangster, or racketeer. The old Mafia, which really doesn't exist anymore. The downfall of Joe Valachi brought everything down, and now there's drugs, and you have no honor among thieves, if there ever was such a thing as honor among thieves.

After the press conference, I had dinner with some friends. We were talking about crime in New York, and a friend leaned over and said, "Listen, Marty, I must tell you. What you said today at the press conference

CHARLES SCORSESE (VINNIE), JOE PESCI (TOMMY DEVITO), AND
FRANK DILEO (TUDDY) IN *GOODFELLAS*.

about the Italian-American gangster and all that nostalgia—you know
what? I find it reprehensible!" He talked about his parents owning a store
and having to pay protection and that sort of thing. I looked at him and I
said, "Listen, you know, a lot of my feeling is that I can't stop loving my
uncle. I just can't." He said, "Is he a gangster?" And I said, "I didn't say
that. It's just that as I get older, I learn certain things about people and how
they behaved in their life." So my friend looked at me and said, "Oh, I see,
it's from the heart then." And I said, "Yes!"

Henry Hill's kids looked on Jimmy Burke as an uncle. If you know the
story, Jimmy Burke [Jimmy Conway in the movie] has to kill at the end,
and he kills a number of people. The kids, though, will always remember
him as Uncle Jimmy. And that's the dichotomy I was interested in.

GoodFellas is an indictment. I had to do it in such a way as to make
people angry about the state of things, about organized crime and how
and why it works. Why does it work? What is it in our society that makes it

work so well and operate on such a grand scale? Major gangsters aren't usually convicted. I have no idea why. It's like the policeman says in the movie, "It's all greed." The gangsters make money and other people make money, too, because of them. "Give me my check and don't cause any trouble." That's the attitude that allows them to exist.

TEN

PREVIEWS

ON MAY 1, 1990, Martin Scorsese, Steven Spielberg, George Lucas, and Sydney Pollack held a press conference at the Creative Artists Agency in Beverly Hills to announce the formation of the Film Foundation, "dedicated," said their statement, "to ensuring the survival of the American film heritage." Film directors Woody Allen, Francis Ford Coppola, Stanley Kubrick, and Robert Redford are the other founding members of the foundation.

While all the filmmakers have worked for film preservation, their choice of Scorsese as president reflects the depth of his personal commitment. In the early 1980s, he spearheaded a campaign to address the problem of color fading in contemporary film stock. Mary Lea Bandy, director of the film department of the Museum of Modern Art and a member of the Archivists' Advisory Council, has said that it was Scorsese's efforts that convinced the Eastman Kodak company to produce a color film stock that would not fade.

Scorsese first made his crusade public at the 1979 New York Film Festival when he screened a scene from *The King and I*, where all the colors had faded into one tone of magenta. "We are committing cultural suicide," he said then. "In the films of the 1968 Apollo space mission, the sky is purple."

MARTIN SCORSESE: Look, the problem is art versus commerce in this business. The print is shown in a theater. It starts to get scratched, it starts to get splicey; what's the sense of keeping it? It will only have a life of six years, anyway. After that, it gets all scratched and beaten-up. They figure, "What's the sense of having one that has beautiful color if it has splices and scratches on it?" I'm saying that even sometimes when something is beaten-up, but has the original color so you can see people's faces and you can see their expressions, it works better than seeing it in pink and then fading to gray, until you can't see it anymore. That's why it's important to search out even damaged prints.

■   ■   ■

In a shocking number of cases, the problem goes far beyond the condition of the prints. "Fifty percent of all the motion pictures produced in the United States prior to 1950 no longer exist in any form, having fallen victim to decay or neglect," says the Film Foundation's fact sheet. Fifty percent! For someone like Scorsese, who has remarked that some of these movies are like members of his extended family, this is unconscionable. "Fifty or five hundred or even five thousand years from now," Scorsese said at the May 1990 press conference, "people will look back to the twentieth century at the first hundred years, the most creative period, in the birth of a new medium. And they'll point a finger and say, 'Why did they allow so much of it to be lost?' We are the they who will be responsible. Time is running out. If we don't do something about it soon, it will be too late."

With Scorsese's archivist Raffaele Donato and CAA agent Jay Moloney acting as co-executive directors, and the National Center for Film and Video Preservation at the American Film Institute playing a coordinating role with the broader archival community, the Film Foundation has already established a number of projects. The first is "to encourage the creation of a Studio Preservation Fund totalling at least $30 million for restoration projects to be undertaken jointly by the studios and the archives." As Scorsese reports, "Steven Spielberg and I have been on an odyssey, traveling from studio to studio. Preservation now seems to be on the front burner for everyone, but each studio context is a little different. Some studios have vast amounts of nitrate; others don't. Studio collections differ in size, and in whether or not some of their holdings are already in an archive."

"Until the early 1950s," the Film Foundation's fact sheet says, "motion pictures were produced on nitrate cellulose film stock. This stock is highly flammable and gradually deteriorates into dust. The major American archives houses more than 100 million feet of film on nitrate stock in need of preservation." In these cases, preservation means transferring fragile materials such as nitrate or fading color film to a more permanent medium.

But the Film Foundation seeks to go beyond preservation, to the actual restoration of works of the creators' original versions. Scorsese and Spielberg worked together to effect the restoration of David Lean's *Lawrence of Arabia*. Francis Coppola sponsored a similar effort for Abel Gance's *Napoleon*. When Stanley Kubrick discovered after a two-year search that the original negative for his 1964 film *Dr. Strangelove* no longer existed, he began restoring the film himself by photographing each frame of a print he owns with a Nikon camera. Martin Scorsese told the press, "The studios did not realize what they had."

The Film Foundation's advisory board will recommend films for restoration. Among the board's members are Dr. Jan-Christopher Horak of the International Museum of Photography at the George Eastman House, Paul Spehr of the Library of Congress's Motion Picture, Broadcasting and Recorded Sound Division, Mary Lea Bandy of the Museum of Modern Art's Film Department, Shirlee Taylor Hazlip of the National Center for Film and Video Preservation at the American Film Institute, and Edward Richmond of the UCLA Film and Television Archive.

But other means of saving films are also needed if the enormous task is to be accomplished. As Scorsese notes, new ancillary markets—broadcast and cable television, home video, and video discs—can encourage preservation. And in some cases, Scorsese himself has undertaken to make new prints of old favorites.

MARTIN SCORSESE: A lot of the old films are being preserved because they are making all new video masters from the old negatives for Ted Turner's station, TNT. The old negatives are being put back into shape. I hope they don't make their videomasters from flat negatives. I hope the cinemascope negatives are all right, and have full composition.

The museums are concerned about every film, but basically they concentrate their time on trying to save the nitrate. I can understand that, and absolutely that has to be done. What I am trying to do myself is to conserve the films of the 1950s and 1960s as well. A lot of people feel the fifties and sixties were a very weak period in American film history. I doubt it! I doubt it strongly. I don't think there ever has been a weak period in American film history. The fifties were extraordinary: Ford, Vidor, and, to a certain estent, Welles, Ray, Fuller, Minnelli—all of them. And then the sixties were very, very important, too, and the seventies, too. There were those thirty years when the negatives were unstable; those are the negatives I'm concerned about.

I am trying to collect, first of all, favorite films of mine. I try to preserve certain films by making new prints of them. At least then there's a print, a positive copy of the film. I have films that ordinarily wouldn't be sought after: certain B films, or certain minor films by major directors. Ordinarily, they will make a new print of Ford's *Mr. Roberts* or *The Searchers*. But they wouldn't do *Donovan's Reef*. Now, that film has got some sloppy things in it, and some silly things, but it's enjoyable—and it really is Ford.

It's really a ridiculous battle, because there's no way I can save every one of the movies I want to save. There are just too many. I would rather save all of them, even some obscure pictures I saw as a child, that don't mean anything to anybody now. But if I can find a print of them and save it and give it to a museum, that's what I'll do.

These movies meant something to me. I had an emotional experience watching them, and I learned a great deal from some of them. There's a certain sentimental attraction to certain pictures, a nostalgia thing. But others I just adored. And, besides being sentimental, others are just important films. And they should be saved.

CAPE FEAR (1991)

"IT'S ABOUT FEAR—FEAR AND ANXIETY AND EDGINESS."
—MARTIN SCORSESE

C *APE FEAR* —Scorsese's first film made in the 1990s, and also his first remake—offers an odd congruence to his preservation efforts. He is remaking just the kind of 1960s genre film he is dedicated to saving. He is also re-creating the J. Lee Thompson film in Anamorphic Panavision, another first for him. The stars of the original version, Gregory Peck and Robert Mitchum, will appear again, in new roles, in Scorsese's film. Gregory Peck, who as Sam Bowden was the target of ex-convict Max Cady's rage, now plays the lawyer who defends Cady when Nick Nolte, the new Sam Bowden, seeks to have him arrested. Robert Mitchum, who was the original Cady, now plays the sheriff. Robert De Niro is the new Cady and Jessica Lange is Sam Bowden's wife, Leigh.

In the 1962 *Cape Fear,* which Peck also produced, the Bowdens are a model family confronted by evil from without. But in Scorsese's version, Sam Bowden has had an affair that has almost destroyed his marriage. In the original film, Sam Bowden merely testified against Max in his trial for a brutal rape. In Scorsese's version, Sam is the public defender who supressed a report on Max's victim's sex life, fearing that the jury might "blame the victim" and allow Max to escape punishment. And in Scorsese's *Cape Fear,* Max sees his vengeance against Sam in religious terms; he has the scales of justice tattooed on his back and quotes from the New Testament on his arm. Perhaps the film is not such a departure for Scorsese, after all.

Scorsese told David Morgan of the *Los Angeles Times* that *Cape Fear* was one of those films that he screened so much, they became "like an old family friend. I felt at home with them." But Scorsese has looked at the old family friend from a different angle. Interestingly, 1962, the year *Cape Fear* was released, was probably the last year in which the myth of the perfect nuclear family could go unchallenged. The assassination of President Kennedy marked an end of innocence, and the end of the unquestioned American dream. Scorsese had also set *Who's That Knocking at My Door?* and *Mean Streets* in the early sixties, when acceptance had just begun to turn to defiance, and "evil" came not only from without but from within: racism, sexism, militarism—all the internal diseases that a generation would seek to expose and expunge.

But now it is 1991, and "evil" is more complex. "Dysfunctional" rather than "perfect" is the adjective of choice to describe American family life. Scorsese will use the same Bernard Herrmann score that hinted at the underlying darkness in the original *Cape Fear*, but now, as in all of Scorsese's movies, we will experience that darkness directly.

For *Cape Fear*, Scorsese reassembled many of the members of his usual team: Barbara De Fina is the producer. Thelma Schoonmaker edited the film. Joe Reidy served as assistant director. There are some new names as well: The cinematography is by Freddie Francis, who recently shot *Glory*, and also worked on the films of Scorsese's artistic mentor Michael Powell. The picture will be presented by Steven Spielberg's production company, Amblin'. The script for the remake is by Wesley Strick, who was also on the Florida set for most of the shooting.

JESSICA LANGE LEIGH BOWDEN) AND NICK NOLTE (SAM BOWDEN)
IN *CAPE FEAR*.

WESLEY STRICK: I think the original movie attempted to turn Peck into a hero, once he became a man of action. But the book [*The Executioner,* by John MacDonald, on which *Cape Fear* was based] did not. The book looked at how this sort of violence brutalizes and degrades everybody, including the so-called righteous man who has been wronged.

When I wrote the script, whether consciously or not, I styled it a little bit for Steven Spielberg's sensibilities. [Spielberg's company, Amblin', had initiated the project.] There were a lot of "movie movie" moments, and some cute touches of Americana in terms of the way the Bowden family was presented. It was a little antiseptic. Because I thought of this as a pop movie—sort of a sleek, modern, big production kind of thriller. A couple of major directors wanted to do it, and then for business and schedule reasons, it didn't work out with them.

Steven Spielberg had always thought that Bob De Niro would be the ideal Max Cady for the nineties, and I agreed. Steven and I had gone to New York to talk to De Niro about it. He seemed interested, although he hadn't really committed. He got Marty involved. He and Steven together sort of twisted Marty's arm—relentlessly, from what I gather. In fact, they staged a reading of the script in New York, for Marty's benefit, which I attended.

Marty said he was interested. Then we had a very intense, four-hour meeting, where Marty just took me page by page through the script, and basically asked me to excise every bit of cuteness. He had quite a radar for every cute detail that I had laced into the thing. And he wanted it out. I mean, he was very diplomatic; he was very sweet about it. It's funny, also, because based on his films and the way he used to appear with his beard, I was terrified of meeting him. And at first I was quite disarmed to find how soft-spoken and funny he was. He didn't offend me in the least; we just went from page to page and he said, "I want this out and I want that out and I want . . ."

One example I remember is, there's a scene in a coffee shop. A private detective is supposed to be tailing Cady. Sam Bowden's hired him. The detective doesn't realize that Cady knows he's around. Cady's way of sending him the message that he's on to him is to send over a platter of food, paid for. The detective looks up and the waitress is standing there with this tray of grits, scrambled eggs, french toast, pancakes, orange

MARTIN SCORSESE IN THE FORT LAUDERDALE PRODUCTION OFFICES OF *CAPE FEAR*.

juice, and coffee. And Marty said, "You've got a platter full of food here. I just want one plate."

It was interesting. Marty's comments focused on the scenes that involved the domestic tensions, mostly between husband and wife. There are two major scenes in the script where they go at each other. The wife, Leigh, discovers her husband on the phone with a girl whom she assumes he is having an affair with. And she just rips into him. I had written what I thought was a pretty big fight, by my standards. It was maybe two-and-a-half pages, which is a long scene for people arguing. Marty wanted more. In another scene they attempt to reconcile, but it blows up into another bitter exchange. Marty called me several times over the next few weeks with more ideas for more bitter, terse exchanges between them. His dialogue was great. He could spin wonderful retorts between husband and wife. He felt that the husband was kind of taking too much from the wife. He wanted Sam to respond along the lines of "Why are we even bothering? Forget it!" He would elaborate that into long wonderful monologues, many of which I wrote, almost verbatim, into the script. I was teasing him; I said, "If they keep fighting in this way, Marty, we're going to have to call this movie *Cape Fear, Cape Fear*."

In an early draft of the script, I refer to an affair Sam had earlier in their marriage. I touched on it only lightly. But Marty, Nick Nolte, and Jessica Lange all seized on that as a wonderful kind of problem in the past that could rear its ugly head and make more problems, as Cady kind of stirred up the pot. Jessica brought a lot of pride to her characterization. She was continually in a state of outrage about this affair, which apparently had occurred years before, but was still a sore subject for her, and something she liked to bring up at the merest excuse. She cuts him no slack. It's quite funny, actually. Marty would always supply those lines for him, like, "I'll never live it down; I can never make amends; one lapse and this is what I get . . ."

I saw the dailies of those scenes, and what struck me was how Marty just did take after take after take after take. And in every one of them, both actors—particularly Jessica, who I think has a real taste for this—pushed themselves farther and farther and harder and more intensely. It was very much like that comment that some people make about Marty's movies, that sometimes you feel uncomfortable, like a voyeur peeking into some-

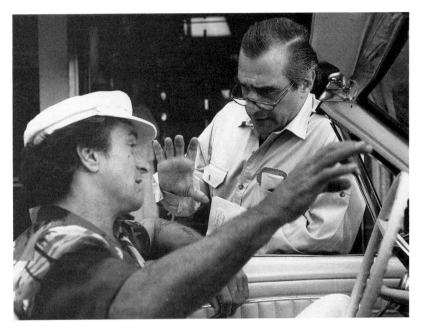

MARTIN SCORSESE DIRECTS ROBERT DE NIRO (MAX CADY) IN THEIR
SEVENTH COLLABORATION, *CAPE FEAR*.

body's home. The rawness of it, the intensity, the emotion, the anger—it just singes you to watch it. Jessica, I think, thrives on reaching those heights of emotion. She was bursting into tears and banging her fists against Nick's chest—things that I could never aproach. I mean, I'm a mild-mannered Jewish screenwriter; what do I know about this stuff? But it was quite thrilling to watch it.

I thought the biggest contribution I could make, as the writer, was to rethink Max Cady. In the original film, Mitchum's performance has something kind of natural and convincing about it. But in that film and in the book, the character was really just a cracker sadist—just a cruel bastard. And that didn't interest me. I think, to me, the most interesting kind of villain is a villain who doesn't believe that he's a villain or that he's evil, but in fact feels justified. That's also the scariest kind of guy to come up against. So that was the place I started from.

I did some research in the South. My main source was called *The Encyclopedia of Southern Culture*, published by the University of North

Carolina, Chapel Hill. It's a wonderful book. One thing that emerged, for me, is something that's expressed in a line that Cady says. He's in the middle of some rant, and he says, "What's the New South, anyway, except the Old South with air conditioning instead of religion?" Here Cady had been imprisoned for I think fourteen years, and when he comes out, what he sees, and what sickens him, is that the New South has become like the rest of the country: gentrified, yuppified, and concerned only with wealth and comfort. The Bowdens, for him, exemplify that change in their complacency and happiness, in their nice house with their nice daughter in their nice town.

Max sees his vendetta in religious terms. He tells Sam something like, "I'm the best thing that's ever happened to you." He quotes from the Bible that it's easier for a camel to pass through the eye of a needle than for a rich man to enter the kingdom of heaven. His message to Sam is, "Yes, I'm going to kill you. You will be dead. But in the process, I will have divested you of all the things that would have prevented you from getting into heaven. Therefore I am your salvation. Because I'm going to take every-thing away from you, and you just might make it through the Pearly Gates, by the time I'm done with you." Some of that was sardonic on the part of Max, but to an extent he truly believed it. He was truly burning with that sense of being the righteous avenger. How pure his motives are, of course, are always subject to debate.

Bob De Niro certainly embraced these ideas. He was constantly looking to embellish his character's dialogue with biblical quotations. The concept was that when Max was imprisoned fourteen years before, he had been an illiterate, with no formal education. He had taught himself to read in prison. One of the first shots in the movie is a slow pan of all the books that he has accumulated in his cell. He has become something of a jailhouse lawyer; he has petitioned the court to let him represent himself in his case. In looking over the files from the case, that's when he realizes that Sam sold him out, that he didn't include a crucial piece of testimony. If you were defending a rapist, you could have a detective check into the back-ground of the victim. And if it was determined that she was, let's say, promiscuous, or had a certain number of lovers within a certain period of time, then that could be used to sort of exonerate the rapist. He could say she was asking for it, whatever it was. Sam had gotten that report that said the victim was promiscuous, and he had buried it.

It raises some interesting ethical questions. From my point of view, what Sam did was right. He perceived Cady as a monster, and he felt that he couldn't be a party to his vindication. He says that after this incident he quit the public defender's office, because he couldn't reconcile what he was doing. That raises a question. There's a difference between an unethical act and an immoral act.

But Cady feels he was wronged. So we're not just dealing with an irrational lunatic here. The man had a point. He lost fourteen years of his life because his own lawyer passed judgment on him—which is surely, in some sense, wrong. But on a higher plane one could say that what Sam did was right, and that he should be honored for it. But in fact, all the terrible things that happen in the film happen as a result of his trying to do, in a sense, something good.

Gregory Peck, in this film, plays a flamboyant southern attorney who turns the tables on Sam. Sam has been, throughout the movie, trying to get a restraining order to keep Cady away from him and his family. But by the time that comes before the court, he has already resorted to hiring a couple of thugs to beat Cady up. Cady has proof of that, and he brings it to court. And in the end the restraining order is granted, but it's granted against Sam—Sam has to stay five hundred yards away from Cady, by order of the court. Peck plays the southern lawyer who pontificates for the judge in a horribly elevated and pretentious rhetorical style.

In my original script, Max was raised in a primitive religious sect, and he made a few direct references to the Bible. I think Bob saw that as a way into the character. He was always looking for more biblical quotes. I was given a biblical concordance that became my best friend during all the rewrites of the script. Every scene of Bob's, he would call me and say, "Can Max say something else here about vengeance, from the Bible?" So I would dutifully go and look up vengeance in my concordance, and go through the twenty-nine quotes about vengeance, and find the best one.

Max takes a position of moral superiority, which is quite disconcerting, given that Sam represents all that is decent and legitimate about the middle class, and Max is a convicted rapist. But in Max's mind he's exposing Sam's hypocrisy. He's bringing to light Sam's continued flirtations with another woman. We're led to believe that Cady has figured out

IN THE NEW *CAPE FEAR* GREGORY PECK DEFENDS MAX CADY, THE MAN
WHO TORMENTED HIM IN THE ORIGINAL FILM. SCORSESE AND NOLTE
WATCH PECK'S PERFORMANCE.

all of the family dynamics and everything that's dysfunctional about this family. So he starts to drive wedges between all of them.

Juliette Lewis, who plays the daughter, is a very interesting actress. She was seventeen, but playing a fifteen year old. There is something girlish about her character, but at the same time, you can sense her sexual awakening. There was this very interesting tension going on within her, between girl and woman. And it was not hard to imagine that Cady, being the pervert and rapist that he is, would see her as a sexual object. And also she, being the kind of nihilistic, rebellious kid, was drawn a little bit toward danger. Plus she had a certain naivete about the world, and an unwillingness to accept that evil is real. Her parents can't seem to convince her; she doesn't want to hear it. So she's intrigued by Cady, too, and denies the worst things that she's been told about him. And when she does meet him, he exudes a certain charm, and a sort of sexual authority as well.

There's a very long and very intriguing scene with them in her junior high school, where he has contrived to meet her alone. It was changed radically from my original script, where the scene was kind of conventional and hokey: He had tricked her into coming down to the basement of the school; she's like a kind of "damsel in distress," and then she makes a corny escape. But in the final version, they end up sitting together in the school auditorium, smoking a joint together, and just sort of rapping about literature. It's the first day of summer school, and his ruse is that he's her summer school drama teacher that she has never met. He's playing the part of the worldly, decadent academic. Max misuses a phrase: She's reading *Look Homeward, Angel* for English class, and he says, "Oh, yeah, that's a *roman à clef;*" and he pronounces the "f." And she just nods, like she's completely entranced by his sophistication.

Marty ran two cameras, just to get the spontaneity of their performances. Bob brought Juliette right up to his level. I remember Marty told me after he shot it that there was such an embarrassment of good footage that he was almost considering dividing the screen in half and just running both of them the whole time.

You don't know whether it's going to end. He's absolutely seducing her, but he's doing it intellectually, by just waving these tantalizing and erotic ideas in front of her. It was Bob's idea to quote from Henry Miller. Max says, "Have you read Miller's trilogy, *Sexus, Nexus, and Plexus?*" But I think he says "Sexus" last, so that it just sort of hangs in the air. And then he goes on to say, "In one of his books, I can't remember which, Miller has a line in which he describes an erection as a piece of lead with wings on it." And she completely blushes. It's the most mortifying moment of her life, but also the most stimulating.

■   ■   ■

In the interview with the *Los Angeles Times,* Scorsese said of the film: "It's about fear, a great deal—fear and anxiety and edginess. Towards the last half, the family threatens to come apart completely at any second . . . . When all the doors are closed, and a guy has no choices, it's fun to see all the different options being closed away. It's almost like some sort of wry moral game that's being played."

The future will see Scorsese returning to New York, but this time, he will be exploring a very different side of the city. His adaptation of Edith Wharton's *The Age of Innocence* will be scripted by Jay Cocks. The picture will star Daniel Day-Lewis as Newland Archer, the prince of the New York social world in the 1870s and 1880s. The milieu is Washington Square, but the action takes place a hundred years before Scorsese's days there at N.Y.U. Still, Newland Archer is a man who, Wharton says, escapes the confines of society and builds a sanctuary "of secret thoughts and longings . . . . Outside it, in the scene of his actual life, he moved with a growing sense of unreality and insufficiency, blundering against familiar prejudices and traditional points of view as an absent-minded man goes on bumping into the furniture of a room." "Familiar prejudices and traditional points of view" exist to be overturned in Scorsese's movies, however much the character bumps around.

IRWIN WINKLER (CENTER) WITH SCORSESE (JOE LESSER) AND ROBERT DE NIRO (DAVID MERRILL) WHO PLAY TWO DIRECTORS FACED WITH BLACKLISTING IN HOLLYWOOD OF THE FIFTIES, *GUILTY BY SUSPICION* MARKED WINKLER'S DIRECTIONAL DEBUT. SCORSESE SHAVED HIS BEARD FOR THE PART.

Scorsese will also continue to produce films he does not direct, as he did with *The Grifters*. One of these, the forthcoming *Mad Dog and Glory* directed by James MacNaughton, tells the story of a reclusive Chicago cop (Robert De Niro), a gangster who secretly wants to be a stand-up comedian (Bill Murray), and a woman they both want.

The future may also bring more acting roles for Scorsese, since his notable performance in *Guilty by Suspicion* (1991), directed by Irwin Winkler. Scorsese's portrayal of blacklisted Hollywood director Joe Lesser—based on real-life counterpart Joe Losey, who prefered exile in London to naming names—gave Robert De Niro, playing fellow director David Merrill, a chance to tease Scorsese/Lesser about his perfectionism.

Whatever Scorsese chooses to do, many of the people in this book will probably appear in the credits, and will have more stories to tell.

MICHAEL CHAPMAN: I remembered something in a poem by W.H. Auden called "In Memory of Sigmund Freud," a eulogy for Freud at his death, that I think really applies to Marty. Auden writes, "[A]ll he did was to remember/ like the old and be honest like children." He goes on to say, "[H]e wasn't clever at all:/ he merely told the unhappy Present to recite the Past/ like a poetry lesson/ till sooner or later it faltered at the line where/ long ago the accusations had begun." The latter part of Auden's poem applies more to Freud than to Marty, but, "All he did was to remember like the old and be honest like children," seems to be exactly what Marty does. In the most complimentary way, it is also true of Marty that "he wasn't clever." He simply focuses on his instincts, on what he feels are his emotions, and allows them to dictate what should happen within the mechanical confines of what film can do.

It's certainly true that the best stuff I've done has been with Marty. I've done some clever stuff on other movies, but the totality comes out best with Marty because the movies were the best. I am way too clever, unlike Marty. You can do all sorts of fancy stuff and make other movies look good, but unless that looking good is at the service of a movie that works as a whole, it's empty.

MICHAEL POWELL: No one chooses to be a director. You are born to it as Marty is.

MICHAEL OVITZ: Marty lives in the apartment above me in New York and if I stop to see him before I go to dinner or on the way home, he's always watching a movie. You can call him at one A.M. and hear a flicking sound—he's watching an old movie on 16-millimeter. Not only can he remember every scene but he can quote the dialogue. His whole life is consumed with film.

MARTIN SCORSESE: There are moments, especially when you work with some very gifted actors like I've been blessed to work with, when certain scenes just come together in the cutting. The music hits, and the camera moves right, and the actors are in there, it's—well, it happens in the cutting. That moment—that's what makes it worth it.

. . .

Here, the boy who grew up in the paradox of priests and gangsters, who still explores "the incessant merciless battle between spirit and flesh," dissolves all contradictions and finds the moments where there are no divisions, only a Real Presence.

CHRONOLOGY

November 17, 1942—Born in Flushing, New York to Charles and Catherine Scorsese.

December 5, 1942—Baptized in St. Leo's Church in Corona, New York.

September 1950—Enters Old St. Patrick's School in Manhattan after family moves back to their original home on Elizabeth Street, Little Italy.

May 26, 1951—Receives his First Communion at Old St. Patrick's Church.

1956—Graduates from Old St. Patrick's School and enters Cathedral College, the seminary for the Archdiocese of New York.

1957—Transfers to Cardinal Hayes High School, Bronx, N.Y. Graduates with honors in 1960.

1964—Graduates from New York University as a film major. Marries fellow student Larraine Brennan.

1965—Daughter Catherine Scorsese born.

1966–1967—Enrolls in graduate studies at New York University Film School.

1968—Wins *Le Prix de l'Age d'Or* for "The Big Shave."

1969–70—Teaches at New York University.

1970—Acts as film program director for the first "Movies in the Park" series sponsored by the Lincoln Center Film Society; represents American independent filmmakers at the International Incontri del Cinema at Sorrento, Italy.

1971—Moves to Hollywood.

1975—Marries Julia Cameron.

1976—Receives the Palme d'Or at the Cannes Film Festival for *Taxi Driver*.

1976—Daughter Dominica Scorsese born, named for Martin's maternal grandmother.

1977—Presents award to director Michael Powell at Telluride, Colorado Film Festival, citing Powell as a major influence on his own work.

1978—Receives David Di Donatello Award in Florence, Italy from the Italian government for his contributions to the cinema.

1979—Marries Isabella Rosellini in Rome.

1980—Nominated for Academy Award, and wins the National Society of Film Critics Award, for Best Director for *Raging Bull.*

1985—Marries Barbara De Fina

1986—Receives the Best Director Award at the Cannes Film Festival for *After Hours.*

1990—Receives the Silver Lion award for Best Director at the Venice Film Festival for *GoodFellas.*

1991—Nominated for the Academy Award, and wins The National Society of Film Critics, New York Films Critics, and L.A. Film Critics Awards, for Best Director for *GoodFellas.*

FILMOGRAPHY

FILMS DIRECTED BY MARTIN SCORSESE:

WHAT'S A NICE GIRL LIKE YOU DOING IN A PLACE LIKE THIS?
(1963)
(16mm, black & white, 9 minutes. Not a commercial release.)

Director/Writer: Martin Scorsese

Producer: New York University Department of Television, Motion Picture and Radio Presentations, Summer Motion Picture Workshop

Editor: Robert Hunsicker

Leading cast: Zeph Michaelis (Harry), Mimi Stark (wife), Sarah Braveman (analyst)

IT'S NOT JUST YOU, MURRAY! (1964)
(16mm and 35mm blow-up, black & white, 15 minutes. Not a commercial release. Premiered at 4th New York Film Festival on September 13, 1966.)

Director: Martin Scorsese

Producer: New York University Department of Television, Motion Picture and Radio Presentations

Writers: Martin Scorsese, Mardik Martin

Cinematographer: Richard H. Coll

Editor: Eli F. Bleich

Leading cast: Ira Rubin (Murray), Andrea Martin (wife), Sam De Fazio (Joe), Catherine Scorsese (the mother)

THE BIG SHAVE (1967)
(16mm, Agfa Color, 6 minutes. Not a commercial release. Made with a grant from the Palais des Beaux Artes, Brussels. Premiered in America at the 6th New York Film Festival on September 28, 1968.)

Director/Writer/Producer/Editor: Martin Scorsese

Cinematographer: Ares Demertzis

Cast: Peter Bernuth (young man)

WHO'S THAT KNOCKING AT MY DOOR? (1965–69)
(35mm, black & white, 90 minutes. Premiered at the Chicago Film Festival in November 1967 under the title *I Call First.*)

Director/Writer: Martin Scorsese

Producers: Joseph Weill, Betzi Manoogian, Haig Manoogian

Cinematographers: Michael Wadleigh, Richard H. Coll

Editor: Thelma Schoonmaker

Leading cast: Harvey Keitel (J.R.), Zina Bethune (the girl), Lennard Kuras (Joey), Michael Scala (Sally GaGa)

STREET SCENES (1970)
(16mm, black & white, color, 75 minutes. Documentary. Not a commercial release. Premiered at the 8th New York Film Festival on September 14, 1970.)

Production supervisor and post-production director: Martin Scorsese

Producer/Director: New York Cinetracts Collective

Cinematographers: Don Lenzer, Harry Bolles, Danny Schneider, Peter Rea, Bob Pitts, Bill Etra, Tiger Graham, Fred Hadley, Ed Summer, Nat Trapp

Editors: Peter Rea, Maggie Koven, Angela Kirby, Larry Tisdale, Gerry Pallor, Thelma Schoonmaker

Cast: William Kunstler, Dave Dellinger, Alan W. Carter, David Z. Robinson, Harvey Keitel, Verna Bloom, Jay Cocks, Martin Scorsese

BOXCAR BERTHA (1972)
(35mm, color, 88 minutes)

Director: Martin Scorsese

Production company: American International Pictures

Producer: Roger Corman

Writers: Joyce H. Corrington, John William Corrington (based on *Sister of the Road*, by Boxcar Bertha Thompson as told to Ben L. Reitman)

Cinematographer: John Stephens

Editor: Buzz Feitshans

Leading cast: Barbara Hershey (Bertha), David Carradine (Bill Shelley), Barry Primus (Rake Brown), Bernie Casey (Von Morton), John Carradine (H. Buckram Sartoris)

MEAN STREETS (1973)
(35mm, color, 110 minutes)

Director: Martin Scorsese

Production company: Warner Brothers

Executive producer: E. Lee Perry

Producer: Jonathan T. Taplin

Writers: Martin Scorsese, Mardik Martin

Cinematographer: Kent Wakeford

Editor: Sid Levin

Leading cast: Harvey Keitel (Charlie), Robert De Niro (Johnny Boy), David Proval (Tony), Amy Robinson (Teresa), Richard Romanus (Michael)

ALICE DOESN'T LIVE HERE ANYMORE (1974)
(35mm, color, 112 minutes)

Director: Martin Scorsese

Production company: Warner Brothers

Producers: David Susskind, Audrey Maas

Writer: Robert Getchell

Cinematographer: Kent Wakeford

Editor: Marcia Lucas

Leading cast: Ellen Burstyn (Alice Hyatt), Kris Kristofferson (David), Alfred Lutter (Tommy), Dianne Ladd (Flo), Vic Tayback (Mel), Jodie Foster (Audrey), Harvey Keitel (Ben)

ITALIANAMERICAN (1974)
(35mm, color, 45 minutes. Documentary. Not a commercial release. Produced as part of the "Storm of Strangers" television series, sponsored by the National Endowment for the Humanities. Premiered at the 12th New York Film Festival on October 3, 1974.)

Director: Martin Scorsese

Production company: National Communications Foundation

Producers: Saul Rubin, Elaine Attias

Writers (treatment): Martin Scorsese, Mardik Martin, Larry Cohen

Cinematographer: Alex Hirschfield

Editor: Bertram Lovitt

Cast: Charles Scorsese, Catherine Scorsese, Martin Scorsese

TAXI DRIVER (1976)
(35mm, color, 114 minutes)

Director: Martin Scorsese

Production company: Columbia Pictures

Producers: Michael Phillips, Julia Phillips

Writer: Paul Schrader

Cinematographer: Michael Chapman

Editors: Marcia Lucas, Tom Rolf, Melvin Shapiro

Leading cast: Robert De Niro (Travis Bickle), Jodie Foster (Iris), Cybill Shepherd (Betsy), Harvey Keitel (Sport), Peter Boyle (Wizard)

NEW YORK, NEW YORK (1977)
(35mm, color, 153 minutes [re-released version: 163 minutes])

Director: Martin Scorsese

Production company: United Artists

Producers: Irwin Winkler, Robert Chartoff

Writers: Mardik Martin, Earl Mac Rauch

Cinematographer: Laszlo Kovacs

Editors: Irving Lerner, Marcia Lucas

Leading cast: Robert De Niro (Jimmy Doyle), Liza Minnelli (Francine Evans), Lionel Stander (Tony Harwell), Barry Primus (Paul Wilson)

THE LAST WALTZ (1978)
(35mm, color, 117 minutes. Documentary.)

Director/Interviewer: Martin Scorsese

Production company: United Artists

Producer: Robbie Robertson

Cinematographers: Michael Chapman, Laszlo Kovacs, Vilmos Zsigmond, David Myers, Bobby Byrne, Michael Watkins, Hiro Narita, Freddie Schuler

Editors: Yeu-Bun Yee, Jan Roblee

Leading cast: The Band (Robbie Robertson, Rick Danko, Levon Helm, Garth Hudson, Richard Manuel), Bob Dylan, Joni Mitchell, Neil Diamond, Neil Young, Van Morrison, Ron Wood, Muddy Waters, Eric Clapton, The Staples, Ringo Starr, Dr. John, Paul Butterfield, Ronnie Hawkins, Emmylou Harris, Michael McClure, Lawrence Ferlinghetti

AMERICAN BOY: A PROFILE OF STEVEN PRINCE (1978)
(35mm, color, 55 minutes. Documentary. Not a commercial release.)

Director: Martin Scorsese

Production companies: New Empire Films/Scorsese Films

Executive producers: Ken Wheat, Jim Wheat

Producer: Bertram Lovitt

Writers (treatment): Mardik Martin, Julia Cameron

Cinematographer: Michael Chapman

Editors: Amy Jones, Bertram Lovitt

Leading cast: Steven Prince, Martin Scorsese, George Memmoli, Mardik Martin, Julia Cameron, Kathy McGinnis

RAGING BULL (1980)
(35mm, black & white, color, 129 minutes)

Director: Martin Scorsese

Production company: United Artists

Producers: Irwin Winkler, Robert Chartoff in association with Peter Savage

Writers: Paul Schrader, Mardik Martin (based on the book *Raging Bull* by Jake La Motta with Joseph Carter and Peter Savage)

Cinematographer: Michael Chapman

Editor: Thelma Schoonmaker

Leading cast: Robert De Niro (Jake La Motta), Cathy Moriarty (Vickie La Motta), Joe Pesci (Joey La Motta), Frank Vincent (Salvy), Theresa Saldana (Lenore), Nicholas Colasanto (Tommy Como)

THE KING OF COMEDY (1983)
(35mm, color, 108 minutes)

Director: Martin Scorsese

Production company: Twentieth Century-Fox

Executive producer: Robert Greenhut

Producer: Armon Milchan

Writer: Paul Zimmerman

Cinematographer: Fred Schuler

Editor: Thelma Schoonmaker

Leading cast: Robert De Niro (Rupert Pupkin), Jerry Lewis (Jerry Langford), Diahnne Abbott (Rita), Sandra Bernhard (Masha)

AFTER HOURS (1985)
(35mm, color, 97 minutes)

Director: Martin Scorsese

Production companies: Warner Brothers; Double Play/The Geffen Company

Producers: Amy Robinson, Griffin Dunne, Robert F. Colesberry

Writer: Joseph Minion

Cinematographer: Michael Ballhaus

Editor: Thelma Schoonmaker

Leading cast: Griffin Dunne (Paul Hackett), Rosanna Arquette (Marcy), Linda Fiorentino (Kiki), Teri Garr (Julie), John Heard (Tom the bartender), Catherine O'Hara (Gail)

THE COLOR OF MONEY (1986)
(35mm, color, 119 minutes)

Director: Martin Scorsese

Production companies: Touchstone, Buena Vista

Producers: Irving Axelrad, Barbara De Fina

Writer: Richard Price (based on the novel by Walter Tevis)

Cinematographer: Michael Ballhaus

Editor: Thelma Schoonmaker

Leading cast: Paul Newman (Eddie Felson), Tom Cruise (Vincent Lauria), Mary Elizabeth Mastrantonio (Carmen), Helen Shaver (Janelle), Forest Whitaker (Amos)

THE LAST TEMPTATION OF CHRIST (1988)
(35mm, color, 163 minutes)

Director: Martin Scorsese

Production companies: Universal Pictures, Cineplex Odeon Films

Executive producer: Harry Ufland

Producer: Barbara De Fina

Writer: Paul Schrader (based on the novel by Nikos Kazantzakis)

Cinematographer: Michael Ballhaus

Editor: Thelma Schoonmaker

Leading cast: Willem Dafoe (Jesus), Harvey Keitel (Judas), Barbara Hershey (Mary Magdalene), Harry Dean Stanton (Paul/Saul), David Bowie (Pontius Pilate), John Lurie (the Apostle James), Gary Basaraba (the Apostle Andrew), Victor Argo (the Apostle Peter), Michael Been (the Apostle John), Paul Herman (the Apostle Philip), Alan Rosenberg (the Apostle Thomas), Verna Bloom (Mary, the mother of Jesus), Peggy Gormley (Martha, the sister of Lazarus), Tomas Arana (Lazarus), Andre Gregory (John the Baptist), Leo Burmester (the Apostle Nathaniel)

NEW YORK STORIES: LIFE LESSONS (1989)
(35mm, color, 44 minutes. Screened as one of three short films. The other parts were *Oedipus Wrecks*, directed by Woody Allen, and *Life Without Zoe*, directed by Francis Ford Coppola.)

Director: Martin Scorsese

Production company: Touchstone Pictures

Producers: Barbara De Fina, Robert Greenhut

Writer: Richard Price

Cinematographer: Nestor Almendros

Editor: Thelma Schoonmaker

Leading cast: Nick Nolte (Lionel Dobie), Rosanna Arquette (Paulette), Patrick O'Neal (Philip Fowler), Peter Gabriel (himself)

GOODFELLAS (1990)
(35mm, color, 146 minutes)

Director: Martin Scorsese

Production company: Warner Brothers

Executive producer: Barbara De Fina

Producer: Irwin Winkler

Writers: Nicholas Pileggi, Martin Scorsese (based on *Wise Guy* by Nicholas Pileggi)

Cinematographer: Michael Ballhaus

Editor: Thelma Schoonmaker

Leading cast: Robert De Niro (Jimmy Conway), Ray Liotta (Henry Hill), Joe Pesci (Tommy DeVito), Paul Sorvino (Paul Cicero), Lorraine Bracco (Karen Hill), Christopher Serrone (Young Henry Hill), Frank DiLeo (Tuddy)

OTHER PROJECTS DIRECTED BY SCORSESE:

MIRROR, MIRROR (1985)
(color, 24 minutes. Episode in the "Amazing Stories" television series.)

Director: Martin Scorsese

Production company: Amblin'

Producer: David E. Vogel

Writer: Joseph Minion (based on a story by Steven Spielberg)

Cinematographer: Robert Stevens

Editor: Joe Ann Fogle

Leading cast: Sam Waterston (Jordan), Helen Shaver (Karen), Dick Cavett (himself), Tim Robbins (Jordan's phantom)

ARMANI COMMERCIAL (1) (1986)
(black & white, 30 seconds)

Director/Writer (treatment): Martin Scorsese

Production company: Emporio Armani

Producer: Barbara De Fina

Cinematographer: Nestor Almendros

Cast: Christophe Bouquin, Christina Marsilach

BAD (1987)
(color, black & white, 16 minutes. Music video for Michael Jackson.)

Director: Martin Scorsese

Production company: Optimum Productions

Producers: Quincy Jones, Barbara De Fina

Writer: Richard Price

Cinematographer: Michael Chapman

Editor: Thelma Schoonmaker

Leading cast: Michael Jackson (Daryl), Adam Nathan (Tip), Pedro Sanchez (Nelson), Wesley Snipes (Mini Max), Greg Holtz, Jr. (Cowboy), Roberta Flack (Daryl's mother)

SOMEWHERE DOWN THE CRAZY RIVER (1988)
(color, 4½ minutes. Promotional piece for Robbie Robertson song.)

Director/Writer (treatment): Martin Scorsese

Production company: Limelight

Producers: Amanda Pirie, Tim Clawson

Cinematographer: Mark Plummer

Cast: Robbie Robertson, Sammy BoDean, Maria McKee

ARMANI COMMERCIAL (2) (1988)
(20 seconds)

Director/Writer (treatment): Martin Scorsese

Production company: Emporio Armani

Producer: Barbara De Fina

Cinematographer: Michael Ballhaus

Cast: Jens Peter, Elisabetha Ranella

SCORSESE'S CREDITS ON FILMS BY OTHER DIRECTORS:

WOODSTOCK (1970)

Produced by Warner Brothers, Bob Maurice

Directed by Michael Wadleigh

Scorsese was an Assistant Director and an editor

MEDICINE BALL CARAVAN (1971)

Produced by Warner Brothers

Directed by François Reichenbach

Scorsese was Supervising Editor

UNHOLY ROLLERS (1972)

Produced by American International Pictures

Directed by Vernon Zimmerman

Scorsese was Supervising Editor

ELVIS ON TOUR (1972)
Produced by MGM
Directed by Pierre Adidge, Robert Abel
Scorsese was Montage Supervisor

THE GRIFTERS (1990)
Director: Stephen Frears
Production companies: Cineplex Odeon Films; released by Miramax Films
Scorsese was Co-Producer, with Robert Harris and James Painten

SCORSESE'S ACTING CREDITS:

WHO'S THAT KNOCKING AT MY DOOR? (1969)
Gangster

BOXCAR BERTHA (1972)
Client in a brothel

MEAN STREETS (1973)
Shorty, Michael's hired killer

ALICE DOESN'T LIVE HERE ANYMORE (1974)
Patron at the diner

TAXI DRIVER (1976)
Passenger in Travis Bickle's taxi

CANNONBALL (1976)
(Directed by Paul Bartel)
Mafioso

RAGING BULL (1980)
Barbizon stagehand

IL PAP'OCCHIO (IN THE EYE OF THE POPE) (1981)
(Directed by Renzo Arbore)
Television director

THE KING OF COMEDY (1983)

Television director

PAVLOVA–A WOMAN FOR ALL TIME (1982)

(Directed by Emil Lotianou)

Gatti-Cassaza, director of the Metropolitan Opera House

AFTER HOURS (1985)

Man with spotlight

'ROUND MIDNIGHT (1986)

(Directed by Bertrand Tavernier)

Goodley, owner of Birdland

GUILTY BY SUSPICION

(Directed by Irwin Winkler)

Joe Lesser, Hollywood director

Photographs courtesy of the following:

Martin Sheerin: frontispiece, pages 6, 8, 28, 240.

Laurie Brockway: page 16.

Mrs. Scorsese: pages 22, 25, 33.

Scorsese Archives: pages 30, 43, 61, 63, 144–145.

American International Pictures/Scorsese Archives: page 66.

Roseanne Leto: page 52.

Twentieth Century Fox: page 157.

M/S Billings Publicity: page 158.

Geffen Company: page 183.

Irwin Winkler: 291.

INDEX